D1431757

NONPROFIT FINANCIAL PLANNING MADE EASY

NONPROFIT FINANCIAL PLANNING MADE EASY

Jody Blazek, CPA

WILEY

John Wiley & Sons. Inc.

Published by John Wiley & Sons, Inc., Hoboken, New Jersey.

Published simultaneously in Canada.

For general information on our other products and services, or technical support, please contact our Customer Care Department within the United States at 800-762-2974, outside the United States at 317-572-3993 or fax 317-572-4002.

Wiley also publishes its books in a variety of electronic formats. Some content that appears in print may not be available in electronic books.

For more information about Wiley products, visit our Web site at http://www.wiley.com.

Library of Congress Cataloging-in-Publication Data:

Blazek, Jody.
      Nonprofit financial planning made easy/Jody Blazek.
          p.   cm.—(Wiley nonprofit law, finance, and management series)
Includes bibliographical references and index.
        ISBN 978-0-471-71527-6 (pbk.)
          1.   Nonprofit organizations—Finance.   2. Nonprofit organizations—Accounting. 3. Nonprofit organizations—Management.   I. Title
        HG4027.65.B553 2008
        658.15—dc22
                                                                                    2007044832

Printed in the United States of America

10 9 8 7 6

Contents

EXHIBITS

About the Author

Jody Blazek is a partner in Blazek & Vetterling LLP, a Houston CPA firm focusing on tax and financial services for exempt organizations and the individuals who create, fund, and work with them. BV provides tax compliance, auditing, and planning services to over 500 nonprofit organizations, including schools, churches, museums, human service organizations, business leagues, private foundations, garden clubs, fraternities, research institutes, civic associations, cultural organizations, and others.

Jody began her professional career at KPMG, then Peat, Marwick, Mitchell & Co. Her concentration on exempt organizations began in 1969, when she studied and advised clients about the Tax Reform Act that completely revamped the taxation of charities and created private foundations. From 1972 to 1981, she gained nonprofit management experience as treasurer of the Menil Interests, where she worked with John and Dominique de Menil to plan the Menil Collection, the Rothko Chapel, and other projects of the Menil Foundation. She reentered public practice in 1981 to found the firm she now serves.

She is the author of six books in the Wiley Nonprofit Series: *IRS Form 1023 Preparation Guide* (March, 2005), *IRS Form 990 Tax Preparation Guide for Nonprofits* (2001, online version, 2004), *Tax Planning and Compliance for Tax-Exempt Organizations*, 4th edition (2004), *Financial Planning for Nonprofit Organizations* (1996), *Private Foundations: Tax Law and Compliance, 2nd edition* (2003), and *The Legal Answer Book for Private Foundations* (2001), coauthored with Bruce R. Hopkins.

Jody serves on the Financial Accounting and Transparency Group created by Independent Sector to support the Panel on the Nonprofit Sector's reports to the Senate Finance Committee. For that project, she also works with Foundation Financial Officers' Group to provide technical assistance and support to the Form 990-PF Reform Committee.

She is past chair of the AICPA Tax-Exempt Organizations Resource Panel and a member of the 990 and 1023 Task Forces. She serves on the national editorial board of Tax Analysts' The Exempt Organization Tax Review. She serves on the Community Service Committee of the Houston Chapter of Certified Public Accountants and is a founding director of Texas Accountants and Lawyers for the Arts and the Houston Artists Fund. She is a member of the board of the Gulf Coast Institute, the Anchorage Foundations, and the Main Street Coalition Council. She is a frequent speaker at nonprofit symposia, including those sponsored by the Conference of Southwest Foundations; Association of Small Foundations; AICPA; Arizona, New York, Washington, Maryland, and Texas Societies of CPAs; the University of Texas School of Law; United Way of the Texas Gulf Coast; Professional Education Systems, and Nonprofit Resource Center, among others.

Jody received her BBA from the University of Texas at Austin in 1964 and took selected tax courses at South Texas School of Law. She and her husband, David Crossley, nurture two sons, Austin and Jay Blazek Crossley.

Preface

Financial planning contributes significantly to the success of a nonprofit organization and allows it to better accomplish its mission. Planning tasks are challenging and too often are overlooked. In this time of shrinking governmental support for nonprofit organizations, astute use of available resources following a well-developed financial plan may be the key to a nonprofit's survival.

The concepts and techniques presented in this book can simplify the efforts of financial managers and board members to be fiscally responsible, or accountable, to the organization's private and governmental funders, to its clients, to the community in which it operates, and to the society benefiting from its work.

The nonprofit world to a great extent embodies selfless groups of persons working to help others in a wide context. The groups through which they work are clustered in three distinct types:

1. Charitable organizations: churches, soup kitchens, universities, museums, and research institutes.

2. Associations and community organizations: civic leagues, business leagues, labor unions, and social clubs.

3. Public sector: governments, municipalities, agencies, and public boards that work with nonprofits.

Hopefully, many people working in this broad range of nonprofits will find in this book a good prescription for their organization's fiscal health.

My experiences as an accountant serving nonprofit organizations inspired me to develop checklists and forms to encourage the use of financial planning. When my firm is engaged to perform traditional accounting services for a nonprofit organization, such as preparation of the annual Form 990 or performance of an annual audit, we often find that the organization needs financial management assistance beyond the specific task we are engaged to perform. Also, when our help is sought to help overcome unexpected financial problems, we often find the nonprofit managers could have averted the crisis with adequate advanced planning.

In Chapter 1, I seek to dispel myths that can hamper a nonprofit's financial success. Nonprofits can profit, or accumulate revenues in excess of expenditures, so long as such resources are devoted to improving the fashion in which the nonprofit accomplishes its exempt purposes. While surpluses shouldn't exceed that amount reasonably needed to assure financial stability, funds can be saved to finance future plans. A nonprofit can set aside funds to expand programs, self-insure risks, build a new building, establish a new location, or simply provide adequate working capital. The primary distinction between a for-profit and a nonprofit is that the latter has no owners. The nonprofit does not distribute its profits, if any, to any private individuals—its creators, insiders, or those who govern it. It can, however, and should accumulate sufficient working capital from surplus income to assure uninterrupted and viable program delivery.

In pursuit of financial stability, a nonprofit can conduct its financial affairs in a business-like fashion as long as its managers understand the ways in which it is different from a for-profit business. Both need strategic plans based on clearly defined goals, with a focus on accountability, productivity, and profitability. To be fiscally successful, both need skilled financial managers. In evaluating a nonprofit's staffing budgets, it is interesting and can be useful to observe whether the organization considers financial personnel equally as important as its program officers. Seeking pro bono volunteer financial services is not always cost effective in the long run.

The fiduciaries of a nonprofit have special responsibilities. Whether labeled as directors, trustees, elders, or commissioners, they are the financial stewards ultimately accountable to those constituents the nonprofit is organized to serve. The common denominator for this stewardship role is selflessness. The beauty of the U.S. philanthropic community is its extensive network of generous volunteers who expect no monetary compensation in return for their efforts. The challenge, however, is to design an organizational structure for the nonprofit within which this great human resource can efficiently function.

Chapter 2 explores the roles of the board members, the staff, and the volunteers. The objective is to define tasks clearly and establish an adequate financial management structure with checks and balances and built-in warning signs to spotlight problem areas. A checklist of issues a fiduciary should consider in fulfilling his or her duty to oversee and guide the organization and its managers is provided. Also, the important distinction between inside and outside accountants is explained to aid in understanding the need for separation of their roles to achieve suitable fiscal oversight and controls. This book should prove particularly useful to the many well-meaning volunteer accountants, lawyers, and other professionals who have little or no experience with nonprofit organizations.

For some years, I have collected examples of poor financial planning by nonprofit organizations. Fundraising events are perfect specimens for such analysis. My favorite example, found some years ago in a now yellowed and undated newspaper clipping, is the story of a small college in Massachusetts. The school spent $40,000 printing 10,000 copies of a cookbook with recipes contributed by local and state politicians; the idea being to raise money and bring some attention to the college. Instead of selling the hoped-for 10,000 copies, only 3,000 copies were sold and the college reportedly was forced to curtail its academic programs to cover deficits from the publishing program.

How could financial planning have improved this situation? First and foremost, the college could have applied the concepts discussed in Chapter 3—it should have prioritized its mission and balanced its available resources. It allocated funds needed for academic programs to "invest" in a risky publishing venture. One can imagine its budgeting procedures were inadequate so that no marketing feasibility study or forecast was conducted in advance and no follow-up promotions were budgeted, as suggested in Chapter 4.

Too many times, I see fundraising events run by well-meaning volunteers with little or no advance planning for financial feasibility. Consider whether fundraising events would actually show a profit if the value of the volunteer time devoted to organizing and presenting such events was quantified. Recently, I saw a group lose money on an event because they were not allowed to serve donated food or drinks as was their past custom. Event planners entered into an agreement to hold the annual gala in a museum without realizing they were required to use approved (and very expensive) caterers. It is often amazing to see, based on the value of fundraising events that the IRS requires the nonprofit to estimate, the narrowness of the margin between the cost of such events and the gross proceeds.

Poorly planned expansion plans can also wreak havoc with a nonprofit's financial situation. A good example of this problem occurred some years ago when the American Center in Paris announced that it was forced to close its doors 19 months after the opening of a new $41 million building designed by American architect Frank Gehry. The building costs used up the Center's entire endowment, leaving too little for running the literature, language, and dance classes that had made the center the preeminent showplace for American artistry in Europe

Investment of the organization's savings, working capital, and permanent funds is a significant, and often troublesome, issue for nonprofit managers and board members. Chapter 5, entitled "Asset Management," addresses the questions involved when a nonprofit accumulates resources beyond its immediate operating needs. In seeking restricted funding and longer-term endowment gifts, a nonprofit must be prepared to respect the covenants and safeguard the property. The prudent investor rules can be applied to safeguard the assets. Luckily, financial returns on investments in the past few years have been positive, but it remains to be seen how hedge funds and other alternative investments will fare during a downturn in the financial markets. If one doubts the need for diversification of investments, the subprime mortgage debacle rocking the investment community during 2007 should be recalled.

In addition to checklists and models to be used in setting financial priorities and allocating precious resources, the reader will find a brief, but thorough, description of the elements of an accounting system in Chapter 6. This chapter should be required reading for all new board members and trustees. To meet their fiduciary responsibility to judge the organization's fiscal condition means they must be able—at least once a year—to read the financial statements. It is not sufficient, in my opinion, for the board treasurer to simply report to the assembled board members that "everything is okay, so you need not read the auditor's report." Post-SOX policies that require an audit committee and thorough review of financial reports to the board are not required for nonprofits, as discussed in Chapter 2, but prudent nonprofits now adopt such governance practices.

I understand that many nonprofit managers and volunteer board members lack financial training and have a fairly high level of avoidance or denial of their ability to understand a balance sheet or cash flow report. To dispel this lack of basic knowledge, Chapter 6 explains the fashion in which financial information is accumulated and presented. Understanding basic terms like *accrual method, restricted funds,* and *receivables* can lead to improved financial decisions. I've noticed that the attitude of persons newly trained to understand financial statements is similar to the mood of clients who deliver their annual income tax data to the firm—a necessary evil has been conquered and overcome.

Beyond basic accounting lies financial analysis applied with the special financial tools explained in Chapter 7. Before approving the cookbook project mentioned above, for example, the board or finance committee members will ask to see the projected sales analysis and marketing plans to hopefully recognize it was grossly inaccurate. When asked to approve a proposed increase in the annual tuition, a private school trustee will ask what the direct per-student cost is and want to know the amount of unapplied variable overhead costs that must be covered. After studying Chapter 7, a financial planner will know why cost accounting is useful in answering such questions. Once one knows how to read the financial statements with an understanding of what makes up each category, ratio analysis can be applied to compare and analyze the numbers. Some financial disasters can be averted when more board members know how to measure the nonprofit's acid test and other financial ratios explained in the section Financial Indicators to Critique Performance.

Financial pressures on nonprofits will continue. Undoubtedly, in the next few years, Congress will be looking for ways to reduce budget deficits resulting from the Iraq war while providing funding for health care for the uninsured. Unfortunately, some federal programs will be reduced, with consequential reduction of many state and local government programs. As nonprofits begin to search for alternative sources of funding, some may be caught in the crossfire. Income-producing activities designed to replace funding cutbacks may be subject to constraints and taxes by the governments that need to raise funds.

Those who govern and manage a nonprofit organization must always be cognizant of the reasons why the nonprofit is permitted tax exemptions for federal and local tax and other purposes. Chapter 8 explains the rationale behind granting tax exemptions and requirements for maintaining the special status. Some associated with a nonprofit organization might want to regularly use Exhibit 8.1, Suitability Checklist for Tax-Exempt Status, to test for ongoing qualification. Before undertaking income-producing programs such as those described in the previous paragraph, the impact of the activity on tax status should be examined.

In completing a marketing questionnaire for this book, I was asked to choose my favorite parts of this book and to describe those that could prove most useful to a nonprofit's financial managers. My answer is that the most unique information is contained in Chapter 1—the notion that a nonprofit organization must "profit" to be financially successful. This concept alone can improve the fiscal health of a nonprofit. Adopting the attitude that the organization can function in a business-like fashion with efficient fiscal systems, well-paid personnel, and balanced resources and vision can improve the results. Certainly, to defend against what some call the "War on Non-profits," the organization's managers can arm themselves with the tools and techniques of financial planning presented in this book.

Some readers know that this book is essentially a second edition of a 1995 Wiley book called *Financial Planning for Nonprofit Organizations*. I am particularly grateful to my audit partner, Kay Walther, for updating the accounting and auditing concepts of Chapter 6. My thanks also go to David Nelson, tax principal in my firm, for his updates for Chapter 2. Finally, I marvel at the continued quality of John Wiley & Sons personnel. I thank my editor, Susan McDermott, for encouraging me to update the book, and Natasha Andrews-Noel, production editor, for bringing it to fruition and making it a useful tool.

Jody Blazek
January, 2008

1

Introductory Concepts

The key to the financial success of a nonprofit
organization is the use of traditional management
tools—forecasts and budgets, well designed and
timely financial reporting system, good governance,
clearly defined line of business (mission), cash flow
planning, fiscal controls, and a lot of goodwill.

Financial planning for nonprofits, like a nonprofit's very purpose for existence, is based on the philosophical aspirations of persons joining together
to accomplish mutual goals. The very purpose for existence of a nonprofit is
based on hope, sometimes on prayer, and almost always on dreams. Dreams
can be unrealistic and can make financial planning a risky venture. The
challenge is to stretch and balance precious resources to best accomplish
the dream. Together, the two functions—performing the mission and providing the requisite resources—work in tandem to sustain the nonprofit's
existence.

   Although idealistic aims guide the planning process and dictate a nonprofit's priorities, accomplishment of the goal can be enhanced with astute
planning. Readers who are familiar with business management will recognize the planning processes discussed in this book. Similar to the income tax
rules concerning tax-exempt nonprofits discussed in Chapter 8, financial
planning for nonprofit organizations requires acknowledgment that the
special character, language, and tools germane to nonprofits be understood
alongside language and concepts applicable to for-profits. When working
with a nonprofit organization, it is useful to ask what would make it prosper and flourish like a business. You can ask how an entrepreneur would
respond if the same situation arose in his or her successful business. You
should wonder whether the stockholders, if the nonprofit had any, would
ratify the recommendations being proposed by management?

The financial activity of nonprofit organizations has been the subject of much scrutiny and criticism during this decade. The IRS Form 990 filed annually by charities, complete with details of revenues, expenses, assets, activities, compensation of officials, and many other disclosures can be viewed on the Internet.[1] Charity Navigator was formed in 2001 to grade charities.[2] During 2002 and 2003, the *Boston Globe* presented a series on the results of its investigation of private foundation abuses.[3] As the Enron scandal also unfolded during 2002, Congress approved new standards applicable to publicly traded corporations. This so-called Sarbanes-Oxley legislation was enacted to prevent a repeat of the Enron misrepresentations by improving rules of governance and oversight of financial matters.

The Senate Finance Committee, then headed by Senator Charles Grassley, next turned its attention to the nonprofit sector. After a series of hearings, the committee in July 2004 issued a 19-page report outlining a wide range of new standards to improve public accountability and governance of nonprofits. In response, Independent Sector assembled a Panel on the Nonprofit Sector consisting of 175 executives and experts with extensive knowledge of and experience with public charities and private foundations. Drawn from organizations of all sizes serving diverse missions and geographic locations, they advise the Panel as it develops recommendations on how to ensure that nonprofits remain a vibrant, responsive, and effective part of American society. These participants, all of whom have volunteered for this important work, joined one of eight groups:

- The Panel. Twenty-four nonprofit leaders who reflect the reach and diversity of the country's nonprofit organizations

- The Citizen Advisory Group. Nine leaders of America's business, educational, media, political, and religious institutions

- The Expert Advisory Group. Eight of the foremost scholars and practitioners in nonprofit operations

- The Work Groups. More than 100 nonprofit practitioners are taking part in five groups: Governance and Fiduciary Responsibility; Government Oversight and Self-Regulation; Legal Framework; Small Organizations; and Transparency and Financial Accountability.

---

[1] At www.guidestar.org.

[2] See www.charitynavigator.org. In June 2007, their site displayed a rating range of one to four stars for over 5,200 charities based on information in their Form 990.

[3] In one example, $250,000 was paid for the wedding of a foundation trustee. On December 30, 2003, in conclusion to its series on foundation practices, the *Boston Globe* reported that "both the Internal Revenue Service and state attorneys general have inadequate resources to provide effective oversight of private foundations."

- The Advisory Committee on Self-Regulation of the Charitable Sector More than 30 leaders examining how to best strengthen self-regulation, including how build on the work of various organizations and subsectors that have already developed standards, accreditation, and training

The Panel's recommendations to strengthen the transparency, governance, and accountability of charitable organizations were first published in June 2005 followed by a supplement in April 2006. The Panel's work continues in the summer of 2007 as comments on its recommendations are reviewed to compile enhanced standards for financial management and governance. Thanks to the work of the Panel and many others, most of the provisions suggested by Grassley's committee were not enacted in the Pension Protection Act of 2006. As the sector works toward new standards, it recognizes that its ability to improve lives depends on the support of the public, which it will receive only if it earns the public's trust.[4]

The American Bar Association Coordinating Committee on Nonprofit Governance has also issued a report recommending reforms.[5] In addition, the IRS issued its list of *Good Governance Policies for 501(c)(3) Organizations* in February 2007.[6] Readers should be alert for new developments, as the scrutiny of the nonprofit sector will undoubtedly continue. Nonprofits and their boards need to take steps to assure their organization is serving its mission in an efficient and cost-effective fashion following the highest possible ethical standards following standards and using checklists in Chapter 2.

If there is any doubt about the need for good financial management and planning, remember what happened to the United Way of America. Even in what one would think was one of the most well-run organizations in the United States; money was misappropriated by an executive director reportedly for personal gain.[7]

HOW TO USE THIS BOOK

This book provides step-by-step solutions to the dilemmas involved in keeping financial resources and the mission in balance. Financial

---

[4] Panel reports, including a draft of the *Principles for Effective Practice*, were released for comments as of June 17, 2007. They are available at www.nonprofitpanel.org/selfreg/Index.

[5] *Guide to Nonprofit Corporate Governance in the Wake of Sarbanes-Oxley*, published by ABA in May 2006.

[6] Available at http://www.irs.gov/pub/irs-tege/good_governance_practices.pdf.

[7] The September 27, 1994, Associated Press report of his trial stated, "William Aramony has pleaded innocent to charges that he diverted United Way money to buy such things as a New York City apartment for his girlfriend."

management tools and techniques for nonprofits are explored and reviewed in some detail, with illustrations, examples, checklists, and model forms. As this chapter explains, the concepts and planning methods used by businesses are germane and can be tailored to suit a nonprofit's needs. The financial planning checklist at the end of this chapter is designed as a comprehensive survey of financial planning issues that face a nonprofit.

Planning for a nonprofit's fiscal health and effective operation is an ongoing and continually evolving process. The mission statement is not necessarily revised monthly, but the current financial data should be. Exhibit 1.1 illustrates the overlapping circles of financial management activities. As a first planning step, the organizational structure is evaluated. It should be clear from the rules of governance and procedures who is in charge, as discussed in Chapter 2. All should understand the function of the board, volunteers, and staff, and the roles of the internal and external accountants in the financial affairs.

Next comes planning and evaluation of organizational objectives, as shown on the right-hand side of the circles in Exhibit 1.1. Before spending a penny, the board members and major supporters in concert with staff define the mission and develop specific performance goals. How can funders or members understand the nonprofit's vision without a description of its activities and financial goals? What will provide the volunteers with a source of direction? Dreams and aspirations must be explored, examined, and written down in a mission statement. This "what if" segment of the planning process facilitates evaluation of alternatives. Chapter 3 explores these concepts and provides suggestions for utilizing critical analyses to test the means of accomplishing the mission.

Once the basic philosophical ambitions are understood, financial management translates the mission into financial terms. Aspirations are expressed in numbers as budget planning begins. The end result should be a financial blueprint for achieving mission-oriented goals. Fiscal performance goals are, after all, merely a means to successful program achievements. Chapter 4 explores the process of preparing and monitoring budgets, incorporating staff participation in the process, and fostering staff support for financial goals. Operational as well as capital-addition budgets are discussed.

Although budgeting is designed to allocate the organization's current resources to achieve program goals, effective asset management maximizes the value of those resources. Plans to monitor cash flow to maximize the yield on cash and other investment assets are formulated in Chapter 5. The investment policies and decisions concerning permanent funds are explored. A checklist for managing and monitoring endowment and restricted funds is provided to serve as a tool in protecting these important resources.

Reporting and monitoring financial transactions as they occur is critical. Chapter 6 discusses financial records and the decisions an organization makes in establishing its accounting systems. Useful journals and ledgers are defined and suggestions made regarding design of charts of accounts.

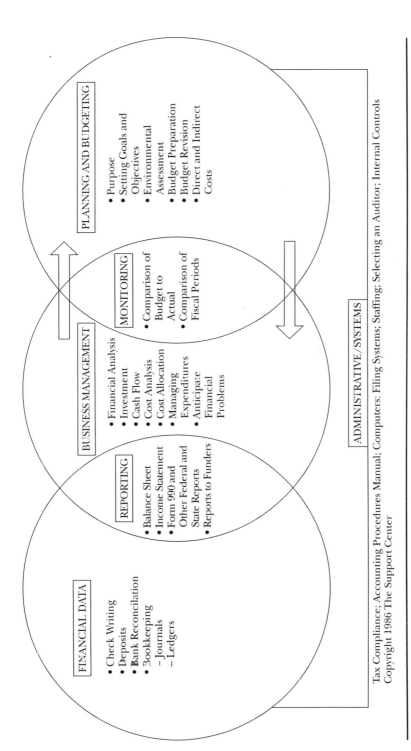

FINANCIAL DATA

- Check Writing
- Deposits
- **B**ank Reconcilation
- Bookkeeping
  - Journals
  - Ledgers

REPORTING

- Balance Sheet
- Income Statement
- Form 990 and Other Federal and State Reports
- Reports to Funders

BUSINESS MANAGEMENT

- Financial Analysis
- Investment
- Cash Flow
- Cost Analysis
- Cost Allocation
- Managing Expenditures
- Anticipate Financial Problems

MONITORING

- Comparison of Budget to Actual
- Comparison of Fiscal Periods

PLANNING AND BUDGETING

- Purpose
- Setting Goals and Objectives
- Environmental Assessment
- Budget Preparation
- Budget Revision
- Direct and Indirect Costs

ADMINISTRATIVE / SYSTEMS

Tax Compliance; Accounting Procedures Manual; Computers; Filing Systems; Staffing; Selecting an Auditor; Internal Controls
Copyright 1986 The Support Center

Exhibit 1.1 Financial Management Activities in Nonprofit Organizations

5

The difference between—and when to use—the accrual method rather than the cash method of accounting is considered. The meaning of FASB and GAAP is explored with an outline of currently applicable pronouncements. A checklist is provided as a guide to computerization and selection of appropriate accounting software. Control and evaluation complete the cycle of financial planning. The task is to monitor, to manage the problems highlighted, and to be aware of how well the reality measures up to the nonprofit's aspirations. The financial planner will want internal controls, such as those described in Chapter 6, installed with the help of the outside accountants to safeguard the nonprofit's resources on a daily basis. The ratio analysis techniques presented in Chapter 7 will be useful in pinpointing any weaknesses and identifying hidden trends. Financial evaluations for purchasing and leasing decisions, employee compliance, and agency agreements implementing strategic alliances are provided. Other financial decisions can be made using the comprehensive checklists and sample forms presented throughout the book.

Because not all nonprofits qualify for tax-exempt status, Chapter 8 explores the criteria for, and the means of obtaining, special tax treatment. Confusion arises because the activities of nonprofits and for-profits are often the same or very similar. Financial planners need to understand the breadth of activity permissible to an exempt organization. Issues pertaining to the use of unrelated business income to support exempt purposes are also discussed. A glossary of tax and financial terms unique to nonprofits precedes the index at the end of the book.

ATTRIBUTES OF NONPROFITS

The world of nonprofits includes a broad range of institutions: charities, business leagues, political parties, schools, country clubs, cities, cemeteries, employee benefit societies, social clubs, united-giving campaigns, and a wide variety of other pursuits. For financial planning purposes, it is useful to distinguish between organizations that direct their efforts outwardly, or externally, and those organizations whose work is focused internally, or toward benefiting their members. Nonprofit organizations share the common attribute of being organized for the advancement of a group of persons, rather than particular individual owners or businesses. Sometimes it is useful for the organization to think of its beneficiaries as clients for planning purposes. Applying this concept, nonprofits can be divided into different groups as follows:

- *Type 1*. Nonprofits that operate to serve the public good by providing health care, education, culture, and social welfare service to the public (hospitals, schools, libraries, and homeless shelters, for example)

- *Type 2*. Organizations that serve both the public and their members (churches, public interest groups, and civic leagues)

- *Type 3*. Nonprofit membership organizations that are member oriented or that focus their activities on fulfillment of member services (social clubs, business leagues, and labor unions)

A nonprofit can utilize the same tools as commercial businesses that perform essentially similar services or sell goods. Likewise, the nonprofit can and should patronize its constituents or customers who fall into basically two groups:

1. *Patrons or investors*. Those who provide resources or money to the nonprofit

2. *Constituents or customers*. Those to whom services and goods are provided.

Type 1 and 2 organizations as described above have both investors and customers. Type 3 organizations primarily have customers. All three types must focus on keeping their investors and customers happy.

Investors want a return on their money. The return that investors in Type 1 and 2 nonprofits receive is mostly intangible and the investment is inspired by compassion for the mission. Their benefit comes through their conscience and knowing they help someone else. Volunteers who invest time must feel important and useful and be shown that their contribution of time is valued and appreciated. Hiring a volunteer coordinator can be an important choice in attracting and maintaining this vital source of financial support.

Type 2 and 3 nonprofit customers choose whether to participate in the nonprofit's programs and use the services or goods proffered. These nonprofits must make every effort to attract customers and give them top priority. The old adage, "Make new friends but keep the old," is a suitable refrain for a membership campaign. Whether one is silver or the other is gold, new and renewing members are an invaluable resource to a wide variety of nonprofits. A nonprofit's attitude toward them can significantly impact its success. Although it is not easy to measure this intangible in the annual budget, it can be invaluable.

For those customers receiving the nonprofit's free or low-cost services, there is an invisible interaction with the investors or contributors. How the nonprofit is perceived or evaluated by its customers can impact the attitude of its investors. The financial planners should ask if the organization treats those to whom it provides services with the highest respect. How does the general public, particularly the nonprofit's contributors, view the value of its services to the community in aiding the sick, poor, uneducated, or other persons in need?

In deciding what to call its investors, some organizations cause confusion by choosing the term *member*. As explained in Chapter 8, a membership organization is one whose members elect the governing board. To avoid this misconception, contributors should be called members only if they actually have this voting right. The name *member* is also tainted by several tax limitations on the income tax deduction of membership dues.

CAN NONPROFITS *PROFIT?*

The pursuit of profit in the normal sense is not the primary motivation of nonprofits, but there are no specific constraints or sanctions prohibiting the accumulation of funds in excess of liabilities, or capital, as long as the mission, or exempt purpose, is served. For many, the term *nonprofit* implies a prohibition against the receipt of revenues in excess of expenditures. Such a view suggests that a nonprofit cannot have a profit and is expected, instead, to lose money. Whatever the result is called, a nonprofit can generate revenues in excess of its expenses and accumulate a reasonable amount of working capital or fund balances. It can save money to build a building, to expand operations, or for any other valid reason serving its underlying exempt purposes. It can borrow venture capital to establish a new project. Basically, a nonprofit can operate without a profit motive and still produce what many think of as a profit.

Meaning of *Profit*

For nonprofit organizations, profit can mean many things, including bringing good; making progress; or being gainful, useful, advantageous, or productive.[8] These terms connote benefit to others and acknowledge the selfless purposes and activities of the organization. Profit for a nonprofit does not always come just from the bottom line. Instead, profit may be measured in terms of the number of books published, increases in attendance or test scores, or enhancement of the profession's public image. Although not necessarily measurable in financial terms, discovering a cure for a disease is the yield, return, or reward for a research organization's efforts.

When a hospital buys a magnetic resonance imaging (MRI) machine to offer better health care, it may reasonably expect the machine to pay for itself plus provide a steady stream of excess revenue, or profit. The hospital may use such profits to improve its diagnostic capabilities or use them to purchase a building, to expand other departments, or for any other valid reason serving its underlying nonprofit purposes. The distinguishing factor

---

[8] *Webster's Deluxe Unabridged Dictionary*, 2nd ed., New York: Simon & Schuster, 1982, p. 1437.

is the motivation for undertaking the activity that might generate the profit. Did the hospital buy the machine simply to make a profit or instead to better improve the health of its patients?

An accurate perspective on the term *nonprofit* focuses on the lack of self-interest in the financial results of the operations. The directors or trustees serve as stewards of the funds to assure they are devoted to meeting the socially desirable goals. The income, or profit, is not distributable to its members, directors, or officers. Just like a for-profit business, the nonprofit can pay salaries and employee benefits to its workers (including its directors), as long as the pay is reasonable in relation to services performed. There are two things it cannot do: (1) distribute the net profit as a return on capital to the people who fund and control the organization, or (2) accumulate profit or capital resources in excess of that needed to accomplish the mission.

Profit Prohibitions

There are few, if any, reasons—legal, ethical, or otherwise—why nonprofits should not accumulate excess funds, or capital, as long as such funds are devoted to the mission. Consider two authoritative interpretations of the term *nonprofit*. The State of Texas says a "nonprofit corporation means a corporation no part of the income of which is distributable to its members, directors, or officers." Similarly, the State of New York provides a two-prong test for determining whether a corporation is qualified to be treated as a nonprofit entity:

1. New York nonprofits must be formed for a nonpecuniary purpose *and*

2. No part of their assets, income, or profit is distributable to, or may inure to the benefit of, its members, directors, or officers with certain exceptions otherwise permitted.

The word *pecuniary* simply means "that which relates to money."[9] Clearly, a nonprofit must receive, hold, and use money to operate. The nonprofit's purpose or reason for having money must not be solely to generate more money. Money can be its means, but not its end. Without specifically saying so, the New York law requires that the nonprofit focus on accomplishing its mission, and that mission must be something other than receiving, spending, and accumulating money.

Note that the second test anticipates the nonprofit may produce a profit; the test simply prohibits insider benefit. The American Institute of Certified Public Accountants' Audit Guide for Not-for-Profits states that the term *not-for-profit* is not intended to imply that a voluntary health and welfare organization cannot obtain revenues in excess of expenses in any

---

[9] Ibid., p. 1420.

particular period; rather, it implies that the organization is not operated for the financial benefit of any *specific individual or group of individuals*.[10]

A nonprofit organization receiving excess revenues, or profit, for the year must decide what level of balances it should reasonably accumulate. Must the money be expended during the coming year? Can the money instead be set aside or saved for a rainy day? A number of different factors influence the answers. For federal tax purposes, the question is whether the organization's nonprofit purposes are served by saving the money rather than spending it on programs. The tax code contains no numerical constraint on the amount of fund balances a tax-exempt organization can maintain. The only specific spending mandate applies to private foundations and requires that 5 percent of the average fair market value of the investment assets be distributed annually for charitable purposes.

Another factor in the decision is the attitude of the organization's funders. A successful nonprofit with money in the bank may meet some resistance to its requests for donations. It may have to justify its need for funding as compared to a nonprofit whose programs may be curtailed unless it receives the funding. The BBB/Wise Giving Alliance standards say an organization should have unrestricted assets available for the following fiscal year of not more than three times the current year's expenses or the next year's budget, whichever is higher.[11] Note temporarily or permanently restricted funds may not be treated as "available for this purpose." See Chapter 5 (Restricted Gifts; Endowments) for consideration of such funding and Chapter 6(FASB, GAAP, and Nonprofits) for accounting definitions.

Why Seek a Profit?

The belief that a nonprofit organization must lack profit motive can limit its success and ultimately its existence. True enough, an organization's top priority is not to produce profits—it dedicates itself to carrying out a mission to benefit others. Yet profit can enhance the ability to perform its mission just as the year-end profit distributed as dividends to shareholders influences a for-profit common-stock market price.

Consider what happens when a nonprofit never generates revenues in excess of expenses. Such an organization cannot finance the expansion of its activities, accumulate a decent level of working capital, retire debt, or meet countless other financial capital needs; its existence might be tenuous, to say the least. Certainly, a newly established nonprofit should plan to

---

[10] *Industry Audit Guide: Audits of Voluntary Health and Welfare Organizations Including Statement of Position 87-2*, 2nd ed., New York: American Institute of Certified Public Accountants, 1988.

[11] According to the 10th standard of the 20 listed in their Standards for Charity Accountability; see www.give.org/standards/newcbbbstds.asp.

generate revenues in excess of expenditures—profit—in its first few years to accumulate sufficient working capital.

DIFFERENCE BETWEEN NONPROFITS AND FOR-PROFITS

A nonprofit organization is distinguishable from a for-profit business in many respects. One distinguishing factor between them is the motivation for undertaking an activity that generates revenue. The fact that a nonprofit charges for the services it performs is not evidence of profit motive. A hospital may pay all of its costs with patient charges. Whether such a hospital is a nonprofit depends on why it was created and how it operates. Is its purpose to promote the general public's health or solely to earn a profit? In other words, does it exist to support an ideal or particular individuals?

A nonprofit decides to adopt a project because of its value to society or its members rather than its potential to generate monetary profits, although one worthy project may be chosen over another based on revenue expectations. Accordingly, the challenges in achieving financial success may be considerably more daunting for nonprofits than for for-profits.

Capitalization: Philanthropists versus Investors

A nonprofit's need for capital, or unrestricted and available-to-spend, funds, to commence and to continue operation is similar to a for-profit's: Capital provides the financial underpinning to bridge gaps in the flow of funds and to ensure that financial obligations can be paid in a timely fashion. Consider, for example, a social club's capital requirements. The typical club has a physical site for its members to congregate and socialize. Whether the club buys and maintains its own building or leases facilities, the club needs capital to do so. Before agreeing to provide the property to the club, the landlady/lord or building seller will require evidence of the club's financial viability, or capital available to finance acquisition and upkeep. The capital may come from the membership assessments or from existing club funds accumulated from profitable club operations in the past. It may also use borrowed capital to buy and operate the property.

The economic rewards customary in business—dividends, interest, and capital appreciation—are not available to those who invest in nonprofits. The standards used by a nonprofit supporter to measure returns on their money are very different from a for-profit investor's. The tools for measuring success, however, are similar. Financial indicators that evidence goals accomplished can be used as a measure. The prosperity of a nonprofit can be evaluated by counting the number of children clothed and fed during the year, by comparing the per-patient costs this year with last, or by studying the number of new professionals qualified due to a business league's training efforts.

Philanthropists who donate capital funds to a nonprofit to obtain buildings or to establish endowments certainly expect the organization to "profit" or benefit from the gift in a sense. In donating capital, the donors are investing in the mission. They recognize and intend their capital to be an unselfish gift directed outward in service of a public purpose. In effect, nonprofits operate on a one-way street. Much of the money they receive is just such one-way money—donations made out of pure generosity, for which nothing is provided or expected in return. Privately owned businesses, in contrast, operate on a two-way street. For-profit organizations generally receive funds from investors who expect something in return.

On a limited basis, a tax-exempt organization is allowed to compete directly with nonexempt businesses. Revenues from unrelated business activities comprise a major source of funding for some nonprofits. The Internal Revenue Code places such a nonprofit on the same footing as competing businesses by imposing a regular income tax on profits they generate from a business. If the unrelated business activity becomes too substantial, the organization can lose its exemption.[12] Chapter 8 considers the question of when a business is "unrelated" and described the level of business activity allowed.

Revenues: Constituents versus Customers

Recipients of a nonprofit's goods, services, or monetary grants in aid are distinct from, but similar to, a for-profit's customers. A prosperous nonprofit most likely treats its program-service constituents—the poor, the sick, the culture seekers, the students—as a business would its customers. It values their patronage and caters to their needs. Whether the nonprofit charges for the goods and services provided or furnishes them on a reduced or no-fee basis, the methods used by a for-profit in purveying similar goods can be observed.

Traditionally, some nonprofits charge for the goods and services they provide to their program service recipients; hospitals and universities are good examples. Churches certainly encourage their congregants to tithe. Many nonprofits provide free services that are financed by a complex variety of donations, grants, and other income sources. Some operate with volunteer labor and sell or distribute donated goods. One important distinction is the fact that it may be impossible for some organizations to charge for the services provided. The public depends on immediate and free response from its firefighters or policemen and women, for instance. Having library doors open in the evening for students to do research is expected.

When a nonprofit does charge, the charge may not necessarily cover costs of the service; for-profits only sell things for less than cost if forced

---

[12] See the author's book entitled *Tax Planning and Compliance for Tax-Exempt Organizations*, 4th ed., Chapter 21 (Hoboken, NJ: John Wiley & Sons, 2004), for a discussion of the unrelated business income tax.

to do so by market apathy. Obviously, it is more difficult for nonprofits to raise prices, partly because of the public's expectations and partly because of the economic need of the organization's constituents. Ironically, the tight budget situation created by cuts in government funding typically comes during depressed economic periods or when new tax rules reduce or remove the tax benefit of contributions, thus discouraging philanthropy. Suffice it to say that a nonprofit is significantly different from a for-profit in many ways, even though its operations and financial decisions may often appear to be similar.

FOR-PROFIT TOOLS

Although businesses do not often show movies for free or feed the poor, they do operate schools, hospitals, theaters, galleries, publishing companies, and conduct other activities that are also carried on by nonprofit organizations. The nonprofit's reason for conducting the activity and the ultimate benefit from the capital are definitely different. Nonetheless, the financial issues look much the same; both types of organization can use similar financial tools. Just as discussed above under the generating-profit issue, there is no reason why a nonprofit cannot use a for-profit model to manage its financial affairs. A nonprofit that operates in a businesslike fashion may be more likely to succeed. Some of the tools that might be useful include:

- *Business plan.* To achieve idealistic goals, nonprofits can develop a long-range plan that looks like what is called a business plan, complete with market surveys, cost projections, and strategic goals. Like a for-profit, a nonprofit can:
  - Accumulate reasonable reserves by earning more than it spends
  - Be clear about who makes decisions
  - Follow sound financial practices for both planning and reporting
- *Critical analysis of decisions.* A nonprofit considers how a for-profit would make a similar financial decision. In considering a question, the nonprofit might ask:
  - What would make this nonprofit prosper and flourish?
  - How would an entrepreneur respond if the same situation arose in his or her business?
  - Last, but not least, if the nonprofit had stockholders, would they ratify the recommendations being proposed?
- *Traditional management tools.* The management tools for achieving organizational objectives are the same whether the objectives are

business oriented or mission oriented. Like for-profits, a nonprofit's management tools include:

- Forecasts, budgets, and ratio analysis
- Well-designed and timely financial reports
- Defined lines of communication and responsibility
- Cash-flow monitoring system
- Efficient organizational structure with fiscal controls
- Identification of the target served (i.e., the customers or constituents)
- Clearly defined line of business (mission)

PURSUIT OF FINANCIAL SUCCESS: SOME OBSERVATIONS

However different the nonprofit is from a business, the methodology for measuring and achieving success is conceptually the same. Before launching into the technicalities of financial planning for nonprofits, readers may wish to consider the following observations regarding the pursuit of financial success.

Be Realistic about Expectations

Nonprofit organizations are created to accomplish a mission—often based on dreams of curing a societal need. Rational, even scientifically determined, projections can be wrong. The polls may say people are worried about feeding children, but they may not respond with contributions needed to do so. The compassion felt toward those with a disease may wane. Fundraising is often successful because of the energy and influence of board members. The nonprofit organization, however, is seldom their top priority; having a great fundraising chair one year does not assure the success of next year's campaign. It is often impossible to find the perfect board chair. A matrix for setting goals with a view to the reality of available resources can be found in Chapter 3.

A healthy dose of realism is also appropriate when the nonprofit's funds are invested. Critical evaluation of the risks inherent in purchasing stocks, bonds, mutual funds, hedge funds, real estate partnership interests, and the like is important. The prudent investor rule and other issues to consider in making such purchasers are presented in Chapter 5.

Make Use of Intangible Resources

A nonprofit's goodwill can be a highly valuable and useful resource. Opportunities abound today for a nonprofit, for example, to allow a credit-card company to use its logo for an "affinity card." Scientific discoveries or symphony performances can be licensed for public distribution. Tangible resources, such as museum spaces, gardens, football stadiums, auditoriums, and similar facilities may also have value outside their use by the organization. The resourceful nonprofit rents or otherwise creates revenues from these otherwise idle assets. Care and careful planning is required. Chapter 5 (Getting Resources) discusses the tax aspects of earning revenue from intangible resources.

Forming strategic alliances to leverage the nonprofit's know-how can also be valuable. Cooperative research projects, educational conferences, and publications, for example, can spread administrative costs and maximize potential for return for all the partners working together on the projects. The business league that recognizes its need for a skilled financial manager it cannot afford to hire might try to find one or more similar leagues with whom to share such a person.

Merging two or more organizations can yield operational efficiencies and enhance the long-term financial viability of the nonprofits joining forces. A photographic exhibition space, sculpture garden, and a children's art center might fare better together rather than in competition with each other. A host of factors might indicate suitable candidates—nature of services provided, economic size, staff skills and longevity, board composition and organizational structure, and so on. Affiliations are discussed in Chapter 7 (Affiliations and Agency Agreements).

Nonprofit Mentality Is Often "Penny Wise and Pound Foolish"

The financial success of some organizations stems from their ability to recruit cadres of volunteers and pounds of donated goods. They tap a wealth of support and goodwill and run on the belief that intangible assets can sustain them. Such resources must, however, be supported by a management structure capable of relieving overworked volunteers and underpaid staff members. Too many nonprofits suffer from classic burnout inefficiencies: lost grants from missed application deadlines, penalties and interest for failures to file returns or deposit payroll taxes, poor program performance, and high employee turnover. Some of a certified public accountant (CPA) firm's most troublesome clients (and often those with the highest fees) will be those organizations who sought volunteer help from somebody's friend who, unfortunately, had little or no experience with nonprofits. In most cases, a nonprofit operates much more efficiently with well-paid staff empowered to hire reputable experts as necessary.

Financial Accounting for Nonprofits Is Different

A nonprofit should engage independent accountants who are both familiar with and experienced in providing accounting services to nonprofits. Expect the CPAs to be responsive to the organization's particular needs, to evaluate fiscal record-keeping systems, and to make suggestions. Ask the CPAs to help to design readable financial reports that can be understood by board members and supporters who are nonaccountants. Expect accountants to translate the meaning of the numbers and the footnotes. Always ask if they have prepared a management letter to report weaknesses in the organization's fiscal management systems, and if so, follow up on the implementation of the suggestions included. Be sure the financials are presented using fund accounting, the preferred system for nonprofits to distinguish restricted and permanent funds from unrestricted moneys as discussed in Chapter 6.

Volunteer service organizations formed to provide assistance to nonprofit organizations exist in many cities throughout the United States. An organization in need of an accountant, lawyer, or other financial advisor experienced in nonprofits should identify such local volunteer groups. The CPA society, the bar association, and the united giving campaign organization typically have such public service programs. Such groups are a good resource for referrals to professionals who work with nonprofits, for educational materials, and information regarding resources available to nonprofits in the area. Some of them provide pro bono or sliding-scale financial management services. Many sponsor educational classes and maintain a library of useful information.

Producing an Audit Trail Benefits the Organization in Many Ways

Being able to connect the source document (for instance, invoice for a hospital stay) with the accounting reports provides the detail required for good budgeting and also facilitates information retrieval (when the patient calls six months later for a copy of the receipt). Fiscal assets are safeguarded by such connections. It only takes a moment to indicate that an invoice has been paid with a particular check number on a particular day. Such a simple step prevents overpayments and provides the answer to many questions.

Well-meaning volunteer bookkeepers and treasurers may not be capable of or have the time to maintain proper records. Although hiring a part-time accounting clerk recommended by auditors may strain the budget at first, overall operational improvement may recoup the cost. Knowing who does what is particularly important for an organization with few or no staff members performing all the accounting tasks. It is critical to develop methods of checks and balances by establishing a good system of internal control. The person who opens the mail and records the financial transactions should never, for example, be permitted to sign the checks. See Chapter 6 (Internal Controls) for a discussion and checklist.

Enhancing Computer Capabilities May Not Cure Financial Ills

Late, incomplete, or incorrect financial reports are not necessarily due to technological deficiencies. If the lack of good financial information is due to poor organizational structure, low personnel skill levels, or volunteer distraction, the problem will not be solved with new technology. Although some checkbook programs, such as QuickBooks, do not contain audit safeguards a CPA might prefer, they may provide a good alternative for the modest nonprofit that lacks a staff person trained in bookkeeping and accounting.

However, the nonprofit should not skimp on the technology acquisition budget. A lot of valuable human resources are wasted on inadequate or ill-suited software. A donor database system is an invaluable fundraising tool that can also enhance volunteer efforts. Better yet (and correspondingly more costly) is an integrated financial reporting system that allows the donor data to be simultaneously entered in the accounting records and the donor database. See Chapter 6 (Computerized Accounting). The acquisition budget should include money to train personnel to effectively use the system. Also keep in mind that computer software designers continually make improvements that obsolete existing systems. The technology budget should always include the purchase of regular upgrades to the software programs. Using the Internet to communicate with the nonprofit's constituents and the public can quickly recoup the cost of designing and maintaining a web site.

Respect the Organizational Structure or Change It

People managing a nonprofit should read and understand the organization's charter and bylaws and then see that the rules are followed. Find out if the board of directors or trustees hold regular meetings documented with reasonably detailed minutes of its decisions. Are new board members and officers chosen annually in accordance with the bylaws? Is proper notice of meetings communicated to responsible parties in a timely manner? Does a board executive committee hold regular meetings with the organization's managers? Does the finance committee meet regularly to review periodic financial reports that reflect comparisons to the approved budget? These issues are discussed in Chapter 2 (The Role of the Board). Determine whether the organization has a special relationship with another nonprofit; specific rules govern the activities of nonprofits established to support another organization.

Know Who's in Charge

Separation of duties is a cardinal rule for fiscal responsibility. Know who's in charge and who's responsible for what. Financial management is more successful when the right mix of people work with a full knowledge of their job and the interrelationships between those jobs. The hierarchy established depends on the form of organization. Most commonly, a nonprofit is managed by its board of directors, which is either chosen by its membership or the existing board members themselves as a self-perpetuating body. The board sets policy; the staff carries out the programs and manages the organization according to the policies. The board must be sufficiently involved so that the staff does not function as the board. Board governance policies, expressed in written procedures, make it possible for all to know their role and work in concert. The written procedures can also facilitate certain tasks that are difficult, for example, firing an ineffectual but well-loved executive director. Always ask if the board sets policy rather than making daily operating decisions? See Chapter 2.

Economic Conditions Must Be Anticipated

Economic conditions influence the nonprofit's revenue and expenditure flows and must be considered during the planning process. An inflationary or deflationary period may have a significant impact. A real-estate price collapse has in the past and may again cause hardships for nonprofits and the demise of those that were not properly prepared for the resulting economic changes. The political climate sometimes demands balanced federal and state budgets and can cause significant changes in the way nonprofits are financed.

Long-Range Planning Is Indispensable

Plotting the future of the organization according to agreed goals and objectives and converting them into definitive steps over a period of three, four, five, or more years greatly improves chances for success. Each program a nonprofit initiates requires energy and financial resources that are more economically recouped when the program functions successfully over a period of years. In other words, a decision to expend funds to launch, or continue, programs should be made in view of their impact over a period of time. Thought of in business terms, the nonprofit invests its resources in each program it sponsors. One of the objectives of long-range planning is to evaluate the return on such investments over a number of years. Similarly, an important part of the planning process plots annual revenues and expenditures. Such budgets approved by the board prior to the beginning of each fiscal year and regularly monitored throughout the year can contribute immeasurably to a nonprofit's financial stability as discussed in Chapters 3 and 4.

Know Why the Nonprofit Organization Has Tax-Exempt Status

Ask to review Form 1023 or 1024, the original application seeking recognition of tax-exemption, to find out why the IRS decided the nonprofit qualified for tax-exempt status. Look at a few years of operational history, such as the annual reports or Forms 990, to see if the purposes of the organization have changed or evolved. Identify the exempt constituency—those persons the organization was formed to serve. Check information about the organization on the Internet at Guidestar.org or on the nonprofit's own web site. Ask whether exempt constituents are in fact being served or if, instead, the private interests of specific individuals are benefited to the detriment of the intended beneficiaries. Find out who's in charge of whatever reports are required by local, state, and federal authorities regulating the nonprofit and be assured they are timely filed. See Chapter 8.

COMPREHENSIVE FINANCIAL PLANNING CHECKLIST

As a prelude to the book, the following checklist (Exhibit 1.2) presents a series of issues with specific questions to be asked in evaluating the financial well-being of a nonprofit organization. Chapters of the book in which the issues are explained in detail are noted. Some issues that are beyond the book's scope, such as insurance and investment manager performance, deserve attention with other references.

Exhibit 1.2   Financial Planning Checklist for Nonprofit Organizations

This checklist poses questions a nonprofit's chief financial officer in concert with the board treasurer or finance committee might review each year. Most answers should be yes, but some questions deserve a no answer or specific information. The objective is to comprehensively survey financial-planning issues that face a nonprofit organization at least annually.

A. Organizational Issues (Chapter 2)

1. Is the organizational mission clearly defined? ☐

   a. Is the mission statement printed? ☐

   b. When was it updated? ☐

   c. What does IRS Form 1023 or 1024 say purposes are? ☐

2. Does the nonprofit organization have a functioning board with members that exercise their fiduciary responsibilities? ☐

   a. Are board meetings regularly scheduled and well attended? ☐

   b. Does the executive committee supervise interim decisions? ☐

   c. Do minutes of directors' meetings reflect efforts to be responsive to exempt constituents by considering the best interests of the community (members or general public) served? ☐

   d. Are decisions made with the view that funds belong to public or members? ☐

3. Should a finance and/or audit committee of the board be established? ☐

Exhibit 1.2   Financial Planning Checklist for Nonprofit Organizations
(continued)

4. Do board and organizational policies ensure management and
   control of the organization's resources?   ☐

   a. Are prudent-investor rules followed?   p. 2

   b. Are personal financial interests monitored?   p. 2

   c. Is there short- and long-term financial and program
      budgeting?   p. 3

   d. Are approved plans evaluated systematically?   p. 4/5

   e. Is satisfaction of funding requirements monitored?   p. 5

   f. Is proper risk management assured?   p. 5/6

   g. Must information be disclosed to the public?   p. 6

5. Are government reporting requirements satisfied?   p. 6

B. Monitoring Self-Dealing (Chapter 2)

1. Are there written policies governing financial transactions
   between the organization and its insiders (and families)?   ☐

2. Should each board member sign a formal conflict-of-interest
   statement?   ☐

3. Were there any financial transactions with insiders this year?   ☐

   a. Are compensation levels reasonable   ☐

   b. How do salaries compare to similar organizations?   ☐

   c. Was anything brought from or sold to an insider?   ☐

   d. If so, was fair market paid?   ☐

   e. Was the value determined by independent parties?   ☐

4. If such a transaction occurred, did private inurement
   (benefit) result?   ☐

5. Does the organization sell products or goods produced by
   volunteers or members?   ☐

6. Did the nonprofit accept gifts that require other organizational
   funds to manage or conserve (a bailout)?   ☐

C. Short- and Long-Term Budgeting (Chapter 4)

1. Is the budgeting process timed properly?   ☐

   a. Do officers of the board change prior to budget approval?   ☐

b. When is the annual meeting? ☐

c. Is budget approved after major funding requests are filed? ☐

2. What type of budget is appropriate for this organization? ☐

   a. Would zero-based budgeting allow critical evaluation of priorities to allow cutback in spending? ☐

   b. Would a functional expense or line-item budget allow for review of program goals? ☐

   c. Are budgets required for fundraising events? ☐

3. Are the proper steps taken in the budget preparation process? ☐

   a. Are goals and objectives for a three- to five-year period developed first (long-range plan)? ☐

   b. Are long-range goals quantified—raising an endowment, financing new facilities, or increasing staff? ☐

   c. Are the prior year's results evaluated? ☐

      i.   Were objectives achieved? ☐

      ii. If not, were they unreasonable? ☐

      iii. What caused variances? ☐

      iv. Were changes indicated by the ratio analyses (Chapter 7)? ☐

   d. Have objectives for the coming year been established? ☐

   e. Are new projects sufficiently documented? ☐

   f. Are estimates of revenues and cost of programs realistic? ☐

   g. Is the budget proposed by staff for approval by board (with intervening steps as the nature of organization dictates)? ☐

4. Are ancillary budgets prepared to implement the overall budget? ☐

   a. Cash flow projections (Chapter 5)? ☐

   b. Investment objective ☐

   c. Membership renewal tracking? ☐

   d. Capital expenditure timing? ☐

   e. Restricted fund budgets? ☐

5. Is a follow-up system for monitoring the budget in place? ☐

   a. Are financial reports timely, with actual expenses and income compared to those budgeted? ☐

Exhibit 1.2   Financial Planning Checklist for Nonprofit Organizations *(continued)*

    b. Are variances analyzed to determine why projects were wrong? ☐

    c. Is the budget revised for recurring changes during the year? ☐

D. Evaluating Performance with Ratio Analyses (Chapter 7)

    1. Is the current ratio or working capital level (cash and other liquid assets compared to debts due in one year) at least 2:1? ☐

    (Note that too low a ratio means short-term liquidity problems; too high sacrifices income for safety.) ☐

    2. Is the acid test or quick ratio at least 11: (Cash today compared to debts due in one month)? ☐

    3. Do contributors or members satisfy pledges on time? ☐

    4. Compare this year's sources of funding to the past five years (has funding base changed?). ☐

    5. Measure activity costs to overall expenses (how much of revenue devoted to exempt purposes?). ☐

    6. Analyze profitability or lack of it for all income-producing activities. ☐

E. Satisfying Donor Restrictions (Chapter 5)

    1. Are all restricted funds accounted for separately?

       a. Endowments ☐

       b. Plant and equipment ☐

       c. Restricted donations or grants ☐

    2. Does the cost of managing and reporting on a restricted fund outweigh its benefit? ☐

    3. Can costs associated with restricted projects be identified? ☐

    4. Are matching-fund grant records available to measure compliance? ☐

    5. Is endowment income sacrificed for capital appreciation? ☐

    6. What is the extent of, and reason for, interfund borrowing? ☐

F. Prudent Investor Rules (Chapter 5)

    1. Is maximum amount of interest earned on short-term cash funds? ☐

       a. Is cash flow planning utilized for liquid funds? ☐

b. Are bills paid on a scheduled basis? ☐

c. Are services invoiced timely allowing efficient collections? ☐

d. Is there a membership renewal system? ☐

e. Are non-interest-bearing accounts kept to a minimum? ☐

f. Can tracing of restricted funds be accomplished through the accounting system rather than separate bank accounts? ☐

g. Are higher long-term interest rates obtained on funds committed for use in over six months or a year? ☐

h. Is short-term borrowing available if needed? ☐

2. Are investment policies prudent? ☐

a. Is priority given to preservation of the endowment or to production of current income? ☐

b. Are provisions made for replacement of the physical plant or facilities or adequate working capital for new projects? ☐

c. Should property be leased or purchased? Mortgaged or not? ☐

3. Is an outside investment manager utilized? ☐

a. Are investment yields measured using a "true" cost basis? ☐

b. Should the organization use two different managers? ☐

c. Are investments sufficiently diversified? ☐

d. Should stocks be sold? Collections deaccessioned? ☐

4. Is the organization prepared for economic change? ☐

a. For disinflation or inflation? For business cycles? ☐

b. How will new tax legislation affect the organization? ☐

c. What are the funding source consequences of such changes? ☐

G. Hazards for Risk Management

1. What measures are needed to protect assets from risk of loss? ☐

a. Does the nonprofit organization have insurance or does it self-insure? ☐

b. Are deductible levels commensurate with working capital? ☐

c. Are properties maintained in good condition? ☐

d. Is adequate data available to identify lost items? ☐

e. Is property labeled and identified with organization's name? ☐

Exhibit 1.2   Financial Planning Checklist for Nonprofit Organizations
(continued)

---

    f. Are personnel required to be trained before using equipment? ☐

    g. What is the condition of physical facilities in which they work? ☐

  2. What types of insurance are appropriate for the organization?

    a. Basic fire, theft, vandalism, and extended coverage? ☐

    b. Liability? ☐

    c. Workers' compensation? ☐

    d. Volunteer/employee auto usage? ☐

    e. Officers and directors' errors and omissions? ☐

    f. Fidelity bond for employees/volunteers? ☐

H. Public Disclosure of Financial Condition (Chapter 6)

  1. Are annual financials issued by independent accountant(s)? ☐

    a. Is positive assurance provided by an audit appropriate? ☐

    b. Would negative assurance provided by review suffice? ☐

    c. Is a compilation report sufficient? ☐

    d. Is an audit required by funding agencies or foundation? ☐

    e. Is a "single-audit" required under OMB A-133? ☐

    f. Do revenue sources, level of internal accounting skills,
      or lack of internal control indicate a need for an audit? ☐

  2. Have recommendations in the auditor's management letter
    been implemented? ☐

  3. Are accounting/business staff and systems adequate? ☐

    a. Are monthly financial reports, including budget
      comparisons, available in a timely manner? ☐

    b. Are they provided to the board? ☐

    c. Would hiring a trained bookkeeper/accountant reduce
      outside accounting fees and/or allow timely reports? ☐

    d. Should records be computerized? ☐

  4. Is a system of internal control in place? (Chapter 6) ☐

    a. Does the bookkeeper or custodian of funds sign checks? ☐

    b. What contracts are approved by a board member? ☐

    c. Is proper documentation required for expenditures? ☐

    d. Are personnel policies in writing? ☐

    e. Must expenditures in excess of the budget be approved? ☐

    f. Are asset records adequate (serial numbers, etc.)? ☐

5. Are archival records evidencing exempt activities kept (theater performance program, student grades, patient records) (Chapter 8)? ☐

6. Is a governmental reporting compliance calendar maintained? ☐

    a. Are Forms 990, 990PF, or 990-T filed timely? ☐

    b. Are payroll taxes withheld, deposited timely reported? ☐

    c. Must Forms 5500 be filed for benefit plans? ☐

7. Is Form 990 made available to public upon request? ☐

8. Are fundraising or lobbying limit tax disclosures made? ☐

9. Must the nonprofit register as a charitable solicitor or file other repors in states in which it conducts activities? ☐

2

Structuring the Organization for Fiscal Strength

Who's in charge? Who's responsible? The answers to such simple questions can mean the difference between a nonprofit's financial success and failure.

The manner in which positions are created and filled, duties are divided, and efforts are coordinated determines the degree to which an organization can carry out its mission in a fiscally sound manner. Financial management is most successful with the right mix of people all knowing what their jobs are. The board, along with the nonprofit's constituents, funders, and regulatory authorities, serve to monitor and help assure that the nonprofit carries out its mission in a fiscally sound manner. The hierarchy depends on the form, maturity, and size of the organization, but together those in charge must:

- Plan for and measure funding needs.

- See that necessary resources are raised.

- Assure that the acquired assets are dedicated to the nonprofit's mission.

- Keep financial records to prepare reports and analyses of financial activity.

- Comply with regulatory and grantor requirements.

- Respect the public nature of resources with good governance and transparency.

A nonprofit organization's hierarchy is illustrated in the organizational charts similar to Exhibits 2.1, 2.2, and 2.3. By showing exactly who will be in charge of what, this chart maps the relationship between the people

Exhibit 2.1   State Association of Nonprofit Managers Organization Chart

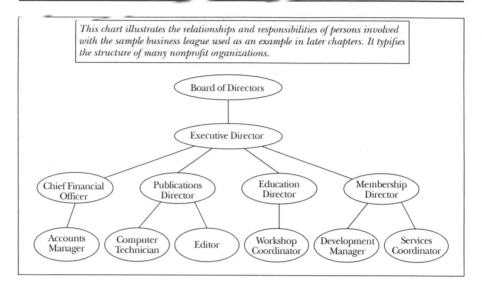

This chart illustrates the relationships and responsibilities of persons involved with the sample business league used as an example in later chapters. It typifies the structure of many nonprofit organizations.

Exhibit 2.2   Endowed Educational Institution Investment Management
Organization

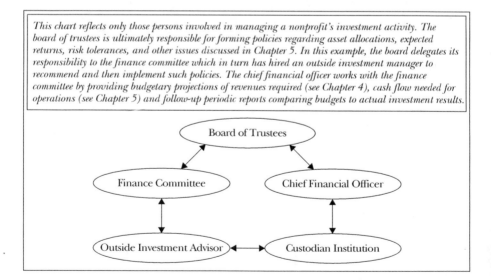

This chart reflects only those persons involved in managing a nonprofit's investment activity. The board of trustees is ultimately responsible for forming policies regarding asset allocations, expected returns, risk tolerances, and other issues discussed in Chapter 5. In this example, the board delegates its responsibility to the finance committee which in turn has hired an outside investment manager to recommend and then implement such policies. The chief financial officer works with the finance committee by providing budgetary projections of revenues required (see Chapter 4), cash flow needed for operations (see Chapter 5) and follow-up periodic reports comparing budgets to actual investment results.

responsible for meeting the objectives listed above. Job descriptions for each position detailing duties, responsibilities, and qualifications supplement the chart. Optimally, organizational and personnel policies are documented in a manual for all to see, understand, and follow.

Exhibit 2.3 SHAPE Organizational Structure for Stabilization and Preservation

This chart, used by SHAPE Community Center in Houston, Texas, portrays another way in which a nonprofit's management structure can be illustrated.

Board of Directors
Community volunteers with ultimate legal and financial authority/responsibility for SHAPE.
Executive Director
Management Staff
Operations; Program; Child Care Administration; Bookkeeping; Community Enterprises Managers: BETA Store, Cafe, Silkscreening Manufacturing and Sales.
Operations and Programs Staff/Contractors
Includes paid staff/contractors and volunteers that perform day-to-day functions in the operation of SHAPE programs and services.
Council of Elders
Leaders of the community with wisdom and experience.
Community
Addressing the ever-changing needs of our community in both a responsive and proactive manner is the mission of SHAPE. What/who is our community in 1996? in 2006?
Advisory Council
Committee volunteers mobilized and working with the board of directors on (1) short-term fundraising/financial/audit and operations matters and (2) long-term development of strategic plan.
Fundraising/Finance/Audit Committee
Community volunteers representing private sector, public sector, and children/families.
Operations Committee
Community volunteers representing private sector, public sector, and children/families.
Strategic Planning Committee

ESTABLISHING THE HIERARCHY

Who's in charge and who's responsible are distinct issues. The governing body—usually the board of directors or trustees—is ultimately responsible for carrying out the nonprofit's mission and safeguarding its resources. The board, however, is entitled to delegate responsibility and the concomitant authority to a chief executive (CEO) and/or operating officer (COO). In other words, the CEO is in charge and manages the day-to-day affairs of the organization. The board should look to the CEO to lead the organization, manage programs that accomplish its mission, and represent the nonprofit organization in its community. The CEO in turn hires, works with, and supervises a chief financial officer, or CFO, and other necessary personnel.

The CFO may have one of many titles, including CFO, vice president for finance, chief financial officer, director of finance, business manager, controller, or even treasurer. The CFO participates in planning and budgeting and then follows up by monitoring cash inflows and outflows, making sure financial resources are actually devoted to planned purposes, and seeing that expenditures remain in balance with available assets.

Typically, a nonprofit organization is focused on its mission and places most emphasis on its programs. For good reasons, precious resources are allocated to hiring the best possible professionals—the teachers, the physicians, or the artists. Those creative individuals often lack financial training and experience. When department heads are selected for other than business skills, the CFO's financial skills may be vital to an organization's fiscal health. Reliance on the CFO also grows with the size and program scope of the nonprofit organization. The financial affairs of a statewide nonprofit organization with branches in 20 towns are necessarily more complicated than the affairs of a church with a congregation of 200 persons.

Who beyond the board, the CEO, and the CFO should be involved in financial planning depends again on the size, breadth, and maturity of the organization. Program managers, department heads, volunteer committee chairs, and other persons actively involved in carrying out the nonprofit's activities can and, some say, should participate in the planning processes. Their input is particularly useful in budget preparation as described in Chapter 4 (Scheduling Budget Process). Outside accountants serve an important oversight and advisory role, as discussed below (Inside and Outside Accountants). The best financial planning team will be unique to each individual nonprofit. For guidance, the planners can consider the fashion in which for-profit businesses organize themselves.[1]

---

[1] A thorough discussion of organizational structure for nonprofit organizations is beyond this book. The Resources section contains references that can be studied by those seeking more information on the subject.

THE ROLE OF THE BOARD

A nonprofit organization is typically governed by its board of directors or trustees. Although the board controls the organization, the board members do not beneficially own the organization and may not operate it to serve their own private purposes or those of their families. Board members are expected to carry out the organization's mission in the best interest of its constituents—the charitable beneficiaries or members. Upon dissolution, a nonprofit organization exempt as a charity must either give its remaining assets to another charitable organization or governmental unit or spend them on charitable purposes. Except for restricted funds donated to accomplish a project not undertaken or completed that might be returnable to the donor, nor can charitable funds may be returned to donors or board members. A business league, a union, and other mutual societies may, under certain circumstances, rebate its accumulated surplus to members if building such a reserve were not a primary purpose of the organization. Nevertheless, the governors of a mutual society must also serve without self-interest.

The board members govern and direct the nonprofit's affairs, but are not expected to operate it. The board selects officers and agents to whom it delegates the job of managing day-to-day activities. This separation of roles is key to allowing the directors to oversee and monitor the organization's activities. In a modest-sized nonprofit with few staff members to manage the organization, some directors may necessarily serve in overlapping positions. Especially in those situations, policies should be established to avoid board interference in operations.

Standards for Directors

Depending on the legal form of organization, a nonprofit's governors may have a variety of titles, including directors, trustees, council members, or elders. Their responsibilities, termed *fiduciary duties* by the legal profession, have evolved through legislation and judicial interpretations. Specific duties are set out in the Model Nonprofit Corporation Act to establish a standard of conduct to which an individual corporate director can adhere.[2] Conducting oneself in accordance with the rules provides a director some protection if a controversy arises due to actions of the organization's personnel. The extent of such legal protection, referred to as *immunity*, varies from state to state and may apply differently to trustees of private trusts. The rules of conduct should serve as a guide in establishing a nonprofit's organizational structure and determining the reliance the management and funders can place in the board.

---

[2] The American Bar Association Business Law Section published a Revised Model Nonprofit Corporation Act in 1987 that has been adopted by some states. Revision of the model was pending as of October 2007.

The model says a director's fiduciary duties fall into two basic catego-ries: the duty of care and the duty of loyalty. These duties require the direc-tor or trustee, including his or her duties as a member of a committee, to exercise caution and prudence in establishing policies and making decisions regarding the organization. Traditionally, board members are also expected to respect and adhere to the organizational documents, the charter and bylaws, of the nonprofit in what has been referred to as the duty of obedi-ence. Attentive management is required. The director's duty of care expects one to act in good faith and fulfill his or her responsibilities by:

- Exercising independent judgment when participating in decisions of the board

- Being informed as to data relevant to board decisions

- Regularly attending meetings

- Monitoring the organization's activities, assessing the efficiency of the organizational structure, and providing for both short- and long-range planning

- Reviewing internal and external financial reports to evaluate fiscal conditions, to assure moneys spent for nonprofit purpose, and to compare actual results to approved budgets

A director may make decisions based on information and reports received from others whom the director reasonably regards as trustworthy. In reviewing information, the director is expected to use good common sense. Decisions should be made using what in a for-profit corporate setting is called the "Business Judgment Rule."[3] The guidelines allow a director to rely on information, opinions, reports, or statements, including financial statements and other financial data, if prepared or presented by:

- One or more officers or employees of the corporation whom the director reasonably believes to be reliable and competent in the matters presented

- Legal counsel, public accountants, or other persons as to matters the director reasonably believes are within their professional or expert competence

- A committee of the board of which the director is not a member, as to matters within its jurisdiction, if the director reasonably believes the committee merits confidence

---

[3] See *Guidebook for Directors of Nonprofit Corporations*, 2nd ed., issued in 2002 by the Nonprofit Corporations Committee, Section of Business Law, American Bar Association, and edited by George W. Overton and Jeannie Carmedelle Frey.

The duty of loyalty requires that a director act with trustworthiness and integrity. Diligent and honest management is essential. The director's actions must be in allegiance to the organization, its mission, and the constituents to be served. A director who takes advantage of the organization's assets, for example, for purposes other than those of the organization violates the duty of loyalty. A conflict-of-interest policy can be adopted to govern a transaction that might cause a violation of this rule. This function is particularly important to avoid the payment of excessive compensation that can subject the director approving such transactions to penalties and result in bad press for the organization.[4] A director whose private interests are in conflict must disclose that fact and absent him- or herself from decisions regarding the conflicted matter. A director also has a responsibility to keep information about the organization's affairs in confidence until it is publicly disclosed.

Each nonprofit director or trustee should be familiar with the specific standards applicable to the state(s) in which the nonprofit operates. Since directors who follow the standards are provided some legal protection, prospective directors will want to be assured the nonprofit has organized itself in a fashion that will enable them to act in compliance with the standards. As discussed in the introductory remarks in Chapter 1, there has been significant criticism of the governance policies of some nonprofits in recent years. Though they do not change the basic concepts outlined in this chapter, specific suggestions from the Panel on the Nonprofit Sector, the American Bar Association, and the IRS are referenced in this chapter.[5]

Impact of Sarbanes-Oxley

Standards applicable to publicly traded corporations were significantly revised by the Public Company Accounting Reform and Investor Protection Act enacted in 2002 in response to the Enron scandal, referred to as *Sarbanes-Oxley*, in attribution to the Congressional sponsors, and *SOX*. Sarbanes-Oxley has limited, but important, impact on nonprofits. The rules intend to create an atmosphere of governance for organizations in which malfeasance and purposeful obfuscation cannot occur. Two provisions apply to nonprofits, the second of which uses amazingly strong language, as follows:

- *Whistleblower rule.* A method for handling complaints about financial improprieties or other misuse of the organization's resources that assures confidentiality for those who report the problem should be adopted. The policy should encourage disclosure and protect the employees who bring incidents to the attention of the board and provide a process to investigate such reports.[6]

[4] See discussion in the introduction to Chapter 1, and this chapter (Filling Board Positions)
[5] See discussion and footnotes 4, 5, and 6 that list the web sites for these organizations in Chapter 1.
[6] Title VIII, Section 802 of the act.

- *Record retention.* Anyone who "knowingly alters, destroys, mutilates, conceals, covers-up, falsifies, or makes a false entry in any record, document, or tangible object with the intent to impede, obstruct, or influence the investigation or proper administration of any matter . . . is subject to imprisonment."[7]

Attention to these provisions is critical and beyond the scope of this book. Each nonprofit will be well served by recruiting the services, either pro bono or for pay, of qualified legal counsel to design and implement these important rules.[8] The enhanced emphasis on the governance and financial transparency of nonprofits will undoubtedly bring additional reforms. Readers must be alert during this evolution of governance standards for nonprofits.

A Director's Duties

A nonprofit director's role is to act on behalf of others. Whether or not called trustees, directors are in a position of trust. Their wards are the members of the general public the organization was established to serve. Their relationship to the organization is somewhat like that of parent to child. As the nonprofit's parents, directors oversee and provide guidance based (one hopes) on their good judgment and integrity. The organization's volunteers and staff (sometimes including the directors) must be left to grow and function independently while relying on the directors to maintain a structure within which the mission can be accomplished.

The actual tasks performed by the director depend again on the size and scope of the nonprofit's activities. At a minimum, a director should regularly attend board meetings for the purpose of reviewing and condoning the activities that are carried out on a daily basis by the managers and staff. Meeting dates should be regular—first Mondays of the month at 5 PM, for example. Minutes of the meetings should be circulated in advance of the succeeding meeting at which their approval is requested. The applicable code of conduct for directors of nonprofit organizations found in state law defining fiduciary responsibility should always be followed.[9] Exhibit 2.4 provides a checklist for visualizing and actualizing the standards applicable to the fiduciary role and contains suggested issues for which the director is responsible.

---

[7] Title XI, Section 1102, dealing with destruction of records.
[8] See Peggy M. Jackson and Toni E. Fogarty, *Sarbanes-Oxley for Nonprofits.* Hoboken, NJ: John Wiley & Sons, 2005, and American Bar Association Coordinating Committee on Nonprofit Governance, *Guide to Nonprofit Corporate Governance in the Wake of Sarbanes-Oxley*, 2005, for guidance on the process.
[9] Ibid., note 2; also see Jack B. Siegel, *A Desktop Guide for Nonprofit Directors, Officers, and Advisors.* Hoboken, NJ: John Wiley & Sons, Inc., 2006.

Exhibit 2.4   A Board Member's Checklist of Fiduciary Duties

This checklist can serve as a board member's guide to meeting fiduciary responsibilities. Some questions have simple yes/no answers for actions taken personally by the director. Others prompt the director to ask if others have carried out responsibilities delegated by the board. References to chapters where the issue is presented appear in parentheses.

The Duty of Care

1. Am I sufficiently informed to perform my director role with prudence and caution (Chapter 2)?

   a. Do I regularly attend board and committee meetings? ☐

   b. Have I read the charter and bylaws? ☐

   c. Did I review the mission statement, long-range plans, basis for tax exemption, and other documents? ☐

   d. Have I become informed about any significant contractual obligations or potential claims on organizational assets? ☐

   e. Are minutes of all board and committee meetings sent to members regularly in advance of meetings? ☐

   f. Are periodic financial reports, compared to approved budget amounts and received on a timely basis (Chapter 6)? ☐

   g. Are the organization's newsletters and other publications reviewed regularly to assure adherence to exempt purposes? ☐

   h. Are meetings of sufficient length and frequency to allow adequate discussion of the issues? ☐

   i. Are independent consultants with adequate knowledge engaged to provide expert advice when needed ? ☐

2. Is the organizational structure adequate to assure an efficient and fiscally sound operation (Chapter 2)?

   a. Are internal financial controls in place (Chapter 6)? ☐

   b. Do independent accountants (Chapter 2) issue financial reports at least once a year? ☐

   c. Are local, state, and federal compliance rules followed (Chapter 8)?

   • Has an exempt status checklist been completed? ☐

   • Is charitable solicitation registration required? ☐

   • Are payroll tax reporting and deposits current? ☐

Exhibit 2.4   A Board Member's Checklist of Fiduciary Duties *(continued)*

- Are ERISA/Labor Department standards followed? ☐
- Do private foundation rules apply? ☐

d. Are personnel policies written, published, and monitored at least annually by a board committee? ☐

e. Have restricted or endowment fund covenants been met? ☐

f. Is investment performance for endowment, working capital, and restricted funds monitored regularly (Chapter 5)? ☐

g. Are duties delegated sufficiently? ☐

h. Should an executive committee be formed? ☐

i. Are other board committees needed? Finance? Audit? Strategic planning? ☐

j. Should staff serve on the board (Chapter 2)? ☐

3. Do long- and short-range financial plans exist (Chapter 4)?

a. Are financial budgets for one- to three-year periods approved before the fiscal year begins? ☐

b. Is ratio analysis applied to periodic financial information to detect problem areas (Chapter 7)? ☐

c. Are staff members required to develop feasibility plans for proposed projects? ☐

d. Are plans monitored after approval to assure accomplishment of both financial and organizational goals? ☐

4. Can I rely on staff and consultants?

a. Are the legal and accounting advisors independent? ☐

b. Is the quality of the service rendered high? Are they sufficiently knowledgeable about nonprofits? ☐

c. Can I satisfy the "business judgment" rule?

d. Is the executive director evaluated periodically? Does she or he conduct regular personnel reviews? ☐

e. Can volunteers be relied upon? ☐

5. Are board members involved, qualified, and dedicated?

a. Is there a good system for seeking new members? ☐

b. Are efforts made to balance skills and interests? ☐

c. Are the interests of the constituents represented? ☐

d. Is there rotation of members or staggered terms? ☐

e. Is there new-member orientation? ☐

f. Are board members provided a written manual of organization documents, policies and procedures? ☐

The Duty of Loyalty

1. Do I have allegiance to the organization? Am I satisfied that the organization is accomplishing its mission and serving its constituents (Chapter 1)?

   a. Am I sure resources are dedicated in accordance with the charter, trust instrument, and funding agreements? ☐

   b. Are exempt purposes being carried out (Chapter 8)? ☐

   c. Are assets preserved and replenished (Chapter 5)? ☐

   d. Is there honest and efficient management? ☐

2. Do I oversee and supervise appropriately with regard to my position?

3. Do I use my position and power to advance personal interests (Chapter 2)?

   a. Am I, my business, or my family involved in a conflict of interest with the organization? ☐

   b. If any self-interested transaction occurs, is due diligence exercised to ensure that no private benefit results? ☐

      i. Did I fully inform other members of the board? ☐

      ii. Did I absent myself from discussion and voting? ☐

      iii. Is there adequate outside evaluation and appraisal of the transaction? ☐

   d. Does the nonprofit organization have a written conflict-of-interest policy? ☐

   e. Are there interlocking directorates or affiliated for-profit or nonprofit entities? ☐

Reviewing Financial Reports

The duty of care requires that a director be informed regarding the non-profit organization's financial affairs. Board members actively involved in the affairs of a modestly sized nonprofit organization may need to receive and review all the reports listed in Exhibit 2.5. It is prudent for board members in nonprofits of all sizes to receive and review the independent

Exhibit 2.5 Inventory of Financial Reports

A suggested list of financial reports needed by board members to oversee a nonprofit's financial affairs follows. The duty to review may be delegated to the finance or executive committee dependent upon the nonprofit's structure. Indicate date of review and whether or not delegated.

Type of Financial Report	Delegated	Date
1. Independent accountants' financial statements		
• Opinion letter	(yes/no)	_____
• Statement of Net Assets	(yes/no)	_____
• Statement of Activity or Statement of Changes in Net Assets	(yes/no)	_____
• Statement of Cash Flows	(yes/no)	_____
• Notes to Financial Statements	(yes/no)	_____
• Management letter	(yes/no)	_____
2. Monthly (quarterly) status reports with actual compared to budget	(yes/no)	_____
• Ratio analyses and statistical program service reports	(yes/no)	_____
• Investment performance	(yes/no)	_____
3. Projected budgets for future periods		
• Operational revenues and costs by function	(yes/no)	_____
• Capital expenditures	(yes/no)	_____
• Cash flow analyses	(yes/no)	_____
• Fundraising projections	(yes/no)	_____
4. Personnel report showing number of permanent, temporary, and volunteer workers; compensation, raises, vacation accruals, benefit costs, compared to the prior year	(yes/no)	_____
5. Insurance/risk management evaluation with associated costs	(yes/no)	_____
6. Financial planning and annual tax compliance checklists	(yes/no)	_____
7. Form 990, Return of Organization Exempt from Income Tax	(yes/no)	_____

accountants' reports and the monthly status reports, items 1 and 2 on the Inventory of Financial Reports. In a larger organization with functioning finance and executive committees, the board may delegate total responsibility to the committee members to oversee financial affairs. If he or she does nothing else, each director should review the Form 990 filed with the IRS, the annual opinion accompanying the financial reports and the management letter, if issued, prepared by outside accountants. It is not sufficient for the board treasurer to simply say to the board members, "Everything is okay, so you need not bother to read the auditor's report or see the 990."

The financial reports are most useful when they are issued and reviewed close to the closing date of the financial information. Unfortunately, nonprofit organizations that receive reduced-fee or pro bono accounting services may not be able to expect timely service. For a calendar-year nonprofit, timely service would mean receipt of the outside accountants' reports by the directors no later than April 30. Monthly activity reports with budget comparisons should be expected by the twentieth of each succeeding month. The time frame for budget planning is discussed in Chapter 4 (Scheduling Budget Process).

Chapter 6 contains brief descriptions of an accounting system's components and explains the fashion in which financial information is accumulated and presented. Accounting terms like *accrual method, restricted funds,* and *receivables* are defined according to the accounting standards and sample financial statements are provided. A nonprofit manager or volunteer board member who lacks financial training can study Chapter 6 to enhance his or her ability to read the financial reports and participate in financial decisions they, as board members, are required to make. The Form 990 filed each year with the IRS is on the list of financial reports important for board members to review because it is available for all to see on the Internet and is often the sole source of information about the organization reviewed by the general public and funders.[10]

FILLING BOARD POSITIONS

There is merit in the view that the board should include a lawyer, an accountant, a banker, a philanthropist, a doctor (for a hospital or medical research entity), a scholar (for a school or literary society), and so on. Ideally, board positions are filled with persons who, in combination, have the requisite skills to promote efficient functioning, maximization of financial resources, and successful performance of the nonprofit's worthy goals. To achieve this objective, begin by defining management positions in the areas

---

[10] Displayed at www.guidestar.org.

of proficiency required for smooth operation, for example, finance, human resources, program development and management, planning, and oversight. Then, seek prospects with knowledge and experience in such areas.

Finding Prospects

The nominating committee's job is to find candidates whose talents will contribute to the organization's success. Suitable candidates also exhibit a personal commitment to, or interest in, the nonprofit organization's mission. Posing a few questions will narrow the selection process:

- Will the nominee spend the time the job requires?

- Has he or she been involved as a volunteer or participant in the nonprofit's activities or in a similar project of another nonprofit?

- How long has the prospect been a member or donor?

- Are his or her friends or business associates involved?

- Will he or she enhance the respect of the community for the nonprofit?

- What technical skills will he or she bring to the organization?

The nonprofit organization should communicate its expectations clearly to prospective board members and organize itself to facilitate the involvement of new members.[11] Policies and procedures that include definitions of duties can be developed in a fashion similar to that discussed later in this chapter (Roles of the Treasurer and the CFO) in the context of the financial management functions.

Staff Representation on the Board

A commonly raised question is whether paid staff members can serve on a nonprofit's board of directors. There is no federal tax prohibition against having a paid staff member as a board member. In Texas, a director may serve in a staff capacity for compensation as long as the pay is reasonable and not in violation of his or her fiduciary responsibility. In California, however, no more than 49 percent of the board members may be staff members. Obviously, this question should be investigated under the laws of the state(s) in which the nonprofit operates.

---

[11] The Nonprofit Management Series Booklets published by Board Source, Washington, D.C., contain a wealth of information on this subject. Booklet 1 (out of 10) of the series is entitled *Ten Basic Responsibilities of Nonprofit Boards* by Richard T. Ingram (49 pages).

Whether it is a good idea to have staff representation on the board is another issue. Strong opinions, usually based on experience, are held on opposing sides. Those that favor staff representation argue that the voice of staff fosters realistic decision making, especially when decisions will impact staff operations. The contrary view is that staff persons are not in a position to exercise the necessary oversight for an impartial decision-making process. Nonprofit organizations should, however, consider including the chief staff person on the board or, at the very least, asking him or her to attend board meetings.

Compensation for Board Service

Another issue is whether board members should receive director's fees or be compensated for serving on the board. This question has several components and is somewhat controversial. Some think directors of charitable nonprofits should—and most do—serve as volunteers to evidence the public service nature of the organization. Again, local law may apply. Texas, for example, permits such payment as long as the amount paid represents reasonable compensation for the work performed. For federal income tax purposes, all types of nonprofit organizations, including private foundations, public charities, and others, can compensate directors so long as the amount paid is reasonable. Penalties, however, can be imposed when excessive benefits are received.[12]

If directors are to be paid compensation, or are involved in any other financial transaction with the nonprofit, organizational protocol for conflicts of interest must be followed.[13] Job description outlining their duties and responsibilities, plus documentation that proves the reasonableness of the amount paid, is necessary. The Panel on the Nonprofit Sector recommends that no fees be paid to board members except to reimburse the cost of board participation.[14] The Internal Revenue Service agrees.[15]

---

[12] Internal Revenue Code § 4941 entitled *Self-Dealing*, prohibits most financial transactions between directors and trustees and the foundation regardless of the benefit gained by the foundation, but allows the payment of reasonable compensation. Similarly IRC §4958, entitled *Intermediate Sanctions*, imposes penalties when excess benefits are paid to those that direct and control the charity or civic association.

[13] See Conflict-of-Interest Policy later in this chapter.

[14] Ibid., note 6, Section III, part 10, p. 662.

[15] Regarding Compensation Practices, their *Good Governance Policies for 501(c)(3) Organizations* issued in February 2007 say, "A successful charity pays no more than reasonable compensation for services rendered. Charities should generally not compensate persons for service on the board of directors except to reimburse direct expenses of such service. Director compensation should be allowed only when determined appropriate by a committee composed of persons who are not compensated by the charity and have no financial interest in the determination." http://www.irs.gov/pub/irs-tege/good_governance_practices.pdf.

Number of Directors

To prevent deadlocks in voting, it is advisable that the organization keep the number of directors to an *odd* number. In deciding on the appropriate odd number, the role the board members will play in governance must be considered. What skills are needed for what committees? How much supervision does the staff require? What amount of work is expected to be accomplished by board committees? Answers to these questions can help arrive at the total number of directors suitable for a particular organization. Keep in mind the bylaws might need to be changed to increase the number. Even though the organizers of a newly established nonprofit expects it can function with 7 or 9 board members, it might be advisable for the bylaws to allow a much larger number, say up to 21, to leave room for future growth. The Panel on the Nonprofit Sector suggests that there should be a minimum of three board members.[16]

Some organizations prefer to limit the number of board members. Many people choose not to accept the responsibility and potential liability of serving as a board member. For these reasons and others, organizations may wish to establish an advisory group auxiliary to their board. This group(s) usually includes persons who bring credibility to the organization through their positions in the community and specialized skills.

ROLES OF THE TREASURER AND THE CFO

As the typical nonprofit organization is conceived and begins its life, activities may be performed and managed by volunteers. Often, there are few, if any, paid staff members. In many cases, the young nonprofit cannot afford to pay independent accountants or even a bookkeeper. The work of paying the bills, preparing the financials, and reconciling the accounts may fall to the board treasurer. Nonetheless, the nonprofit should adopt policies and procedures that define the roles that will, as the organization matures, be performed by different people. Exhibit 2.6 provides a model for establishing duties appropriate to the separate roles of a board treasurer and a CFO.

INSIDE AND OUTSIDE ACCOUNTANTS

A certified public accountant (CPA) is trained to evaluate the financial condition of an entity and issue reports to explain such condition. A CPA will also evaluate the systems for maintaining financial records and securing internal

---

[16] *Strengthening Transparency Governance Accountability of Charitable Organizations,* a final report to Congress and the Nonprofit Sector, June 205, Section III, part 13, p. 75.

Exhibit 2.6   Roles of the Treasurer and the Chief Financial Officer

> *The separate roles of the board treasurer and the chief financial officer are outlined in this checklist. The attributes, duties, and distinctions between the positions should be respected and written, even if the organization in its earliest stages has one person performing both roles.*

The Board Treasurer

Exercise of Fiduciary Responsibility

- Attend meetings and actively participate in activities. ☐
- Assure development of short- and long-term policies/plans. ☐
- Monitor policies/plans with regular financials. ☐
- Review financial transactions among insiders and the nonprofit. ☐

Assurance of Financial Accountability

- Oversee inside/outside accountants. ☐
- Establish financial committee of board, if organizational size dictates. ☐
- Monitor internal controls and procedures. ☐
- Depending on staff size and capability, the board treasurer may also:
  - Cause to be prepared or prepare regular financial reports and budgets. ☐
  - Sign checks. ☐
  - Negotiate contracts/purchases. ☐
  - Oversee compliance filings and public information. ☐
  - Manage or cause investments to be managed. ☐

Chief Financial Officer

Responsibility for Financial Data

- Process primary financial documents (bills, payments, bank statements, donor information, etc.) as they are received into the organization. ☐
- Monitor investments, receivables, payables, inventories, and other financial matters requiring supervision. ☐
- Follow internal control procedures and accounting systems manual. ☐

Exhibit 2.6   Roles of the Treasurer and the Chief Financial Officer
(continued)

- Produce accounting journals and ledgers. ☐
- Maintain filing system. ☐
- Create efficient audit trail. ☐
- Label files for record retention purposes. ☐
- Identify restricted fund transactions. ☐

Produce Financial Reports.

- Basic financials, including Statement of Net Assets (Balance Sheet), Statement of Activity (Support, Revenue, and Expenses), Statement of Cash Flows, Statement of Functional Expenses (by program) ☐
- Supplemental planning reports for:
  - Event income/expense, cash flow projection, investment yield reports ☐
  - Daily sales/attendance/contributions reports ☐
- Maintain compliance with governmental regulations and reports.
  - Maintain payroll system and deposit taxes timely. ☐
  - File all reports due according to a compliance calendar (Exhibit 8.2). ☐
  - Compliance with granting agency reporting/application deadlines. ☐
- Coordinate timing and work with outside auditors, both CPAs and governmental/agency.
  - Prepare workpapers and detail analyses requested. ☐
  - Respond timely with information requested. ☐
- Plan for, develop, and coordinate approval of budget(s). ☐

Facilitate Flow of Financial Information

- Work with and train staff and/or volunteers. ☐
- Work with the board treasurer. ☐
- Prepare any financial analyses requested by finance committee and board; and attend meetings when invited. ☐
- Review policies/procedures and provide recommendations to the board regarding fiscal management. ☐
- Maintain technical skills required to perform the job and seek qualified advisors when needed. ☐

control over the entity's funds. The CPA's technical skills and experience are also useful in budgeting, financial planning, computer system design, and other financial aspects of a nonprofit organization.

Although CPAs bring valuable skills to a board of directors, the American Institute of Certified Public Accountants (AICPA) code of ethics stipulates that the CPA must be independent of an entity to issue an audited opinion. An independent CPA does not serve on the board of directors or have a financial interest in the nonprofit. Other levels of financial reporting may be issued by a CPA who serves on an organization's board. However, it is advisable for all organizations to adopt a policy of retaining independent accountants for financial reports including reviews and compilations as well as audits. The levels of service a CPA may perform is discussed later in this chapter (Selecting Financial Reporting Services).

Financial Management Team

Ideally, the complete financial management team consists of the board finance committee headed by the treasurer, outside advisors (investment managers or bankers), the chief financial officer, the staff (the inside accountants), and the advice of the independent CPAs (the outside accountants). In reality, a nonprofit's resources or circumstances may not allow it to engage all desirable members for the creation of such a team. In such cases, the organization should identify and analyze the consequence of overlapping or combined roles.

Some combinations of duties simply cannot be performed effectively by a single member of the financial team. Consider a church treasurer who also serves as the church bookkeeper and essentially functions as the chief financial officer. In such a situation, another board member (elder) should sign checks and oversee and review the financials, although this duty would, if the team were complete, be the treasurer's.

As the functions involved in evaluating the nonprofit's financial affairs become complicated, the finance committee can be fragmented. The new parts might include a budget committee, an audit committee, and an investment committee, and others devoted to specific issues, such as budgeting, new building construction, or salary review.

Defining Inside and Outside Accountants

Inside accountants are primarily responsible for financial reporting and planning on a daily basis. They pay the bills, collect the money, and keep the books. They plan, prepare, and monitor budgets, see that sufficient resources are available for the tax-exempt mission, and maximize the use of available resources for the benefit of the organization's constituents.

The *outside* accountants evaluate financial reports prepared by inside accountants and inform the public regarding the validity of the financials by issuing a formal opinion. The treasurer, with the help of the finance committee, coordinates the work of both inside and outside accountants. To provide a credible evaluation, the outside accountants must be truly independent, or impartial. They must be free of any vested interest in the organization. Appropriate fiscal control can be achieved only with the division of these duties. The prudent organization will not rely on a single volunteer treasurer to serve as both its inside accountant, by keeping its books, and its outside accountant, by issuing an opinion about the periodic financial statements stemming from such records.

SELECTING FINANCIAL REPORTING SERVICES

CPAs perform three levels of financial reporting service: audits, reviews, and compilations. The highest level of reliance can be placed on audits, though all three services can be used to present the nonprofit organization's financial statements. For all three services, the starting point in the CPA's evaluation process is the nonprofit organization's internally produced financials, which the organization is responsible for maintaining. The nature of the work performed by the accounting firm in providing different levels of service is discussed below.

Some organizations adopt a policy of rotating their accounting firm periodically. For public companies, the Sarbanes-Oxley Act mandates rotation of lead audit partners (or firms) at least every five years.[17] Those recommending rotation seek a different or fresh look at the organization's financials.[18] Conversely, many organizations find the wealth of information accumulated over time by their auditors serve them well in evaluating financial practices and decisions. Certainly knowledge of the nonprofit's history allows more informed recommendations as the nonprofit evolves. Discussions on this issue will undoubtedly continue.

Understanding the Auditing Process

An audit provides the highest degree of assurance an accountant can offer that the financial statements are a fair presentation of the data shown. The CPA examines the financial records for the reporting period and

---

[17] Jack B. Siegel points out in his book *A Desktop Guide for Nonprofit Directors, Officers, and Advisors,* "This has caused a number of nonprofits to consider whether they should adopt auditor rotation as a best practice."
[18] The *IRS Good Governance Policies for 501(c)(3) Organizations,* issued in February 2007, recommend rotation every five years. See www.irs.gov/charities/charitable/article/0,id=167626,00.html.

certifies that the information is reliable. The accountant's report includes a reminder that the financial statements are the representations of the organization's management.

In performing an audit, the CPA conducts tests and procedures designed to ascertain the accuracy of the reported financial information. By no means are all transactions audited or examined. The CPA looks at a representative sample to determine whether one can reasonably expect that the procedures and documentation maintained for those selected items are indicative for all records. The CPA considers the level of internal auditing inherent in the nonprofit's organizational structure. The internal controls are reviewed to determine whether the nonprofit's system of checks and balances and its division of duties function to prevent misstatements or diversions of resources. See also Chapter 6 (Internal Controls) for further discussion of this matter.

The most distinguishing element of an audit as compared to a review or compilation is the process of obtaining outside verification of the organization's reported transactions for the year. The auditor writes to a sampling of the nonprofit's contributors and creditors, asking them to confirm the transactions by sending verification or explanation of differences directly to the CPA. Similarly, the auditor requests the nonprofit's bank(s) and financial institutions holding their assets to confirm or deny the existence of the accounts and the accuracy of the balances stated in the organization's balance sheet. Grantees may also be contacted to verify the receipt and purpose of the grants. The responses to such requests for outside verification are to be returned directly to the CPA firm.

The objective of this confirmation process is to go beyond the nonprofit organization's own record of the transactions. Independent validation enables the CPA to offer its assurance that the reported amounts are correct. Such validation creates an important distinction in the level of reliance that can be placed on an audit as opposed to either a review or compilation. The types of opinions that may be issued by the auditor are:

- *Unqualified.* An unqualified opinion says the financials clearly reflect the nonprofits financial position and operating results. It is also referred to as a *clean* opinion.

- *Qualified.* In a qualified opinion, the CPA says "except for_____," all is accurate. In situations where, for example, branch offices were not audited, appraisals were not obtained for a significant asset, or an inventory count was not performed in a timely manner at year-end, a qualified opinion will be required.

- *Adverse.* The financial statements do not fairly present the financial situation or there is a question as to whether the nonprofit is a going concern (i.e., debts exceed assets).

- *Disclaim.* The CPA is unable to express an opinion.

When to Audit

Nonprofits seek audited financial reports for a variety of reasons. Many governmental funding agencies and grantor foundations require an audited financial report. The Office of Management and Budget requires a separate *Single Audit* of certain federal grants. Some national or statewide organizations require their branches or chapters to obtain audited financial statements.

Without an imposed requirement that the organization seek an audit, many organizations consider the expense involved worth the result. The persons responsible for the nonprofit's financial affairs may recommend an audit to satisfy their duty of care, discussed in this chapter (The Role of the Board). Situations that may indicate a need for an audit, rather than a review or compilation, include:

- The nonprofit's funding sources allow for misappropriation. Donations collected by volunteers, sales of donated goods, individual ticket sales for public performances or trade shows are all examples of such funding sources.

- The sheer number of financial transactions deserves outside verification.

- Activities are conducted in a number of different locations.

- Internal control procedures are poor and need scrutiny and suggestions for improvement.

Review and Compilation Processes

In performing a review, the CPA evaluates the reasonableness of the financial information provided by the organization and discusses questions with the internal accountants. No outside confirmations are obtained and, therefore, no opinion is given as to the validity of the figures. The review opinion simply offers the negative assurance that the CPA found nothing wrong. Depending on the nonprofit's size and the complexity of its financial assets and transactions, an annual review may suffice to meet the board's fiduciary duty to oversee fiscal management.

A review might, for example, be an appropriate level of CPA service for a smaller organization with modest assets whose board members monitor the financial affairs regularly. An appropriate review candidate might be a nonprofit with a good internal control system and an active CPA treasurer who reconciles the banking records and prepares monthly financials throughout the year. A review may also serve the interests of a grant-making private foundation whose endowment is held in marketable securities, managed by a professional investment advisor.

In compiling, the CPA takes information from the nonprofit's accounting records and arranges them in financial statement format. No outside verifications, inquiries, analyses, or tests occur. Compilations are usually prepared for internal purposes only or as a by-product of the preparation of a tax return. Basically, the CPA preparing a compilation functions as an internal accountant. In larger organizations, a monthly compilation might be prepared by outside accountants for the board in addition to the year-end review or audit.

Requests for Proposals for Accounting Services

When seeking the services of an accounting firm for an audit, review, or compilation, organizations customarily request proposals from one or more firms. Exhibit 2.7 presents a model proposal letter.

Exhibit 2.7   Request for Proposal for Audit

The following letter requests a proposal from an accounting firm for an audit. Sending such letters to more than one accounting firm enables the organization to make comparisons before it makes its selection.

Community Benefit Projects Hometown, Texas
John J. Adams, Partner
Adams, Banks, & Coffee, CPAs
1111 National Bank Building
Hometown, Texas 77777

Dear Mr. Adams,

COMMUNITY BENEFIT PROJECTS (CBP) services the people of Hometown in many ways. We help the underprivileged by conducting training classes for the unemployed and after-school programs for sports and tutoring for our youths. We aid senior citizens with shut-in visits and transportation services. We greet newcomers to town with information and referrals. CBP invites you to submit a proposal to conduct audits of our financial statement and related information for the year 20XX. The audits must be in accordance with generally accepted accounting principles and meet governmental reporting requirements.

Audits: We are required to have two audits as follows:

- Audit of Statement of Net Assets, Statement of Activity and Functional Activities, and Statement of Cash Flows

- Single audit of our grants required under OMB Circular A-133, *Audits of Institutions of Higher Education and Other Nonprofit Institutions*, and the U.S. General Accounting Office's *Government Auditing Standards*

Tax Work: In addition to the annual audit, we require the following tax returns be prepared for filing in a timely manner:

- Form 990, Return of Organization Exempt from Income Tax

- Form 990-T, Exempt Organization Business Income Tax Return

Exhibit 2.7   Request for Proposal for Audit *(continued)*

Work schedule: Our staff is available to provide support and preparation of the underlying schedules based on your guidelines. We would prefer that you arrange a planning meeting in December prior to our year end. We expect the books will be closed by February 12, so that you could schedule the field work after that time. The report must be completed in draft form for presentation to the finance committee on March 20. The final report must be completed by March 31, the date of our annual meeting.

Qualifications: Please provide a description of your firm's qualifications to serve a tax-exempt organization such as ours, resumes of key personnel, and a list of other nonprofit organization clients.

Fee: Your audit proposals should reflect the total fee and include the time budgets for audit and tax work reflecting the number of hours and rate per hour for assigned personnel. (Note many nonprofit organizations request reduced rates in recognition of their nonprofit status.)

Site visit: We would welcome you to visit our offices in the coming weeks to obtain information necessary to make an accurate proposal. You can call our controller, Ms. Joan Levy, to schedule an appointment.

Proposal deadline: The proposal must be submitted by October 10. The finance committee will meet October 20 to review proposals and make a recommendation to the board of directors regarding the choice of auditors.

If you have any questions or would like further clarification of any aspect of this request for auditing services, please contact me or our Finance manager, Harry Smart. We look forward to receiving your proposal.

Sincerely,

John J. Hay, CFO

CONFLICT-OF-INTEREST POLICY

The Model Nonprofit Corporation Act requires that the directors of a nonprofit corporation abide by a duty of loyalty. As explained more fully under The Role of the Board above, the director must act in the best interest of the organization, not in his or her own interest. The federal tax law specifically requires that no profits or assets of an exempt organization inure to the benefit of officers and directors or other private individuals. Private foundations are also specifically prohibited from most financial transactions involving their directors and major contributors.

A fiscally prudent nonprofit organization will adopt a conflict-of-interest policy to ensure that personal benefit is not given to insiders as financial decisions are made. The policy expresses the nonprofit's ethical obligation to use resources solely for the benefit of constituents (or members). Transactions involving insiders are not necessarily prohibited, but they must be fully disclosed and subjected to scrutiny. All relationships and possible self-interest must be revealed and examined in a document similar to Exhibit 2.8.

The Forms 990 now ask whether the nonprofit has a conflict policy, and the IRS, in connection with the Form 1023, Application for Recognition of Exemption, asks if their version of the policy, shown in Exhibit 2.9, has been adopted.

Exhibit 2.8   Conflict-of-Interest Questionnaire for Board Members

A questionnaire similar to the one below may be used to make directors aware of the nonprofit's policy regarding conflicts of interest. The answers provide disclosure, identify, and explore the potential for self-interest arising in financial transactions.

Nonprofit organization (name the organization) is a tax-exempt organization which operates to benefit the general public (or the XYZ profession, certain workers, or church congregants or other suitable description of exempt constituents). We intend to avoid any possible conflict between the personal interests of those that govern our organization and operate it and our constituents. Therefore, we ask each of our board members and responsible staff persons to complete and sign this conflict-of-interest policy questionnaire.

*Name:*_____

*Position in nonprofit organization:*_____

Relationships: List any businesses in which you or members of your immediate family (parents, siblings, grandparents, children) have a financial interest through employment or private ownership.

Name of Business	Nature of Relationship
_____	_____
_____	_____
_____	_____

Permitted transactions: Circumstances may arise in which it would be financially beneficial to do business with you, your relations, or friends. Our policy allows transactions that are clearly shown to benefit our organization based on the information indicated below and approval by a two-thirds majority of the directors, not counting the interested party(ies).

Proposed sale or service: Describe a proposed financial transaction:

	Related Party	Bidder 1	Bidder 2
Suggest price:	_____	_____	_____
Payment terms:	_____	_____	_____
Delivery date:	_____	_____	_____
Other terms:	_____	_____	_____

Exhibit 2.8   Conflict-of-Interest Questionnaire for Board Members *(continued)*

To the best of my knowledge and belief, except as disclosed above, neither I nor any person with whom I have or intend to have a personal or business relationship is engaged in any transaction or activity or has any relationship that may represent a potential competing or conflicting interest as defined in the statement of policy.

Date: _____   Signature: _____

Exhibit 2.9   IRS Version of Conflict-of-Interest Policy

Conflict-of-Interest Policy

Article I

Purpose

The purpose of the conflict of interest policy is to protect XYZ CHARITY's interests when it contemplates entering into a transaction or arrangement that might benefit the private interest of an officer or director of the organization or might result in a possible excess benefit transaction. This policy is intended to supplement but not replace any applicable state and federal laws governing conflict of interest applicable to nonprofit and charitable organizations.

Article II

Definitions

1. Interested Person

Any trustee, principal officer, or member of a committee with governing board delegated powers, who has a direct or indirect financial interest, as defined below, is an interested person.

2. Financial Interest

A person has a financial interest if the person has, directly or indirectly, through business, investment, or family:

    a. An ownership or investment interest in any entity with which the organization has a transaction or arrangement,

    b. A compensation arrangement with the organization or with any entity or individual with which the organization has a transaction or arrangement, or

    c. A potential ownership or investment interest in, or compensation arrangement with, any entity or individual with which the organization is negotiating a transaction or arrangement.

Compensation includes direct and indirect remuneration as well as gifts or favors that are not insubstantial.

(A financial interest is not necessarily a conflict of interest. Under Article III, Section 2, a person who has a financial interest may have a conflict of interest only if the appropriate governing board or committee decides that a conflict of interest exists.)

Article III

Procedures

1. Duty to Disclose

In connection with any actual or possible conflict of interest, an interested person must disclose the existence of the financial interest and be given the opportunity to disclose all material facts to the directors and members of committees with governing board delegated powers considering the proposed transaction or arrangement.

2. Determining Whether a Conflict of Interest Exists

After disclosure of the financial interest and all material facts, and after any discussion with the interested person, he/she shall leave the governing board or committee meeting while the determination of a conflict of interest is discussed and voted upon. The remaining board or committee members shall decide if a conflict of interest exists.

3. Procedures for Addressing the Conflict of Interest

   a. An interested person may make a presentation at the governing board or committee meeting, but after the presentation, he/she shall leave the meeting during the discussion of, and the vote on, the transaction or arrangement involving the possible conflict of interest.

   b. The chairperson of the governing board or committee shall, if appropriate, appoint a disinterested person or committee to investigate alternatives to the proposed transaction or arrangement.

   c. After exercising due diligence, the governing board or committee shall determine whether the organization can obtain with reasonable efforts a more advantageous transaction or arrangement from a person or entity that would not give rise to a conflict of interest.

   d. If a more advantageous transaction or arrangement is not reasonably possible under circumstances not producing a conflict of interest, the governing board or committee shall determine by a majority vote of the disinterested directors whether the transaction or arrangement is in the organization's best interest, for its own benefit, and whether it is fair and reasonable. In conformity with the above determination it shall make its decision as to whether to enter into the transaction or arrangement.

Exhibit 2.9   IRS Version of Conflict-of-Interest Policy *(continued)*

4. Violations of the Conflicts-of-Interest Policy

a. If the governing board or committee has reasonable cause to believe a member has failed to disclose actual or possible conflicts of interest, it shall inform the member of the basis for such belief and afford the member an opportunity to explain the alleged failure to disclose.

b. If, after hearing the member's response and after making further investigation as warranted by the circumstances, the governing board or committee determines the member has failed to disclose an actual or possible conflict of interest, it shall take appropriate disciplinary and corrective action.

Article IV

Records of Proceedings

The minutes of the governing board and all committees with board delegated powers shall contain:

a. The names of the persons who disclosed or otherwise were found to have a financial interest in connection with an actual or possible conflict of interest, the nature of the financial interest, any action taken to determine whether a conflict of interest was present, and the governing board's or committee's decision as to whether a conflict of interest in fact existed.

b. The names of the persons who were present for discussions and votes relating to the transaction or arrangement, the content of the discussion, including any alternatives to the proposed transaction or arrangement, and a record of any votes taken in connection with the proceedings.

Article V

Compensation

a. A voting member of the governing board who receives compensation, directly or indirectly, from the Organization for services is precluded from voting on matters pertaining to that member's compensation.

b. A voting member of any committee whose jurisdiction includes compensation matters and who receives compensation, directly or indirectly, from the Organization for services is precluded from voting on matters pertaining to that member's compensation.

c. No voting member of the governing board or any committee whose jurisdiction includes compensation matters and who receives compensation, directly or indirectly, from the Organization, either individually or collectively, is prohibited from providing information to any committee regarding compensation.

Article VI

Annual Statements

Each director, principal officer and member of a committee with governing board-delegated powers shall annually sign a statement, which affirms such person:

a. Has received a copy of the conflicts of interest policy,

b. Has read and understands the policy,

c. Has agreed to comply with the policy, and

d. Understands the organization is charitable and in order to maintain its federal tax exemption it must engage primarily in activities that accomplish one or more of its tax-exempt purposes.

Article VII

Periodic Reviews

To ensure the organization operates in a manner consistent with charitable purposes and does not engage in activities that could jeopardize its tax-exempt status, periodic reviews shall be conducted. The periodic reviews shall, at a minimum, include the following subjects:

a. Whether compensation arrangements and benefits are reasonable, based on competent survey information, and the result of arm's length bargaining.

b. Whether partnerships, joint ventures, and arrangements with management organizations conform to the organization's written policies, are properly recorded, reflect reasonable investment or payments for goods and services, further charitable purposes and do not result in inurement, impermissible private benefit or in an excess benefit transaction.

Article VIII

Use of Outside Experts

When conducting the periodic reviews as provided for in Article VII, the organization may, but need not, use outside advisors. If outside experts are used, their use shall not relieve the governing board of its responsibility for ensuring periodic reviews are conducted.

Adopted by Trustees on____20____   Officer

3

Financing the Dream

Nonprofit organizations are based on hope,
sometimes on prayer, and almost always on dreams.
Optimum planning can turn dreams into
realizable goals.

A nonprofit's reason for existence or its primary goals are mission-based—
to cure the sick, to advance a profession, to discover new technologies, to
educate the public, and to do other tasks of benefit to others. The nonprofit's financial goals are secondary to its mission and not the top priority.
Financial success, though, can enhance an organization's ability to provide
services. A nonprofit's managers need to ask this *chicken-and-egg* question:
What comes first, the mission and programs designed to accomplish the
mission or the cash to finance the program? Actually, it is useful to realize
that aspirations and financial resources intertwine as management works
to coordinate the two. Both goals must be recognized and coordinated to
identify results in both fashions. Attention to this unruly pair is the process
that turns dreams into realizable goals.

BALANCING MISSION AND FINANCES

The nonprofit organization's dual goals may make its planning processes complex. Most for-profit entities can focus on their single-minded profit motive.
While the for-profit exists to enrich its owners, the nonprofit has the twin
purpose of accomplishing its mission and meeting the financial goals necessary to do so. Financial planning for a nonprofit, therefore, must be thought
of as a cycle of intertwining philosophical and financial concerns as shown in
Exhibit 3.1. Evaluation and development of organizational goals and ambitions are critical, but assessment of available resources and past results is an
equal part of the process. The work of keeping the pair in coordination never

Exhibit 3.1   Financial Planning Cycles

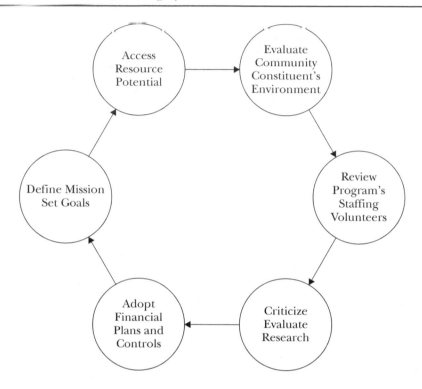

really stops. It is always useful to translate and study the results attained by nonprofits in terms of mission-oriented goals and financial goals.

Mission-oriented goals and financial goals may also be viewed as concurrent objectives that advance each other. The two sets of goals should interact in a complementary fashion. Each should facilitate the other.

Certainly, the trust an organization's constituents place in its programs can only enhance the likelihood of financial success. A community center that is recognized for the worth of its programs has a far easier time gaining financial support than a center with great ideas but no accomplishments. In other words, resource acquisition or fundraising is most successful when program presentations are successful. At the same time, the converse is true. The best of programs may fail if a nonprofit's financial management is poor. Overextended programs quickly earn a negative reputation with financial constituents. It is much harder to raise funding to cover a deficit in a struggling or discontinued program than to seek support for a prospective program.

The relationship between the mission-oriented goals and financial resources is critical. Exhibit 3.2 illustrates the connections that should be made between mission-oriented goals and its financial ones.

Exhibit 3.2   The Balance Between the Mission and Financial Resources

---

This chart is deliberately simple to clearly reflect the connections that exist between a mission-oriented goal and its financial counterpart. Each goal on the left is matched with a related financial solution or means to attain the necessary resources for program performance.

Goal to Accomplish Mission	Financial Resource
Feed more children to relieve the suffering of the poor.	Get donations of outdated food from grocery stores and cafes.
Double the congregation to spread the church's spiritual message.	Market the church through weekly gospel programs on public radio.
Publish more training manuals to better educate our league members.	Replace overworked staff with skilled writers to update and expand manuals.

DEFINING THE MISSION

Prior to spending the first penny, the organization must understand its dreams and define its mission and the accompanying mission-oriented goals. Equally important, of course, is translating those goals into realizable steps using a process that can be called *quantifying the mission.* How many children would the organization hope to serve? How many papers can be presented?

Ideally, the board, the staff, and possibly major supporters convene in an annual or biannual meeting to develop a consensus on what exactly the aim of the organization will be. What needs to be accomplished as the end result of the organization's activities and efforts must be established? Many nonprofit organizations engage trained facilitators to guide these meetings to develop what are often called *strategic plans*. The facilitator brings impartiality to the deliberations and can help balance the many versions of the organization's dreams in the minds of the participants. A thorough discussion of the mission side of the long-range planning process is beyond the scope of this book, but a wealth of information is available on the subject.

Mission Statement

The consensus reached at the planning meeting is most often referred to as the mission statement. This statement succinctly presents the organization's reason for being. A business league's mission statement, for example, might read as follows:

> The Association of Nonprofit Managers is a league of chief operating and financial officers of nonprofit organizations formed to provide professional training, assistance, and career support, and to enhance communications among its members.

A new organization's creators write the first version of its mission statement when completing IRS Form 1023 or 1024 to seek recognition of tax-exempt status. Plans for the programs will flesh out the expressed statement of purpose, or mission. Financial projections are presented to reflect the available (or expected) financial resources. Questions such as how the programs will be supported, who will be served and where, how recipients will be charged, what assets will be used to conduct the programs, and other relevant details must be answered. These answers are considered and, if necessary, the mission program will be revised as a part of an ongoing planning process.

Prioritizing Goals

Using the system suggested earlier in this chapter for identifying connections between the mission and financial resources is not always easy. But planners must assure that sufficient financial resources can be made available to accomplish the mission. Although tough choices will have to be made at times, it is always important to keep aspirations high. The process of prioritizing goals should be performed with the full extent of the mission in mind. The steps involved in achieving the mission must first be stated before they can be arranged in a logical manner. Exhibit 3.3 illustrates a chart to be used as a model for listing organizational objectives.

Exhibit 3.3   Prioritizing Organizational Objectives

A chart such as the one below may be used to weigh organizational objectives. Each nonprofit's list of goals being considered as a part of the annual planning process and mission-statement update would be compiled as shown, for example, in the right column. Participants would then weigh, or prioritize, the choices by grading the objective on a scale ranging from 9 (highest) to 1 (lowest).

Priority Level 1–9	Goal	Organizational Objective
	A	Expand number of persons served, locations where services are provided, hours or days on which service offered.
	B	Increase type or scope of services offered to existing clientele.

Priority Level 1–9	Goal	Organizational Objective
	C	Decrease scope of or eliminate services, seek another organization to perform the services or fill the need, or teach the service recipients self-sufficiency (conduct self-extinguishing projects).
	D	Improve quality of services provided (supplement nurse practitioner with weekly physician; change hiring criteria to require higher education or experience level).
	E	Create new projects or expand existing ones.
	F	Phase out organization's existence by developing decentralized units to conduct now centralized programs.
	G	Enhance visibility in community and with constituents.
	H	Increase number of and services provided by volunteers and hire a volunteer coordinator.
	I	Raise standards for program—for graduation, for certification, for permanent or senior membership, or for participation.

ASSESSING THE RESOURCES

The next step is to assess financial resources with respect to the priorities for organizational objectives. A viable organization is one that continually assesses resources. The staff is alert to coming changes and prepares for them. How well the organization serves its constituents should be foremost in the minds of planners during the annual evaluation.

Did the membership or volunteers grow in number? Did the nonprofit receive public recognition for its accomplishments? Is there a need to seek new volunteers or to engage consultants to measure the organization's performance? Are sufficient liquid assets available to initiate a new program? The information gathered during the budgeting process, discussed in Chapter 4, may be used to make both micro and macro resource decisions.

Making Micro Resource Decisions

Micro resource questions focus on the mission-oriented program rather than the nonprofit's fiscal health as a whole, but the best answers to micro questions will keep the connection between mission-oriented goals and financial ones in view. For example, the mission-oriented goal of doubling the number of hungry children fed by an organization may necessitate an increase in financial resources as shown in Exhibit 3.2. In such a case, the additional children are much more likely to be fed if the organization planners translate the mission-oriented goal into related financial goals, such as hiring additional staff, buying more food, and receiving more contributions or grants.

However, when a nonprofit needs to limit, rather than increase, its use of financial resources, financial issues should first be explored in terms of the mission. The selection of the best financial solution will depend on the mission-oriented objectives that may still be achieved.

A symphony society that faces budget cuts needs to view all aspects of its choices to determine which programs best serve its mission and what may still be accomplished. The planners must ask whether the primary goal is to present formal concerts in the civic hall. Should they capture the finest rendition of a great symphony on an electronic medium for public distribution and sale? Do they want outreach into the community by performing chamber music in schools? Should they hire the most highly qualified director to teach and develop the finest musicians?

Once the planners have reexamined and redefined the symphony society's mission-oriented goals, they can begin the process of matching the mission with the best financial solutions. Exhibit 3.4 outlines various financial alternatives.

Macro Resource Analysis

A critical look at the organization's big financial picture is also part of the planning process. An overall view of the nonprofit's macro financial condition provides an opportunity to evaluate its long-term fiscal stability. The planners first study financial reports similar to those found in Chapter 6 (Design of the Financials), beginning with the Statement of Financial Position (also called Balance Sheet). Questions are asked, such as, "Are the unrestricted fund balances sufficient to survive a change, temporary or otherwise, in funding sources?" The financial information can be evaluated using the financial indicators and ratios discussed in Chapter 7 (Financial Indicators to Critique Performance).

Depending on the results of the financial analysis, the nonprofit would adopt specific financial steps to be taken to improve its macro, or overall, financial situation. This process can be explored by studying the fiscal attributes of a model church presented in Exhibit 3.5.

For planners who look only at the bottom line, the church's financial picture may seem healthy. The model church has $108,510 in *unrestricted net assets* (formerly called *fund balances*), on its balance sheet. The church has $390,000 of assets and $281,490 of debt. This situation indicates that, during its life, the church has accumulated assets well in excess of the money it owes. If the church was a for-profit company, its stockholder's equity would equal $108,510.

But a closer examination of the balance sheet reveals an entirely different picture. The church simply does not have the money to pay the bills that

Exhibit 3.4   Chart for Weighing Choices: Financial Solutions for Tight
Budgets

*This chart may be used by a nonprofit faced with revenue reductions and/or need
to reduce spending. The financial solutions for each organization will be different. The CFO or financial committee might prepare this list of possible actions as
a worksheet to guide a discussion to evaluate the choices. Each person would rate
the financial steps with a V for Viable or a U for Unacceptable.The steps can also
be weighted by assigning priorities as in Exhibit 3.3.*

Financial Step	Rating V or U
Research public perception of accomplishments; interview recipients of services or participants to evaluate their needs/ideas.	
Establish a development department to increase contributor/ member base.	
Raise membership prices, service fees, publication rates.	
Charge for services now offered for free.	
Eliminate programs or downsize staff.	
Merge with or absorb another organization.	
Sell off underutilized assets.	
Improve marketing, hire development specialist, publish magazine, sponsor public events, involve celebrities, and so on.	
Reallocate resources to realign strengths and weaknesses.	
Establish new measurement systems to evaluate performance.	

will soon be due. Compare the top asset line of $20,000 (which represents the
assets currently available to pay bills) with the top liability line of $81,490.
They show a negative current ratio of 1:4. In other words, the debts coming
due in the next year amount to four times the current assets.

First glances at the bottom line of a financial statement can be mislead-
ing. The church's unrestricted net assets of more than $100,000 might appear
reasonable for an organization of its size. However, after looking at the various categories of assets, one observes that the fund balance is comprised of
noncash assets, that is, the church's equipment and buildings. Because these
assets are used daily in conducting services, they certainly are not available
for sale to pay bills. This condition leaves the church vulnerable. A delay of

Exhibit 3.5   Holy Spirit Church Statement of Financial Position
(December 31, 20XX)

This exhibit is designed for use in connection with the discussion of macro resource decisions and is based on the financial report shown in Exhibit 6.6.

Current (liquid) assets	$20,000
Operating equipment and furnishings	120,000
Buildings	250,000
Total assets	390,000
Current liabilities	81,490
Long-term debt	200,000
Total liabilities	281,490
Unrestricted net assets	108,510
Total liabilities and net assets	$390,000

a few days or weeks in funding can produce such havoc as late creditor payments, missed paychecks, and/or delinquent employee tax deposits, among other financial embarrassments and failures.

Once the church planners have recognized their financial problem, they can develop macro resource goals to correct the situation. Over the course of the next few years, the church should particularly focus on *financial goals A, B, C, and D* shown in Exhibit 3.6. No doubt those four would all be given top priority on the chart used to prioritize macro resource goals. To facilitate realization of the macro goals, the church would also establish specific steps to balance its mission and financial goals using the chart shown in Exhibit 3.2.

In facing its financial problem, the church would implement a formal financial planning system. First, it would prepare a budget for the coming year following the guidelines in Chapter 4. Next, it would convert the budget into a monthly cash flow projection as illustrated in Exhibits 5.3 and 5.4. The church's financial managers would study Chapter 6 to evaluate the existing accounting system. If necessary, the system would be upgraded to ensure they will receive timely and informative financials, compared to the approved budget, each month throughout the year. Finally, one hopes the church would begin to use ratio analyses as explained in Chapter 7 (Financial Indicators to Critique Performance) to currently evaluate and improve the current funding situation.

Exhibit 3.6   Prioritizing Macro Resource Goals

This chart lists the nonprofit's Macro Resource Goals. The CFO or financial committee would prepare the list of goals as a part of the annual planning process. Each nonprofit's list would be unique but similar to the examples shown in the right column. Planning participants would then weigh, or prioritize, the choices by grading the objective on a scale ranging from 13 (highest) to 1 (lowest).

Priority Level 1–13		Macro Resource Goal
	A	Establish working capital base.
	B	Maintain three (or more) months' operating cash balance (improve cash flow).
	C	Retire debt or reduce accounts payable.
	D	Seek endowment funding to provide investment income to offset annual fluctuations in grant funding?
	E	Buy or build permanent facilities.
	F	Establish branches statewide or citywide.
	G	Increase portion of exempt function revenues.
	H	Conduct marketing campaign (to expend membership, to educate public about mission, sell tickets, and so on).
	I	Raise salaries or increase the number of personnel.
	J	Improve employee benefits—retirement, medical, education, child care, cafeteria plan.
	K	Establish a volunteer guild.
	L	Replace major governmental funding source or be prepared if funding is cut or eliminated.
	M	Hire chief financial officer to improve financial reporting, monitoring, and planning.

4

Budgeting

A budget is the numerical expression of an organization's dreams that serves as a guide or measure of acceptable financial performance.

After the organization has examined its priorities and refined its mission in view of expected financial resources, it is time to prepare the budget. The budget charts a direction for allocating and maximizing the use of resources and ideally identifies any financial problems that could arise in the coming year. The budget itself can also provide indicators for evaluating employee performance and gives the staff goals to reach and steps to achieve them.

BUDGET-PLANNING ISSUES

As a financial measure of the nonprofit's goals, a budget compiles programs planned for the coming year in some detail based on assumptions. It shows how many students the nonprofit expects to enroll next year, how much money it plans to spend to save which endangered species, or the number of members expected to become new and renewing dues-paying constituents next year. The scope and size of a nonprofit's programs and asset base dictates the complexity of its budget(s). One or more years of projected revenues and expenses might be suitable dependent on the sophistication of the nonprofit's long-range planning and its computerized accounting system. In its most complete form, a budget is a compilation of plans and objectives of management that covers all phases of operations for a specific period of time.[1] Exhibits in this chapter illustrate budget workpapers for a model business league, State Association of Nonprofit Managers.

---

[1] Robert Rachlin and H. W. Allen Sweeney, *Handbook of Budgeting*, 3rd Ed. New York: John Wiley & Sons, 1993.

It is important to distinguish between the portion of the budget based on reality and that stemming from dreams. The budget planner needs both a healthy skepticism and optimism. Necessarily, the process involves uncertainty; decisions are made about the indeterminate future that the organization cannot control. Should the financial planners simply assume that a nonprofit's existing programs will continue? Which, if any, of the nonprofit's programs are essential? How will the organization face the unknown? Before developing the budgets, the planners must make the specific policy decisions outlined below.

Balancing

The nonprofit must decide whether the budget is to be balanced. Should the budget reflect sufficient revenues to pay expenses? An organization that needs to build up its working capital might want to project a budget imbalance of revenues over expenses (a profit). Program priorities are also balanced in an effective budget. The nonprofit's capabilities and resources are allocated or balanced to impact the maximum audience or beneficiaries. Those programs to continue and those to close are balanced. The wrenching debate over balancing the federal budget each year illustrates the complexity of the task.

Most nonprofits cannot afford the luxury of an imbalanced budget and fewer still have the accumulated surpluses or financial stability to borrow money to finance a deficit year. Organizations that charge for their services may not be able readily to increase the price of programs. Nonprofits are not like the lettuce growers who seem to simply announce, "Sorry folks, the weather was bad, so we are doubling the price of your leafy salad greens."

Timing

Budgets need to be completed within a time frame that allows for planning in advance of the applicable period. As discussed in more detail later in this chapter (Who Participates in Budgeting?), the lead time required for grant requests and multiyear projects make it imperative that the budget process be properly timed. Realizable target dates for the completion of the planning should be established for all to follow. Some aspects of the budget process—accumulation of statistical data and client evaluations—are timeless and are ongoing tasks constantly feeding the budget system and keeping it current.

Evolution

Although not a common practice, some organizations might adjust the budget throughout the year as changes are indicated. The budget establishes criteria that signal the need for change or identify the need to refine or alter the course of action. Although it may be difficult to modify once it is adopted, a budget found to be unrealistic or inaccurate can be changed. In its original or unaltered state, it continues to signal a problem even though the issue has been addressed and changes have been made to correct it. A budget updated for the new situation might better serve as a monitoring system as it is tailored to respond to unforeseen conditions. Most nonprofits choose to continue to compare current financial information with the originally approved budget and provide footnotes, as shown in Exhibit 6.6, explaining changing conditions that have caused the results to be less or better than originally expected (or hoped).

Accountability

The people expected to accomplish the program(s) and financial goals expressed in the budget are identified and actively involved in the budgeting process. Responsibility is associated with those that are actually capable of realizing the goals. A budget developed, monitored, and revised in the controller's office is of little value to the program staff. Without the active awareness and participation of those actually carrying out the activities, a budget's usefulness is diminished as discussed later in this chapter (Who Participates in Budgeting?).

Zero Basis versus Incremental

The budgeteers adopt either a zero-based system or an incremental methodology for preparing the financial guideline for the coming year. Zero-based budgeting essentially incorporates the planning process for setting organizational objectives as part of the budgeting process. Starting from a zero base, the financial planners assume no program is necessary and no money need be spent. The programs to continue will have to be proven worthy, as well as fiscally sound, following an orderly evaluation of all elements of revenue and spending. Each program is examined to justify its existence and is compared to alternative programs. Priorities are established, and each cost center is challenged to prove its necessity. The worthiness of a program justified with abstract terms is tested and must be proven to be financially sound to be adopted. For this reason, program managers may feel threatened by and not participate as fully in the zero-based method.

An incremental budget, however, treats existing programs and departments as preapproved, subject only to increases or decreases in financial resources allocated. Essentially, the nonprofit's historical costs are the base from which budget planning starts. The focus of the budgeting process is on the changes anticipated in last year's numbers; the planning process has already been completed and program priorities established. Incremental budgeting is, therefore, often less time consuming and also felt by some to be less threatening to program managers.

Forecasting

The organization must decide whether its budget is to be based on measurable and predictable statistics or only on good guesses. Although it is useful for program officers to have a healthy dose of optimism about predicting the future results, outside opinions may prove to be more accurate. When the organization can afford the expense involved, business marketing tools, such as statistical sampling of previous donors or program participants, can be applied to forecast or predict a reasonable level of donations for the coming year. The effort to maintain peripheral data systems that capture statistical information such as renewal rates, source of renewals, results of marketing campaigns, and other historical profiles must also be considered as discussed later in this chapter (Statistical Operational Data) and illustrated in Operational Indicators found in Exhibit 7.1.

TYPES OF BUDGETS

Before the budget process begins, the nonprofit considers the type of budgets that are best suited to its planning and monitoring needs. The basic budget is a comprehensive look at the entire organization's overall projection of the revenues or financial support and its expected expenditures for the coming year. An endless number of varieties of this basic form can be created for particular planning and assessment needs.

Specialized or supplemental budgets can provide a pinpoint focus on fragments of financial activity germane to individual programs or revenue centers. For example, a membership organization establishes goals for its various categories of members. The number of members and the amount of funds received from members can be quantified according to useful information including (1) new, renewing, and nonrenewing; (2) unsolicited versus solicited or (3) zip code, religious preference, age, and so on, as shown in Exhibit 4.5. Such quantification of membership serves to guide not only the business office in monitoring cash flow projections, but also the development, and possibly the program department throughout the year as membership projections are matched up with the unfolding reality. Exhibits 4.6 through 4.15 illustrate of a model business league's budgets and worksheets. A listing of all potential budget reports would be extensive, but a brief look at the possibilities includes at least the following:

- Annual, quarterly, and/or monthly projections of income and expense for the entire organization as well as each of its divisions, departments, branches, and so on

- Revenue projections by type, such as contributors or student tuition

- Individual project, department, branch, or other cost center projections

- Service delivery costs by patient, by student, by member, or other client

- Capital additions (building or equipment acquisition)

- Investment income (and/or total return)

- Cash flow (short and long)

- Fund-raising event revenue and expenses

- Bookstore, pharmacy, or resale shop sales

- Personnel projections

ADVANTAGES AND DISADVANTAGES

The budget is a tool to allocate resources and to implement strategic plans effectively. It can be a useful tool that produces a spectrum of beneficial results. Significantly it serves as a guideline for program personnel directly involved in carrying out activities enabling them to numerically measure their accomplishments and respond to unexpected changes. Management personnel can use it to evaluate staff performance. Like any tool, the budget can produce either advantages or disadvantages, depending on the skill and diligence with which it is used. The chief advantages and benefits of effective budgeting include:

- A thoroughly planned and implemented budget enhances the likelihood a nonprofit will be financially successful.

- A budget is a tool that translates abstract goals into determinable bites or bits; it stipulates performance goals.

- The planning and preparation process leading to a budget force the organization to look at itself, to set priorities, and to narrow its choices.

- A budget facilitates coordination and cooperation between the various programs and financial departments.

- Periodic budget comparison to actual financial performance can signal trouble and allow for response to changing conditions in a timely manner.

- A budget measures financial performance in relation to the non-profit's expectations.

The chief *disadvantages or difficulties* with the budgeting process include:

- The karma or presence of controls may stifle creativity.

- There is a natural tendency to emphasize cost control due to a myriad of unknowns at the time of budget preparation.

- A budget based on historical information alone can fail to keep up with a rapidly changing society.

- Too often, nonfinancial personnel do not participate in the budgeting process resulting in operational blueprints approved without the input of program personnel.

- A budget is not easy to implement and may require extra enthusiasm among the management personnel to be accepted as useful.

WHO PARTICIPATES IN BUDGETING?

A good budget cannot assure its own success and will not take the place of responsible management. Almost everyone involved with a nonprofit may suitably participate in the budget planning. At a minimum, the organization's top administrators, program heads, and board members or trustees contribute to the final result. The budget ultimately should be a compilation of information furnished by all the responsible program and administrative personnel who have in turn factored in the input of the people with whom they work. No one person should be responsible for the budget. The organization's financial (also called accounting or business) office compiles and monitors the budget. How far into the organizational chain the leaders seek input depends upon each nonprofit's circumstances.

Ideally, the budget process is participatory and involves input from all the nonprofit's program staff and volunteers devoted to accomplishing its goals. Outside funders sometimes influence the process. The budget allocation panel of a united giving campaign often coordinates their projected funding levels with the nonprofits they support. Such funders want to know if the organization plans to provide services that are already being provided by another organization in the community. They may try to influence a grant recipient to conduct programs to accomplish the funder's goals.

A budget imposed from the top down hampers staff enthusiasm and can negatively influence realization of the expressed goals. A non-profit may need to curtail the vociferous program officer seeking more money for his or her pet projects. The input of the volunteer case workers, for example, may yield a more realistic and realizable budget for a social service program and enhance volunteer enthusiasm. During the process, compromise and trade-offs will naturally occur. The participation of the staff from the outset makes them more enthusiastic about alternations not initiated by them. Optimally, it

Exhibit 4.1   Who Works on the Budget When?

	Who	**What**	**When**
Step 1	Accounting department	Provide budget worksheets	Sixth month of year (or before)
Step 2	Responsible program officers and administrative personnel based on input of all	Do research; solicit and compile ideas, prepare projections	Next two months
Step 3	Chief executive and financial officer	Combine all budgets into one, balance any conflicts, verify impact on strategic plans	Three months before year-end
Step 4	Chief executive and operating officer, subject to board or trustee approval	Review and finalize budget	Two to three months before year-end
Step 5	Board of directors or trustees	Formally adopts budget	Before year begins

may also make them more understanding or accepting of changes, including budget cuts that impact them personally (low or no raise). The participation of the board, officers, staff, and volunteers in the goal-setting process enhances the nonprofit's chances of reaching its goals. The whole budget process should motivate personnel and inspire the organization's performance. Everyone should be informed of the plan with a chart similar to the one in Exhibit 4.1.

SELLING THE BUDGET

The most effective budget is one prepared with broad and informed input from many personnel in the organization, including the chief executive, operating (if appropriate), and financial officers; administrative staff; program people; and volunteers (if appropriate) as discussed above. To achieve success, communication among all participants is encouraged during the whole process.

Budget Policy Manual

A formal budget manual containing written procedures and guidelines governing the process, budget models, checklists, and other aids to preparation is desirable to document the process. At a minimum, the organization should prepare a budget policy statement to stipulate the following:

- *Philosophy.* How the nonprofit uses the budget is described to encourage ongoing participation in the process. Folks need to know what to expect. They want to know how the nonprofit plans to respond to variances and whether the budget evolves or changes during the year.

- *Responsible persons.* Who does what when during the budget process is outlined.

- *Time frame.* A schedule of the expected steps.

- *Forecast guidelines.* Guidelines can indicate the economic assumptions to be applied, methodology to be used for making projections, independent sources of information, and circumstances under which outside professionals can be engaged to perform forecasts.

- *Report design.* A standard or suggested form for input by various programs or departments is furnished with clear instructions as to amount of detail desired, explanation of assumptions, and so on.

- *Follow-up.* The ongoing budget monitoring system and its recurring time frame is described. See periodic financial reports shown in Exhibits 6.6 and 6.7.

Communicating the Process

All involved in the budget preparation should be informed well in advance of how the process will work. They receive a copy of the budget policy manual if one is prepared. At a minimum, an office communication similar to Exhibit 4.2 is suggested.

Exhibit 4.2   Interoffice Memo on Annual Budgeting

TO: Program and administrative officers (suitable titles used, such as chief, head, manager, and so on)

FROM: Chief financial officer

RE: Annual Budgeting Schedule and Guidelines

I invite your contribution to our annual financial planning process. Our continued success depends on the accomplishments of your program. This package is a follow-up to the strategic long-range planning sessions you participated in last month. Now it is time to translate our goals into the specific activity we expect in both a financial and narrative fashion. Additionally, we ask you to compose a narrative description of your plans.

> **Worksheets** reflecting the actual results of your program for the past year, and the six months to date in this year broken down as follows are enclosed:
>
> - Revenues
> - Operating expenditures
> - Capital additions
>
> **Assumptions:** Projections should factor in the following assumptions:
>
> - Overall price increase will average 2.3%.
> - Salary increase for all will equal 3%.
> - Meritorious raises should not exceed 7%.
> - Membership revenue should increase 10%.
>
> **Narrative:** Please explain changes your department plans to make in response to changing economic conditions, grant funding, constituent needs, and so on. Explain any major differences between the past and projected financials.
> **Time Frame:** The deadline for submission is July 1 (one month hence).

SCHEDULING BUDGET PROCESS

In the best situation, budgeting is an ongoing process repeating itself in a cyclical manner. Also ideally, the philosophical basis for budget decisions is established in consideration of the nonprofit's long-range plan. To reach this optimum budget condition, the participants described in Exhibit 4.1 must allow sufficient time for the plans to be fully developed. The steps to follow include:

Step 1.	Set goals.	Perform long-range/strategic planning	Six to eight months before year end
Step 2.	Establish objectives.	Identify programs and activities to accomplish goal	Four to six months before year end
Step 3.	Design programs.	Describe method of actualizing the goals	Three to four months before year end
Step 4.	Budget prepared.	Quantify revenues and expenditures based on forecasts and program services accomplishments	Two to four months before year end
Step 5.	Budget approved.	Responsible person(s)	One to two months before year end
Step 6.	Monitor progress.	Compile reports comparing budget to actual financial results	As periodic financial report are issued

Prior to the accumulation of the financial aspect of a budget, the planning process occurs as described in Chapter 3. Goals are critiqued, evaluated, and established. Programs that can accomplish the goals are examined, compared, and studied. Past successes are considered and compared to failures or results falling short of desired goals. Finally, program planning and development are complete and the financial aspect begins.

Exhibit 4.1 suggests that the actual budget preparation process begins essentially six months prior to the date to which the budget applies. An organization whose fiscal year ends December 31—the calendar year—starts the process for the coming year by July, if not before. Enough time is allowed before the fiscal year starts to gather reliable forecasting information and to provide a reasonable period for an orderly approval process. Keep in mind that the board of directors ultimately approves the final product. Also consider a longer time frame possibly needed to coordinate the budget with grant-funding proposals, as discussed later in this chapter (Timing Dilemmas).

Changing Budget Midyear

The astute project manager is alert to outside forces that will impact fiscal performance of the organization and regularly catalogs new information that is useful in preparing the next year's budget. Networked personal computers can facilitate the accumulation of information on an ongoing basis. Some organizations may find a "living" budget that regularly changes throughout the year as circumstances change to be preferable to a fixed and unchanging budget.

The reasons the budget needs to change are endless. Forecasts may prove inaccurate for reasons of inadequate information or circumstances beyond the organization's control—an expected grant renewal is cut back or denied, a major funder defaults on a pledge, a natural disaster compounds demand for aid to the public, or the cost of newsprint doubles. Holy Spirit Church certainly did not expect the results shown in Exhibit 6.7 when it approved its original budget.

The issue when unforeseen changes occur is whether the approved budget should be altered or updated to reflect the changing conditions. Alternatively, as shown for State Association of Nonprofit Managers in Exhibit 6.6, the monthly financial statements can use footnotes to explain significant variances from the approved budget. The attributes of a "living" or constantly changing budget are compared to a static budget.

Static Budget	Living Budget
Compares dreams at a point in time to reality of current situation	Presents realistic statistics in view of changing circumstances or conditions
No time spent on revisions	Requires continual updating
Wastes funds expended on program to be discontinued or found to be ineffective	Constant maximization of resources
Allows unreasonable expectations	Positive context for accomplishment

Timing Dilemmas

Certain aspects of a nonprofit's financial life span years or involve years different than its fiscal year. Projects with multiyear time frames must be coordinated with the annual budget planning cycle. Consider, for example, the scheduling dilemma posed when an organization seeks funding from the state arts council that operates on a different fiscal year. Say the council funds programs for the state's fiscal year beginning on October 1 and requires grant applications no later than February 1 with awards approved by July. The calendar year nonprofit's normal budget approval date may be the end of November.

The gap in time between the grant submission deadline and budget approval date in the above example requires at least a two-step process. First, the grant budget is prepared for approval essentially six months in advance of the organization's overall budget approval date. Only nine months of the grant period, January through September, will impact the upcoming calendar year budget. The budget should provide contingency plans in case the grant award for the subsequent year is significantly different.

Too often, in my experience, grant requests are not approved as part of the normal budget cycle. Submission of a grant request essentially commits the nonprofit to carry out the program. The grant funds may not be sufficient to pay for all the costs involved, including the time and effort to apply and monitor the grant. It is prudent, therefore, for all grant requests to be subject to the same advanced approval system and be a part of the annual operating budget planning as discussed in this chapter (Who Participates in Budgeting?). Alternatively, the nonprofit could function under a two- to three-year budget plan.

Retiring board members or executive directors should never approve the coming year's budget as their last official act. The most effective budget is one developed and approved by the persons with a vested interest in its execution. Timing the annual change in officers or board members optimally occurs well in advance of the nonprofit's year end. For example, a calendar year budget ideally is approved in November or December with plans complete before the new year begins on January 1. To facilitate that time frame, the board members could take office in October or November to allow them time to study and approve the budget for which they will be responsible.

PREPARING FORECASTS

A nonprofit organization may face unique problems in forecasting its revenues. Those nonprofits supported by contributions and grants face the most difficult task. Voluntary donations are often based solely on the giver's compassion or support for the organization's mission and their personal generosity. The public's concern about a particular social problem—AIDS or disaster relief, for example—may wane. Other intangible factors compound the degree of difficulty in making projections for a nonprofit. Unfortunately, human psychology seems to make people place a higher value on those services for which they pay more. Fundraising activities are for some a social activity that can lose its cachet—the celebrity appeal of the organization may fade.

A service-providing nonprofit, such as a school or a business league, may have a slightly easier task in forecasting future revenue. Fees for services are motivated by the payor's perceived or actual need for the services the nonprofit is offering. As long as the services are of high quality and meeting the needs of the students, the sick, or the members, the nonprofit can reasonably project repeat or renewed participation. The adage, "You value what you pay for," is a factor. In planning training seminars for the Texas Accountants and Lawyers for the Arts, we discovered that those registrants who paid a fee, even a modest $5 fee, were much more likely to show up for the class than those required to pay no fee.

A forecaster first studies current revenue and spending levels and asks if the amounts can be sustained. If unusual and nonrecurring events occurred in the past year or two, will they reoccur? Is it instead reasonable to expect an increase in revenues? What level of increase does the nonprofit expect due to some action taken in the past, such as last year's establishment of a development department? What increases might result if some new marketing scheme is added to the expense side of the budget?

Information about the nonprofit's demographics and the conditions in its community are factored into the projections. National and local reports of economic activity can be studied on the Internet, in the public library, local city planning office, small business administration office, university, referral agencies, and similar resources. In view of the prevailing and predicted economic conditions, the forecaster then asks how the nonprofit may be affected by those uncontrollable outside forces. The nature of the nonprofit's constituents is also evaluated. Are they getting older, more educated, healthier, and so on? If the data is unclear, the nonprofit may need to test its internal projections or have them validated by outside consultants. Uncertainty may indicate the need to perform market surveys.

Donations and Memberships

Forecasting voluntary contributions and membership support is a job that becomes easier as the organization matures. The best source of data on which to predicate the future is the organization's own history. In making projections, statistical charts reflecting several years of revenue can serve as a guide. This is illustrated in Exhibit 4.5. Some nonprofits have a high level of goodwill generated after years of operation, such as a 50-year-old church or CPA society. A new or young organization may need to be more careful in weighing the past and evaluating the likely success of development plans.

Service Delivery Fees

Again, the organization's age impacts the predictability of the revenue projection. The mature organization knows the average number of students, attendees, research reports, or other services delivered in the past year and years. Presumably, the need for the services and policy decisions about their delivery have been reviewed as a part of the long range planning process. The budgeteer's job may simply be one of translating those goals into a financial format. The number of persons to be served and the expected prices are coordinated with the planners.

Absent guidance from some goal-setting procedure, the person(s) compiling the budget may need to perform market analysis—evaluate the need and past effectiveness of the service(s), changing constituency base, or demand for the services. On the basis of these planning steps, the nonprofit projects the numbers to be served and price to be charged in order to arrive at the predicted service revenue.

Grants and Contracts

Predicting the renewal or approval of grants from governmental funding agencies, private foundations, and business sponsors is a difficult and troublesome task. Uncertain facts and unanswerable questions must be faced. Will some legislative body reduce or eliminate the program? Will the foundation's asset values fall, causing a reduction in money allotted to grants? (The annual payout requirement for a private foundation equals 5 percent of value of its investment assets.) Are priorities among funders changing?

Corporate sponsorship levels are usually tied to the sponsor's profit levels—a fact often unknown at budget preparation time. Renewal of a government research contract may depend on an incomplete project or preliminary data that makes a prediction impossible at budget time. Governmental regulations concerning cost reimbursements or bidding process may affect the forecast.

Particularly where a portion of the nonprofit's operating overhead or administrative funds are paid for with grant funds, very cautious projecting is prudent. Think about the consequence when the grant that funds half of the executive director's salary is not renewed. Where a good possibility exists for nonrenewal, the uncertain forecast indicates the need for a flexible or evolving budget as discussed in this chapter (Evolution; Timing Dilemmas). Employment arrangements with staff members funded by a grant (and the corresponding expense budget) should be tailored to fit any contingency that the funds may cease.

Investment Income

The care required in projecting investment income is determined by the portion of the organization's revenues expected to be provided by such income.

For many nonprofits, the portion is modest. The higher the portion, the more significant the methodology and expertise used in making predictions. For an endowed grant-making foundation, all of whose revenues come from investment returns, for example, the forecast is vital to establishing funding levels for the coming year. Endowed institutions customarily establish a spending level based on the expectation that actual investment income will vary from year to year.

To appreciate the task an organization faces in projecting investment income, recall the significant market declines when the Silicon Valley tech bubble burst. In some years, interest rates have moved up or down more than 100%. Generally, a nonprofit's working capital should be sufficient to withstand fluctuations in short-term interest rates without serious impact on its overall financial picture.

The importance of forecasting rises for the nonprofit with long-term investment funds. If the organization funds are administered by a professional investment manager, the manager should provide investment income projections. Otherwise, the nonprofit must do its best to predict the unpredictable while keeping a healthy level of skepticism about the unknown. The fact is that no banker, governmental official, or country on earth controls the interest rates, price of equity investments, inflation or deflation rates, relative currency values, or other economic factors that will influence a particular nonprofit's return on investment in the coming year. To complicate the matter, what constitutes expendable income from investment assets is a much debated subject. The budgeted revenues may be suitably based on concepts of total return. Where this forecast is significant, consult Chapter 5 (Prudent Investment Planning; Restricted Gifts) for more information useful in projecting investment income.

Expenses

For most nonprofits, expenditure levels can be predicted with a fair degree of certainty partly because the nonprofit has more control over expenses than revenues. The compensation arrangements with personnel are known, for the most part. Facility costs may be relatively stable under the terms of a lease agreement or mortgage note. Historical expense reports form the basis for the expense budget subject to adjustment for the expected rate of growth or decline in prevailing prices according to the Federal Reserve Bank or other economic predictors.

One major issue in forecasting costs is identifying those that are variable in relation to revenue stream or client demand. A disaster relief agency may know how much it costs to clothe and house flood victims, but it cannot know when the storm or storms might occur. Again, historical records may be useful. For example, the government's hurricane bureau predicts how many storms will confront the Gulf of Mexico each year and where they will occur.

A contingency based on client demand for the nonprofit's services is sometimes as difficult to predict, but the same crystal-ball judgments can be applied. It can be very important to acknowledge the uncertainty and submit a flexible budget. The prudent budget preparer seeks the best possible information to prepare and submits projections subject to change. Another way to view or face the job of forecasting costs is to identify costs according to those that are controllable versus those that are uncontrollable.

If expected costs are too high, the financial planners consider alternatives. Sometimes a nonprofit needs people with skills to supervise a project, but the suitable person's expected compensation level would skew the nonprofit's overall pay scale. In such a situation, the organization has many alternatives:

- Outsource the job to another nonprofit or company (may be able to receive some fee for selling the program's goodwill).

- Hire the skilled consultant on a part-time or hourly basis to operate the program and have him or her train a permanent person.

- Eliminate or reduce the scope of the program or enter into a joint venture with another nonprofit to conduct the program.

Projected expenses must also be matched to the expected revenue flow. The proposed expenditure budget should be tested by preparing a cash flow report as illustrated in Exhibits 5.3 and 5.4. Although the State Association of Nonprofit Managers' overall budget projections looked well balanced and reasonable, a marketing campaign planned early in the year would have caused cash flow deficits. The second version of the exhibit shows how the plans were changed to match the monthly spending with the expected revenue flow.

Choosing which programs to continue is a decision made in light of their effect on incoming resources. Sometimes the program is simply one the nonprofit itself shouldn't attempt to sponsor or conduct. A variety of questions can be asked to assess the impact of program planning decisions on the nonprofit's resources, as shown in Exhibit 4.3.

STATISTICAL OPERATIONAL DATA

On a regular basis, the nonprofit needs to gather statistics and information relevant to the budgeting and planning process. Each organization needs a mechanism to measure its overall and individual program effectiveness. How can it determine whether its goals are being reached? What are the results of its efforts? Successes and failures and weaknesses and strengths should be regularly evaluated and quantified. The information can form

---

Exhibit 4.3   Resource Assessment Checklist

Question	Comments
How secure are the funding sources?	_____
How many people attend or benefit from the activity?	_____
What does the activity cost per person?	_____
How much revenue does it produce?	_____
Does the activity appeal to volunteers?	_____
Is the program readily fundable with grants?	_____
Does the program produce peripheral or ancillary benefits or costs?	_____
What portion of the nonprofit's overhead is funded by the activity?	_____
How dependent are the nonprofit's grantees on its funding?	_____
Is the activity performed by some other organization?	_____
Should the budget include a marketing campaign to broaden public support and public awareness of the program?	_____

---

the basis for decisions, establishing priorities, and making choices. The sophistication and scope of the self-assessment process will vary by organization. To be effective, not only program performance and accomplishments of the organization itself are measured, but staff, volunteer, manager, and board performance as well.

Sample Customer Survey

To facilitate evaluations, the organization can develop written documents to compile information. The response of constituents—members, donors, and service recipients—is solicited and accumulated. Some call constituents *customers* and recommend that customer satisfaction be emphasized. The response measurements for a nonprofit's customers will be different from a business, but they are equally important to consider.

For each situation, a suitable follow-up system should be used to implement changes indicated by the data. Why gather data if they are not studied and if changes indicated are not implemented? The steps the organization takes in reaction to constituent suggestions should also be shared or reported back to them. The type of questions about the nonprofit's resources and costs that are useful to include on a customer or constituent survey are shown in Exhibit 4.4.

Exhibit 4.4 Service Delivery Evaluation

This survey is intended to serve as an example of the type of questionnaire a nonprofit might use to seek evaluations of its program service delivery. The survey could be completed at the time one is served or could be mailed to a sampling of participants or members.

STATE ASSOCIATION OF NONPROFIT MANAGERS

Member (Constituent) Survey

Name of Member (patient, student, donor, or such)   _____

Address   _____

Phone   _____

Fax, E-Mail, or Net Path   _____

Date   _____

Are you happy with SANM?   [ ] (yes)   [ ] (no)

If not, please explain.   _____

_____

_____

Why do you value services
received from SANM?   _____

How could SANM be of
better service to you or your
organization?   _____

Would you pay more?   _____

Please tell us more!   _____

Useful Statistics

A myriad of data can be organized and presented in a manner that aids the nonprofit's planners to predict or forecast the future. National surveys of the compensation levels of nonprofit personnel can be consulted to see if projected levels are in line with outside trends.[2] The examples in Exhibit 4.5 should serve only to inspire creativity for designing statistical summaries germane to each particular organization.

---

[2] The Council on Foundations publishes an annual survey of compensation levels of various positions for foundations of varying sizes. Towers Perrin, an international human resource and management consulting firm, compiles an annual *Management Compensation Report for Not-for-Profit Organizations*.

Exhibit 4 5   Typical Nonprofit Organization Membership History

Membership Renewal Statistics

Membership Categories	Members Renewing	New Members	Total for Year 20XX	Nonrenewing Members	Original Forecast	Prior Year Actual	Forecast for Year 20XX
Basic	5,000	2,000	7,000	1,800	7,500	6,800	7,200
Family	2,000	500	2,500	600	2,800	2,600	2,600
Friend	500	50	550	20	500	520	540
Supporter	70	10	80	30	75	100	90

Membership Profiles

Member, patient, student, etc. Characteristics	Forecast for Year 20XX	Actual for Year 20XX	Forecast for Next Year 20XX
Total of all served	10,875	10,020	10,430
Gender:			
Female	6,075	5,840	6,030
Male	4,800	4,200	4,400
AGE (use brackets suitable for the nonprofit):			
Under 10 years	700	780	800
Age 11–18	1,200	1,010	940
Age 19–25	2,475	2,200	2,180
Age 26–40	3,800	3,600	3,910
Age 41–64	2,000	1,820	1,940
Over 65	500	510	460
Age unknown	200	100	200
	10,875	10,020	10,430

Other possibilities:

Zip code

Ethnic origin

Profession

Category of member

Angels

Saints

Patrons

Disciples

Revenue Source History						
	Four Years Ago	Three Years Ago	Two Years Ago	Last Year	Average	Forecast Next Year
Individual Contributions	520	640	780	1,000	735	1,200
Grants from Private Foundations	100	200	300	400	250	500
Government Grants	1,200	1,200	1,000	600	1,000	400
Program Service Revenue	40	80	200	600	230	700
Income from Endowment	30	−10	80	100	50	80
Operating Revenues	1,890	2,110	2,360	2,700	2,265	2,880
Endowment or Capital Gifts	120	200	50	10	95	0
Total Revenues	2,010	2,310	2,410	2,710	2,360	2,880

Expenditure Levels						
	Four Years Ago	Three Years Ago	Two Years Ago	Last Year	Average	Forecast Next Year
Direct Program Service Costs:						
Program 1	1,200	1,100	1,000	800	1,025	800
Program 2	200	300	300	300	275	320
Program 3	200	350	700	1,000	562	1,200
Management and General	200	260	280	410	287	420
Fundraising and Development	10	30	40	50	32	80
Property and Equipment Acquisitions	200	50	0	10	65	40
Total Expenditures	2,020	2,060	2,320	2,570	2,246	2,860

CAPITAL ADDITIONS BUDGET

Beyond the operating budget lies the capital budget shown in Exhibit 4.12. Here, plans are developed for spending funds to acquire assets, such as equipment and buildings, that will benefit the nonprofit over a period of time. Because the capital spending benefits the organization in a more tangible and often longer-lasting fashion, the nonprofit may arrange to pay for the acquisition over a period of time, sometimes many years. Therefore, in capital budgeting, several distinct issues are considered:

1. Will the new asset improve our performance and enable the organization to better accomplish its mission?
2. How will the acquisition be financed?
3. What will it cost to obtain and maintain the asset throughout its life?

The issues in answering question 1 are the same as described for considering an operating expense budget. Procedures and forms to use in making such purchase decisions are suggested in Chapter 7 (Purchasing Procedures). The type of statistical data gathered to propose capital additions is illustrated in Exhibit 7.7. Issues to consider in deciding to acquire or purchase capital assets versus leasing them is illustrated in Exhibit 7.8. In the following sample budgets, the capital additions are incorporated into the overall nonprofit budget and treated much like other operating expenses.

Questions 2 and 3 add another dimension—that of financing the acquisition. Should the nonprofit buy the equipment for cash? Should it lease or buy under an installment purchase agreement? Equally important is question 3—what will the asset eventually cost in total for the time the organization uses it? Chapter 7 (Purchasing Procedures) suggests some tools for answering these difficult questions.

MONITORING VARIANCES

Once the budget is approved for the upcoming year, a monitoring system is in order. Computers can certainly make this process easier. Even the most basic accounting software packages available over the counter today contain modules for budget reports. As a part of the routine monthly financial reporting, the actual financial transactions to date are compared to the budget, as shown in Exhibits 6.6 and 6.7 for State Association of Nonprofit Managers and for the Holy Spirit Church.

The report design should deliver the information succinctly so that variances reflecting situations that require action or changes are clear and apparent. A variance is the difference between the expected or projected outcome and what actually happened. When they occur, they must be interpreted and analyzed. Holy Spirit Church's variances certainly show that its financial condition is not as expected, and it should cause alarm. The report reflects a serious problem that the church's financial managers must face.

MODEL BUDGETS

This section contains illustrative budgets for a mock business league, State Association of Nonprofit Managers, also known by its acronym, SANM. The design of the budget workpapers follows the format of SANM's monthly financial statements shown in Exhibit 6.6. The intention is to make it easy to prepare monthly variance reports and to facilitate understanding of the comparisons. A variety of formats, however, are successfully used by nonprofit organizations. Briefly, SANM's budget workpapers shown in Exhibits 4.6 through 4.13 serve the following purpose in their budget planning process and can serve as a model for varying types of nonprofits.

Proposed Overall 20XX Budget Compared to 20XX Actual

The overall budget comprehensively reflects all resource flow to be approved by the board and to serve as a blueprint to measure accomplishment of financial goals for the coming year (Exhibit 4.6). Note that the proposal is prepared, as suggested earlier in this chapter (Scheduling Budget Process), midyear, or almost six months before the budget period begins. The actual financial results for the prior year and the current six months form the basis for projecting both the current year's and the upcoming year's results. The overall budget is a compilation of the information contained in SANM's seven other budget segments illustrated.

Exhibit 4.6   Proposed Overall Budget Compared to Actual

STATE ASSOCIATION OF NONPROFIT MANAGERS

PROPOSED OVERALL BUDGET COMPARED TO ACTUAL

	Actual 20XX	Actual to Date (6 months)	Projected 20XX	Proposed 20XX
Revenues				
Chapter member dues	$238,000	$102,000	$249,700	$270,000
Members-at-large dues	76,000	47,000	78,600	80,000
Information services	40,000	76,000	120,000	150,000
Publication sales	180,000	89,000	204,000	230,000
Continuing education	98,000	62,000	106,000	110,000
Annual meeting	42,000	28,000	28,000	20,000
Royalty income	1,000	32,000	42,000	52,000
Interest income	3,000	600	1,000	1,000
Total revenues	678,000	436,600	829,300	913,000
Expenses				
Salaries and payroll taxes	310,000	178,000	363,000	360,000
Retirement and medical benefits	26,000	11,900	25,300	30,000

Exhibit 4.6   Proposed Overall Budget Compared to Actual *(continued)*

Professional fees	30,000	4,000	32,000	32,000
Supplies	20,000	10,900	24,000	26,400
Telephone	12,400	9,700	18,000	20,000
Postage and shipping	16,800	10,100	18,000	20,000
Building costs	43,200	14,500	36,000	38,000
Equipment repair and insurance	9,600	8,500	12,000	14,000
Printing and publications	140,000	68,400	120,000	137,000
Travel	15,000	4,200	17,000	30,000
Meetings and classes	26,000	9,600	22,000	32,000
Information services	32,000	44,000	57,000	80,000
Depreciation on equipment and furnishings	36,000	21,000	42,000	47,000
Marketing	13,000	8,700	17,000	46,600
Total expenses	730,000	403,500	803,300	913,000
Excess of revenues over expenses	($52,000)	$33,100	$26,000	$0

Functional Revenue and Expense Budget

This report, Exhibit 4.7, compiles the detailed projections prepared by each department. Note that the six-month numbers do not appear on this sheet because the column totals are calculated on the following worksheet.

Member Services Budget Worksheet

SANM's program officers each suggest a desired functional, or departmental, budget for the respective activities for which they are responsible, similar to the one shown in Exhibit 4.8 for the member services department. This worksheet is the type to attach to the interoffice memo (Exhibit 4.2), to invite participation of the department in the budget process. The financial information shown in the two left-hand columns—actual 20XX and actual to date—would be completed by the business or accounting office prior to distribution. For large organizations, there could be layers of such workpapers for segments within the department or activity center.

Exhibit 4.7   Functional Revenues and Expense Budget

STATE ASSOCIATION OF NONPROFIT MANAGERS

FUNCTIONAL REVENUES AND EXPENSE BUDGET

	Projected Actual 20XX	Proposed 20XX	Member Services	Publications	Meetings and Classes	Administration
Revenues						
Chapter member dues	$249,700	$270,000	$270,000			
Members-at-large dues	78,600	80,000	80,000			
Information services	120,000	150,000	150,000			
Publication sales	204,000	230,000		$230,000		
Continuing education	106,000	110,000			$110,000	
Annual meeting	28,000	20,000			20,000	
Royalty income	42,000	52,000	42,000			
Interest income	1,000	1,000				$1,000
Total revenues	829,300	913,000	542,000	230,000	130,000	1,000
Expenses						
Salaries and payroll taxes	363,000	360,000	128,000	82,000	32,000	118,000
Retirement and medical benefits	25,300	30,000	8,000	5,000	2,000	15,000
Professional fees	32,000	32,000	12,000		8,000	12,000
Supplies	24,000	26,400	8,800	4,400	6,600	6,600
Telephone	18,000	20,000	8,500	4,500	2,500	4,500
Postage and shipping	18,000	20,000	4,000	11,000	2,500	2,500
Building costs	36,000	38,000	6,500	12,500	6,500	12,500
Equipment repair and insurance	12,000	14,000	2,000	4,000	2,000	4,000
Printing and publications	120,000	137,000	10,000	98,000	26,000	3,000
Travel	17,000	30,000	20,000		5,000	5,000
Meetings and classes	22,000	32,000	6,000		26,000	
Information services	57,000	80,000	80,000			
Depreciation	42,000	17,000	4,600	2,800	1,600	8,000
Marketing	17,000	46,600	25,000	5,000		
Total expenses	$803,300	883,000	323,400	229,200	120,700	191,100
Excess of revenues over expenses	$26,000	$30,000	$218,600	$800	$9,300	($190,100)

Exhibit 4.8   Member Services Budget Worksheet

STATE ASSOCIATION OF NONPROFIT MANAGERS

MEMBER SERVICES BUDGET WORKSHEET

	20XX Actual	Actual to Date (6 months)	20XX Projected Actual This Year	20XX Proposed Next Year
Revenues				
Chapter member dues	$238,000	$132,600	$249,700	$270,000
Members-at-large dues	76,000	28,200	78,600	80,000
Information services	40,000	38,000	120,000	150,000
Royalty income	1,000	220,800	42,000	42,000
Total revenues	355,000	220,800	490,300	542,000
Expenses				
Salaries and payroll taxes	108,000	60,000	126,000	128,000
Retirement and medical benefits	6,480	2,900	6,000	8,000
Professional fees	15,000	4,200	12,000	12,000
Supplies	10,000	3,840	8,000	8,800
Telephone	12,800	5,020	8,000	8,500
Postage and shipping	3,600	2,290	4,000	4,000
Building costs	6,200	5,800	8,000	6,500
Equipment repair and insurance	1,800	1,100	2,000	2,000
Printing and publications	6,250	2,300	5,000	10,000
Travel	19,000	4,800	10,000	20,000
Meetings and classes	1,760	800	2,000	6,000
Information services	22,900	26,100	61,000	80,000

Depreciation on equipment and furnishings	12,400	7,000	14,400	4,600
Marketing	500	2,000	4,600	25,000
Total expenses	226,690	128,150	271,000	323,400
Excess of revenues over expenses	$128,310	$92,650	$219,300	$218,600

Budget Increases (Decreases) Projected for 20XX

This report shown in Exhibit 4.9 calculates the actual dollar increases or decreases in the overall revenue and expense categories and shows the percentage of change. Many versions of this report, including graphs and other financial or economic information, could be designed to translate and best explain the budget for those who must approve the proposals.

Exhibit 4.9   Budgeted Increases (Decreases) Projected for 20XX

STATE ASSOCIATION OF NONPROFIT MANAGERS

BUDGETED INCREASES (DECREASES) PROJECTED FOR 19X7

	Expected Actual 20XX	% Change	Increase (Decrease)	Projected for 20XX
Revenues				
Chapter member dues	$249,700	8%	$20,300	$270,000
Members-at-large dues	78,600	1%	1,400	80,000
Information services	120,000	12%	30,000	150,000
Publication sales	204,000	10%	26,000	230,000
Continuing education	106,000	2%	4,000	110,000
Annual meeting	28,000	−3%	(8,000)	20,000
Royalty income	42,000	4%	10,000	52,000
Interest income	1,000	0%	0	1,000
Total revenues	829,300	34%	83,700	913,000

Exhibit 4.9   Budgeted Increases (Decreases) Projected for 20XX *(continued)*

Expenses

Salaries and payroll taxes	363,000	−1%	(3,000)	360,000
Retirement and medical benefits	25,300	19%	4,700	30,000
Professional fees	32,000	0%	0	32,000
Supplies	24,000	10%	2,400	26,400
Telephone	18,000	11%	2,000	20,000
Postage and shipping	18,000	11%	2,000	20,000
Building costs	36,000	6%	2,000	38,000
Equipment repair and insurance	12,000	17%	2,000	14,000
Printing and publications	120,000	14%	17,000	137,000
Travel	17,000	76%	13,000	30,000
Meetings and classes	22,000	45%	10,000	32,000
Information services	57,000	40%	23,000	80,000
Depreciation on equipment and furnishings	42,000	−60%	(25,000)	17,000
Marketing	17,000	174%	29,600	46,600
Total Expenses	803,300	10%	79,700	883,000
Excess of revenues over expenses	$26,000	15%	$4,000	$30,000

Personnel Budget

SANM's expected personnel costs for the upcoming year is shown on Exhibit 4.10. This report customarily is kept confidential and prepared in the accounting department in consultation with department heads rather than being broadly circulated.

Program Cost Analysis

SANM evaluates the viability of its member dues, publication prices, and class fees with the calculations shown in Exhibit 4.11. This exhibit report shows the meetings and classes revenues barely cover the direct cost of this activity; in

Exhibit 4.10   Personnel Budget

STATE ASSOCIATION OF NONPROFIT MANAGERS

PERSONNEL BUDGET

Projected Compensation for the fiscal year 20XX, compared to 20XX

Position and/or Name	Base Compensation	Fringe Benefits	Payroll Taxes	Actual Comp. This Year	Budgeted This Year	Budgeted for 20XX
Full time						
Executive director	$60,000	$7,600	$5,000	$72,600	$72,000	$78,000
Chief financial officer	48,000	5,400	3,800	57,200	57,000	60,000
Career counselor/ referrals	40,000	3,000	3,200	46,200	38,000	48,000
Publications director	40,000	3,000	3,200	46,200	46,000	48,000
Computer/Internet guru	30,000	1,800	2,400	34,200	34,000	36,000
Assistants (4)	88,000	4,100	7,000	99,100	108,000	90,000
Part time						
Editor (1/2 time)	20,000	400	1,600	22,000	25,000	20,000
Assistant	10,000		800	10,800	10,000	10,000
Totals	$336,000	$25,300	$27,000	$388,300	$390,000	$390,000

Exhibit 4.11   Program Cost Analysis

STATE ASSOCIATION OF NONPROFIT MANAGERS

PROGRAM COST ANALYSIS

	Program Services			
	Member Activities	Publications	Meetings and Classes	Total
Total direct program costs	$267,000	$229,600	$122,000	$618,600
Supporting service costs	$92,350	$36,940	$55,410	$184,700
Total cost of program	$359,350	$266,540	$177,410	$803,300
# of members	2,500			
Publications sold		23,860		
Hours of education			12,000	
Per-unit direct cost	$106.80	$9.62	$10.17	
Total program cost per member	$143.74	$11.17	$14.78	

other words, the revenue does not pay any portion of the association's administrative cost burden—it needs to control the cost or raise the price for meetings and classes. The per-participant direct and total program costs for the service provided should enable SANM to reevaluate its class and meeting fees.

Many variations on this theme could be utilized for fundraising event costs, student or class-hour costs, per-patient costs, and so on. The concepts and methodology used in cost accounting, outlined in Chapter 7 (Cost Accounting), can be consulted for guidelines on cost analysis.

Other Reports and Analysis

SANM's relatively simple capital acquisitions budget is shown in Exhibit 4.12. For some organizations this report and the accompanying cost analyses, including competitive bids and other plans, can be quite extensive. The insurance coverage report in Exhibit 4.13 serves two purposes. For budgeting purposes, the premiums for the coming year are reflected. For risk analysis purposes, the types and limits of coverage are reported for review by those fiscally responsible for protecting the organization's resources as explained in Chapter 2. For a list of other financial report and statistical information that might prove useful to other nonprofits, see Types of Budgets earlier in this chapter.

Exhibit 4.12   Capital Acquisition Budget

STATE ASSOCIATION OF NONPROFIT MANAGERS

CAPITAL ACQUISITION BUDGET

Description of Asset	Total Cost thru 20XX	New Adds to Date 20XX	Projected thru Year-end	Sales or Dispositions	Total Cost thru 20XX	Proposed Next Year
Buildings	$300,000				$300,000	
Computers and statewide network	62,000	$18,000	$12,000	($12,000)	80,000	
Upgrade memory (8 computers)						6,400
New computers (3)						6,000
Office Furnishings	80,000	12,000	2,000	(4,000)	90,000	
Publication storage racks						3,000
New classroom furniture						12,000
Totals	$442,000	$30,000	$14,000	($16,000)	$470,000	$27,400

Exhibit 4.13 Insurance Coverage Report

STATE ASSOCIATION OF NONPROFIT MANAGERS

INSURANCE COVERAGE REPORT

Type of Coverage	Insurance Company	Period of Coverage	Premium This Year	Premium Next Year
Property and casualty:				
Building	ABC Casualty	August–July	$3,600	$4,200
Equipment	ABC Casualty	August–July	1,400	1,800
Liability:				
Umbrella	ABC Casualty	August–July	3,000	2,800
Officer/director	ABC Casualty	August–July	1,600	1,600
Malpractice	Natl NPO Assn	Calendar–renew Dec.	2,000	2,400
Staff related:				
Worker's compensation	ABC Casualty	Calendar–report due Nov.	4,600	4,800
Health (1/2 pd by employees)	Best HMO	Month to month	14,000	12,000
Disability (pd by employees)	Natl NPO Assn	Month to month	none	
Fidelity bond	ABC Casualty	August–July	800	800
Total all insurance			$31,000	$30,400

A BUDGETING CHECKLIST

Exhibit 4.14   Short-and Long-Term Budgeting Checklist

This checklist would be completed by the chief financial officer or other party responsible for organizing the budget effort and compiling the information. It could also be reviewed by the board finance committee to determine if all suitable steps in the process have been taken.

1. Why is a budget useful?

   a. It outlines in financial terms the goals and policies approved by the board. ☐

   b. It is a tool for monitoring adherence to and deviations from plans throughout the year. ☐

   c. Its preparation causes the organization to focus on planning, evaluation of programs, and accomplishment of its mission. ☐

2. Is the budgeting process timed properly?

   a. Can proposed staff or project changes realistically be implemented before the fiscal year begins? ☐

   b. Is board membership scheduled to change prior to budget approval? (Avoid having a new board be responsible for a budget they didn't approve.)

   c. If the budget is approved by members, when is the annual meeting? ☐

   d. Must major grant funding requests be submitted in advance of approval of the overall budget? If so, consider the need for a two- or three-year plan. ☐

3. What type of budget is appropriate for this organization?

   a. Is a zero-based budget needed for critical evaluation of priorities to force a serious cutback in level of expenses? ☐

   b. Are existing programs examined as closely as proposed projects? ☐

   c. Will functional or line-item budget allow proper review of program goals? ☐

   d. Is the budget based on existing operations, with incremental increases or decreases for economic conditions? ☐

4. Who prepares the budget?

  a. Is a budget committee needed? ☐

  b. Would a budget committee made up of accounting department staff, board members, and outside advisors be effective? ☐

  c. If each department does initial preparation, are standard formats and instructions furnished to lend consistency? ☐

  d. Is the final budget comprehensive, including restricted funds, endowments, capital improvements, and all financial aspects? ☐

5. What are the steps in the budget preparation process?

  a. Develop goals and objectives for a three- to five-year period first (long-range plan, dreams). ☐

  b. Quantify long-range goals, such as raising an endowment, financing new facilities, or increasing staff. ☐

  c. Evaluate last year's results.

    i.   Were objectives achieved? ☐

    ii. If not, were they unreasonable? ☐

    iii. What caused variances? Were midyear revisions appropriate? ☐

    iv. Were changes indicated by ratio analyses? ☐

  d. Establish objectives for the coming year. ☐

  e. Prepare program justifications. ☐

  f. Prepare estimates of revenues and cost of programs. ☐

  g. Compile, evaluate, and balance the results. ☐

  h. The budget should be approved first by the staff, then by the board (with intervening steps as nature of organization dictates). ☐

  i. Amend the budget when the monitoring process shows a need for change. ☐

6. Evaluate programs and services rendered.

  a. Who are the constituents? ☐

  b. Is the organization reaching them? ☐

  c. Should promotion be budgeted? ☐

  d. Is the cost per person too high? ☐

  e. Is a competing organization providing the same services? ☐

Exhibit 4.14   Short-and Long-Term Budgeting Checklist *(continued)*

---

7. Evaluate the pricing of services.

   a. Should charges be made? Prices increased or decreased?   ☐

   b. Would audience/membership/students/etc. increase with a decrease in prices, resulting in more revenue?   ☐

   c. Are funding sources available to cover free or reduced-cost services?   ☐

8. Evaluate fund-raising activities.

   a. Can board members and other volunteers devote sufficient time to reach fund-raising goals? If not, should consultants or new staff be hired?   ☐

   b. Is an annual special giving campaign in addition to the membership campaign necessary? Would it drain membership?   ☐

   c. Can project sponsors or cosponsors be found?   ☐

   d. Should a planned giving program be established?

      i. Charitable remainder or trusts?   ☐

      ii. Pooled income fund or charitable gift annuities?   ☐

   e. Can investment capital rather than gifts be sought for asset major acquisitions?

      i.   Limited partnership?   ☐

      ii. Subsidiary corporation?   ☐

      iii. Joint venture?   ☐

9. Evaluate expenses.

   a. Could alternative approaches improve efficiency and thus reduce costs?   ☐

   b. Is the use of volunteers effective?   ☐

   c. Would "investing" in a paid development director or volunteer coordinator more than pay for itself?   ☐

   d. Are computers used effectively?   ☐

      i. To save money, are cheaper but time-consuming or inadequate programs in use?   ☐

      ii. Would networking, e-mail, or web page pay for itself through saved time and mailings?   ☐

e. Are fixed and variable expenses segregated? If so, are they properly allocated to programs? ☐

f. Are salary level changes factored into benefit costs? ☐

10. Consider outside forces.

a. Is funding likely to be cut due to the depressed state of the economy nationwide or in the area? ☐

b. Has there been a shift in population? Have plants closed? Are the standards of the profession changing? Is there a new university in town? ☐

c. Has there been a drought, pollution increase, or stock market crash? ☐

d. Are accreditation or granting requirements changing? ☐

11. Before final approval, consider these issues.

a. Is there any doubt about the reliability of projections? ☐

b. Do sufficient cash reserves exist to cover shortfalls/overages? (If not, increase working capital in the budget.) ☐

c. Reevaluate policy goals if cuts must be made. ☐

d. Could projects be carried out in cooperation with or by another organization? ☐

e. Would charts or graphs illustrate trends and make decisions clearer? ☐

f. Reconcile short-term resource needs with long-range growth. ☐

12. Prepare supplemental budgets to implement the overall budget.

a. Cash flow projections. ☐

b. Investment objectives. ☐

c. Capital expenditure timing. ☐

d. Restricted fund budgets. ☐

13. Devise a follow-up system for monitoring the budget.

a. Use timely financial reports to compare actual expenses and income with those budgeted. ☐

b. Revise budget to reflect recurring changes during the year. ☐

5

Asset Management

A nonprofit's planners should view its finances from a "going concern" perspective, meaning the nonprofit is alive and prepared to conduct its activities for an indefinite period of time into the future.

A nonprofit's resources, or assets, are best managed from the perspective of a *"going concern,"* that is, without assuming any limit on the organization's existence. Although financial planners strive to get the best return from invested assets, they must be sure the organization has sufficient liquid assets available to finance current operations. The goal, in brief, is to maintain the optimum balance between available assets and those that are invested, or growing, assets. A going concern operates in a fiscally solvent fashion. Solvency in this context means the ability to pay the organization's debts in a timely manner or to meet its financial responsibilities—not to dissolve like sugar.

This chapter will consider how a nonprofit's resources flow and interact. Tools for managing that all-important resource—cash—are illustrated and explained. Issues to consider in accepting and protecting restricted and permanent funds are explored in depth, along with discussion of the total return concept for measuring investment income.

MAXIMIZING RESOURCES

To be fiscally solvent and operate as a going concern, the nonprofit's managers, after the budgets are developed, focus on two more objectives:

1. Smoothly financing current operations by making the most efficient use of current, or liquid, funds.

2. Maximizing available and obtainable resources to enhance return on the resources, or capital.

101

Conceptually, the task of accomplishing these objectives can be entitled either *asset management* or *resource allocation*. All the nonprofit's resources—from its volunteers and members, to the cash in the bank, to its bricks and mortar—are assets that can be fiscally managed. Such assets not only provide a benefit and contribute to accomplishing the overall organizational goals, they also add to costs. The financial manager continually seeks to balance the forces of benefit and inherent cost. True, a planned giving campaign seeking long-term pledges of support and may be desirable; but the financial costs associated with the campaign and with monitoring and collecting the pledges must be assessed to evaluate the ultimate overall increase in available resources. Similarly, a plan to keep cash balances fully invested must take into account the salary of the person who oversees the effort in calculating the net interest return anticipated.

A nonprofit's overall resource flow is depicted in Exhibits 5.1 and 5.2. The sources and uses of resources for a business league and an educational institution are illustrated. Although the labels may be different, the flows of resources are prototypical and may be found in a wide variety of nonprofit organizations. The resources of a church supported by its members, for example, would look very much like the business league. Similarly, a museum's resource flow would resemble that of the educational center once visitors were substituted for students, art collectors for alumni, and art exhibitions for academic programs.

Exhibit 5.1   Resource Flow for Business League

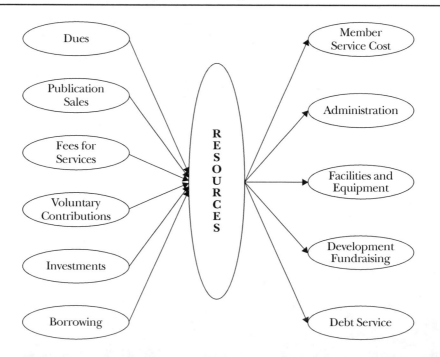

Exhibit 5.2   Resource Flow for Academic Institution

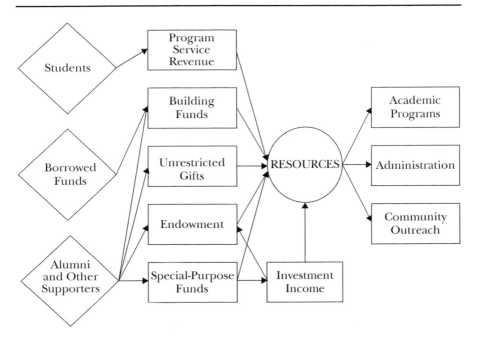

The prominent center, labeled "RESOURCES," represents the funds available to finance operations or pay the bills. Theoretically, the flow of funds coming from the sources on the left side of the chart is sufficient to finance the outflows on the right. Some argue that the successful nonprofit focuses first on the left—the sources of funds. They would say that it is easy to spend the money; the difficult part is obtaining it. Others reason that excellent programs draw the support of a nonprofit's natural constituency and, therefore, should be the focus. One way to dissect the illustration is to ask which comes first. In other words, "Should we authorize the expenditure of funds before the funds are in the bank?" It may now be apparent that in resource management, the objective is to look at the organization holistically and to capture the benefit of its resources—from sources to programs and back again—with a balanced perspective.

GETTING RESOURCES

To further examine the resource picture, the planners consider the choices in obtaining those resources. A nonprofit's funding typically comes from one or more of the following sources:

- Contributed funds (general support, grants, and restricted gifts)
- Membership dues

- Exempt function (related) income (charges/fees for mission activity)
- Investments or business ventures (unrelated) income
- Intangibles, such as alliances with other organizations
- Indebtedness

There is much written and a wealth of data and assistance available about fundraising that is beyond the scope of this book. My intention in this section is to provide a bit of information to whet a financial planner's appetite by exploring resources that might be overlooked and about which there is a fairly high degree of misinformation.

The U.S. political milieu cannot be forgotten in evaluating future resource sources. Federal and state legislators continually struggle to balance those budgets in view of competing needs and opinions. Nonprofits dependent upon government funding must be attentive to proposals that impact their funding. The contribution deduction permitted by the federal tax code, combined with the donor's tax rate, is thought by some to significantly impact the donor's generosity and, thereby, a nonprofit's ability to raise contribution dollars. Although some gifts to nonprofits stem from pure generosity, the elimination of the charitable deduction would remove a traditional incentive for giving. One can only hope that the philanthropic impulses unique to Americans will survive any transformation and budget balancing acts of Congress.

Forming Alliances

Most organizations have a valuable intangible resource—their know-how and accomplishments, as mentioned in Chapter 1 (Pursuit of Financial Success: Some Observations) and illustrated in Chapter 7 (Affiliations and Agency Agreements). Financial planners should seek to recognize these resources and the possibilities for using them to replace evaporating government funding and for other reasons. As an example, alliances can be formed among groups of nonprofits providing similar or overlapping services. During the past 10 years in Houston, Texas, coalitions have been formed by nonprofits that focus on child care, public education, mental health, areas of the city, such as Main Street and the Medical Center, and many more community issues. These consortia compare notes and study delivery systems, existing funding sources, elimination of duplicated services, and in several instances the need to merge organizations. The hope of these consortia is to identify and stretch citywide resources available to those in need. To inspire the consideration of such resources, the following suggest intangible resources that might be identified:

- Can the cost of our talented programmers be leveraged by sharing their knowledge with similar organizations?
- Could the exemplary after-school program conducted on the town's north side serve as a model for centers in other locations?

- Could the award-winning stage production be taken on the road?

- Could our organization cosponsor this year's seminar with similar organizations throughout the state?

- Is there a market to circulate the children's art exhibition we have approved for next year?

- Can the curators design the teaching materials in a fashion suitable for bookstores and teacher supply houses?

- Can we seek other cultural groups to join us to more fully utilize our theater?

- Should our loosely affiliated local organizations seek a national group exemption to save each individual group the need to seek IRS approval and make annual filings?

These questions could result in plans to achieve economies to scale that enhance and maximize a nonprofit's existing resources. The attitude can be: "Why should all the arts organizations in town have individual web pages? Why not have an art site accessible on the Internet for all?"

Business Income

Most nonprofits have resources, such as their name, their mailing list, their buildings, and their knowledge and volunteers, among other assets, that can be commercially exploited for their benefit. It is very important to point out that most exempt organizations are permitted to conduct business activities for income-producing purposes as long as that activity does not subsume them and become the organization's primary focus. The rules concerning business income are highly complex and represent a very good example of why some people think the income tax system as we know it should be discarded.

Fees for rendering services or selling goods are referred to as *business income*. Business income earned by a nonprofit must be distinguished between that earned in pursuit of its mission—called *related income*—and that earned from an activity undertaken simply to make money—called *unrelated income*. Just a few examples of related income are student tuition paid in return for education provided, fees for continuing education seminars sponsored by a business league, charges to hospital patients, and sales of books on topics germane to the organization's mission. This type of income is an expected and currently tax-free source of nonprofit revenues.

However, income from operating a public restaurant, selling advertisements in the quarterly newsletter, or providing health insurance programs are not considered to advance the mission or to be unrelated. For federal purposes, the net profit from unrelated business activity is subject to income tax just as if the nonprofit were a for-profit company. The rules are designed to eliminate unfair competition to businesses by putting a nonprofit on the same footing as a for profit.

The unrelated business income tax rules have been a healthy target for lobbying groups for and against them. As a result of successful lobbying by nonprofits, the rules exclude from tax a business that is operated with volunteer labor, one that sells donated goods, one that is operated irregularly (the annual bazaar), and one that produces passive investment income, including dividends, rents, royalties, and interest. The small business lobby continually insists these special exceptions are unfair and should be eliminated. The IRS and nonprofits argue about the rules on a regular basis, making them unclear and difficult to understand. Suffice it to say, business income can provide a good resource for the nonprofit that is willing to study the rules and possibly pay tax on the profits.[1] The fourth edition of my tax book now has 73 pages on this subject.

Planned Gifts

The term *planned gift* refers to a gift that is paid over a period of years or at some time in the future. For a variety of reasons, such gifts may sometimes afford the giver a considerable economic advantage over an immediate, direct gift of cash or property. A brief description of the types of planned gifts the organization might solicit follows:

- **Split-interest trusts** are attractive giving techniques because they provide for both charitable and noncharitable beneficiaries. A charitable remainder trust pays income for a term of years to the giver or other private individuals and eventually pays the trust principal to a charity. Its economic benefit is split between the donor and the nonprofit charity. A charitable lead trust functions conversely and pays the income to charity for a period of years and ultimately gives the property to individuals. The lead trust created under Jacqueline Kennedy's will reportedly allowed her to give a substantial sum to each of her children 35 years hence tax free. Split interest trusts may be created either during life (called intervivos) or at death (called testamentary).

- **Retirement plan** property held in an individual retirement account (IRA) or other qualified retirement plan account is accumulated income that has never been taxed. This characteristic makes such a plan a good choice for a planned gift. When someone dies with retirement assets still in the plan, a heavy (sometimes double and

---

[1] The chapter on this subject in Blazek, *Tax Planning & Compliance for Tax-Exempt Organizations*, 4th ed., Hoboken, NJ: John Wiley & Sons, 2004, Chapter 21. Supplemented annually.

possibly higher than 70 percent) tax burden is imposed. If the plan is given to charity instead, a charitable deduction allows escape from the estate tax and the charitable recipient does not pay the income tax when it receives the assets in the plan. Effective for 2007 and 2008, a person over 70 years old could receive a tax deduction for a donation of up to $100,000 from an IRA account to charity.[2]

- **Life insurance policies** can also be a good choice. The annual premium is an affordable gift for many benefactors and attractively provides a much greater gift upon the insured's death. Under the existing tax rules, a charitable income tax deduction is allowed for the gift of an existing whole life insurance policy equal to the cash surrender value at the time of the gift.

For organizations interested in learning more about planned gifts, the web site of the National Committee on Planned Giving (NCPG) can be studied. The NCPG has chapters in major cities throughout the country. An Internet search on the words *planned giving* yields an amazing list of institutions that have planned giving programs and are ready to provide information on the subject.

CASH FLOW PLANNING

Often, the most important resource for a nonprofit is its cash. To maintain solvency, financial viability, or plainly said, *the ability to pay its bills*, the organization must have sufficient liquid assets. Certain noncash assets, such as donations receivable, eventually contribute to liquidity and are a part of the cash-management process. Such assets are commonly called current assets on a financial statement and include those assets with potential to become liquid within a short period of time—monthly student tuition receivable, bookstore inventory for sale, and the like. One way to conceptualize the cash management process is to think of the cycles of cash that continually flow through the organization. To maintain solvency, the cash must flow smoothly and be readily available when it is time.

Understanding CPAs' Cash Flow Statements

Certified public accountants (CPAs) designed the cash flow statement because the financial reports may reflect an excess of revenues over expenses when there is no money in the bank. This situation arises, for example, when the organization spends cash to acquire equipment. Assuming the equipment will be useful over a number of years, only part of its purchase price

---

[2] There is hope, in 2007, that this provision will be extended.

is expensed (depreciated) for the year of purchase but cash equal to the full price was spent. A charitable pledge is reported as income in the year pledged, and it likewise may produce a noncash profit. On the other side, a nonprofit showing a deficit might have money in the bank from collecting a prior year's pledge or from selling obsolete equipment. Using the accrual method accounting, as explained in Chapter 6 (Choosing a Method), may exaggerate this result. This method presents resources earned, such as a student's obligation to pay tuition monthly, as current income, even though the money is not in the bank. Similarly, supplies purchased but not yet paid for are shown as an expense. The statement is designed to fully explain the differences in resource flow and cash in the bank. The cash flow report reconciles the impact on the nonprofit's resources from its current operations, its borrowing or financing activity, and finally its investment activity. The statement calculates the sources of increase or decrease in cash to arrive at the total change in cash as shown in Exhibit 5.3.

Exhibit 5.3   Statement of Cash Flows for the Year 20XX

Cash flow from operations:

Excess of revenue over (expenses)	$26,000
+ Add back noncash depreciation:	52,000
Adjust for accrual items:	
+(−) (Increase) in accounts receivable	(9,000)
+(−) Decrease in inventory and prepayments	24,000
+(−) (Decrease) in accounts payable	(32,000)
+(−) Increase in deferred revenues	14,000
= Net cash provided from (to) operations	75,000

Cash flow from investments:

Net proceeds of sale (purchase) of securities	0
+(−) Sale of equipment	16,000
+(−) (Purchase) of equipment	(44,000)
= Net cash from (used for) investment	(28,000)

Cash flow from financing:

+ Proceeds of new loan	0
− Payments of mortgage principal	(4,000)
= Net cash provided from (to) financing	(4,000)
Sum of net increases (decreases) in cash for year	43,000
+ Beginning cash balance	17,000
= Ending cash balance	$60,000

Cyclical Fluctuations

The other side of cash flow planning addresses timing cycles. Cash inflows and outflows for most nonprofits fluctuate throughout the year for many reasons other than the accounting ones illustrated in Exhibits 5.4 through 5.7. Churches typically receive high tithes during the Christmas season and experience lighter collection plate receipts during the summer vacation season as illustrated in Exhibit 5.8, which is based on the financial statements of Exhibit 6.7. Schools require (or encourage by charging interest) parents to pay a full year's tuition before the school year begins. Some business leagues or unions collect member dues once a year rather than throughout the year.

For those many nonprofits funded in an uneven fashion throughout the year, cash flow planning is a must. The fluctuations in cash probably cannot be entirely controlled. Instead, the planners become aware when cash shortfalls are likely to occur and prepare to bridge the gap with delayed expenditures, borrowing, or some new fundraising projects. Postponed expenditures or acceleration of payment terms for constituent billings are typical options to solve the problem.

Designing Cash Flow Budgets

Once the annual operating and capital budgets are authorized, they can be converted into a cash flow budget to verify availability of resources, to see if the nonprofit can finance the plan. The cash flow budget is prepared on a monthly basis to pinpoint possible cash shortfalls that do not appear in the annual compilation of numbers. The task is to summarize the projected sources and uses of cash for the coming year, according to the actual months of receipt and expenditure.

To do so, first estimate when collections on year-end receivables will occur. Next, calculate the normal time lag, if any, between the invoicing or billing for services or pledges (the point at which the income is recorded under an accrual system) and depositing the money in the bank. Use this statistic to convert the budget into expected inflow of cash from revenue-producing activity on a monthly basis.

Correspondingly, chart the expected expenditure of cash according to the month the payment is required, as shown in Exhibits 5.4 through 5.7. The prediction is based on past experience and educated guesswork. Expected capital expenditures, sales of assets, borrowing, debt repayment, and other financing transactions are then factored in.

In view of any deficits revealed by the cash flow budget, the need to borrow or redesign the entire budget can be considered. Note that the model cash flow budget reflects a policy decision to maintain a minimum cash level. Monitoring the cash flow budget is an ongoing process. Constant vigilance is critical. Close attention is especially needed if cash flows fluctuate widely or if months of deficit funding are expected. The need to closely monitor cash

Exhibit 5.4 Business League's Cash Flow, Version 1

STATE ASSOCIATION OF NONPROFIT MANAGERS

CASH FLOW PROJECTED FOR YEAR 20XX

VERSION 1

	January	February	March	April	May	June	July	August	September	October	November	December	Total
REVENUES													
Chapter member dues	$10,000	$40,000	$20,000	$30,000	$10,000	$5,000	$3,000	$2,000	$30,000	$40,000	$30,000	$50,000	$270,000
Members-at-large dues	3,000	10,000	8,000	12,000	6,000	2,000	1,000	800	1,200	5,000	11,000	30,000	90,200
Information services	14,000	14,000	12,000	12,000	12,000	10,000	10,000	8,000	16,000	14,000	14,000	14,000	150,000
Publication sales	20,000	20,000	20,000	20,000	20,000	10,000	10,000	10,000	25,000	25,000	25,000	25,000	230,000
Continuing education	8,000	8,000	20,000	8,000	8,000	2,000	2,000	2,000	22,000	8,000	16,000	6,000	110,000
Annual meeting	10,000	5,000	5,000										20,000
Royalty income		6,000		8,000		20,000			8,000				42,000
Interest income	200	200	200	200	200								1,000
Total revenues	65,200	103,200	85,200	90,200	56,200	49,000	26,000	22,800	102,200	92,000	96,000	125,000	913,000
EXPENSES													
Salaries and payroll taxes	30,000	30,000	30,000	30,000	30,000	30,000	30,000	30,000	30,000	30,000	30,000	30,000	360,000
Retirement and medical benefits	2,500	2,500	2,500	2,500	2,500	2,500	2,500	2,500	2,500	2,500	2,500	2,500	30,000

													Total
Professional fees	1,000	1,000	12,000	10,000	1,000	1,000	1,000	1,000	1,000	1,000	1,000	1,000	32,000
Supplies	2,200	2,200	2,200	2,200	2,200	2,200	2,200	2,200	2,200	2,200	2,200	2,200	26,400
Telephone	1,667	1,667	1,667	1,667	1,667	1,666	1,667	1,666	1,667	1,666	1,666	1,667	20,000
Postage and shipping	1,667	1,667	1,667	1,667	1,667	1,666	1,667	1,666	1,667	1,666	1,666	1,667	20,000
Building costs	2,000	2,000	12,000	2,000	2,000	2,000	2,000	2,000	2,000	3,000	4,000	3,000	38,000
Equipment repair and insurance	1,100	1,100	1,100	1,100	1,200	1,200	1,200	1,200	1,200	1,200	1,200	1,200	14,000
Printing and publications	12,000	8,000	12,000	9,000	12,000	9,000	11,000	9,000	20,000	9,000	10,000	16,000	137,000
Travel	1,000	1,000	6,000	1,000	3,000	3,000	1,000	1,000	3,000	3,000	3,000	4,000	30,000
Meetings and classes	500	500	18,000	500	2,500	500		1,000	2,000	2,000	1,500	3,000	32,000
Information services	4,000	15,000	15,000	9,000	5,000	4,000	4,000	4,000	5,000	5,000	5,000	5,000	80,000
Marketing	11,650	11,650										23,300	46,600
Purchase of equipment	10,000										7,400	10,000	27,400
Total Cash Outlay	81,284	78,284	114,134	70,634	64,734	58,732	58,234	57,232	72,234	62,232	71,132	104,534	893,400
Excess (deficit) of CASH	(16,084)	24,916	(28,934)	19,566	(8,534)	(9,732)	(32,234)	(34,432)	29,966	29,768	24,868	20,466	19,600
Cash at beginning of month	60,000	43,916	68,832	39,898	59,464	50,930	41,198	8,964	(25,468)	4,498	34,266	59,134	60,000
Cash at end of month	$43,916	$68,832	$39,898	$59,464	$50,930	$41,198	$8,964	($25,468)	$4,498	$34,266	$59,134	$79,600	$79,600

Exhibit 5.5 Business League's Cash Flow, Version 2

STATE ASSOCIATION OF NONPROFIT MANAGERS

CASH FLOW PROJECTED FOR YEAR 20XX

VERSION 2

	January	February	March	April	May	June	July	August	September	October	November	December	Total
REVENUES													
Chapter member dues	$10,000	$40,000	$20,000	$30,000	$10,000	$5,000	$3,000	$17,000	$15,000	$40,000	$30,000	$50,000	$275,000
Members at large dues	3,000	10,000	8,000	12,000	6,000	2,000	1,000	800	1,200	5,000	11,000	30,000	90,000
Information services	14,000	14,000	12,000	12,000	12,000	10,000	10,000	12,000	12,000	14,000	14,000	14,000	150,000
Publication sales	20,000	20,000	20,000	20,000	20,000	10,000	10,000	20,000	15,000	25,000	25,000	25,000	230,000
Continuing education	8,000	8,000	20,000	8,000	8,000	2,000	2,000	2,000	22,000	8,000	16,000	6,000	110,000
Annual meeting	10,000	5,000	5,000										20,200
Royalty income		6,000		8,000		20,000			8,000				42,300
Interest income	200	200	200	200	200								1,300
Total revenues	65,200	103,200	85,200	90,200	56,200	49,000	26,000	51,800	73,200	92,000	96,000	125,000	913,300
EXPENSES													
Salaries and payroll taxes	30,000	30,000	30,000	30,000	30,000	30,000	30,000	30,000	30,000	30,000	30,000	30,000	360,000
Retirement and medical benefits	2,500	2,500	2,500	2,500	2,500	2,500	2,500	2,500	2,500	2,500	2,500	2,500	30,000

Professional fees	1,000	1,000	12,000	10,000	1,000	1,000	1,000	1,000	1,000	1,000	1,000	1,000	32,000
Supplies	2,200	2,200	2,200	2,200	2,200	2,200	2,200	2,200	2,200	2,200	2,200	2,200	26,400
Telephone	1,667	1,667	1,667	1,667	1,667	1,666	1,667	1,666	1,667	1,666	1,666	1,667	20,000
Postage and shipping	1,667	1,667	1,667	1,667	1,667	1,666	1,667	1,666	1,667	1,666	1,666	1,667	20,000
Building costs	2,000	2,000	12,000	2,000	2,000	2,000	2,000	2,000	2,000	3,000	4,000	3,000	38,000
Equipment repair and insurance	1,100	1,100	1,100	1,100	1,200	1,200	1,200	1,200	1,200	1,200	1,200	1,200	14,000
Printing and publications	12,000	8,000	12,000	9,000	12,000	9,000	11,000	9,000	20,000	9,000	10,000	16,000	137,000
Travel	1,000	1,000	6,000	1,000	3,000	3,000	1,000	1,000	3,000	3,000	3,000	4,000	30,000
Meetings and classes	500	500	18,000	500	2,500	500		1,000	2,000	1,500	1,500	3,000	32,000
Information services	4,000	8,000	8,000	8,000	8,000	8,000	8,000	8,000	5,000	5,000	5,000	5,000	80,000
Marketing		10,000									13,300	13,300	46,600
Purchase of equipment	10,000									10,000	7,400	10,000	27,400
Total Cash Outlay	69,634	69,634	107,134	69,634	67,734	62,732	62,234	61,232	72,234	72,232	84,432	94,534	893,400
Excess (deficit) of CASH	(4,434)	33,566	(21,934)	20,566	(11,534)	(13,732)	(36,234)	(9,432)	966	19,768	11,568	30,466	19,600
Cash at beginning of month	60,000	55,566	89,132	67,198	87,764	76,230	62,498	26,264	16,832	17,798	37,566	49,134	60,000
Cash at end of month	$55,566	$89,132	$67,198	$87,764	$76,230	$62,498	$26,264	$16,832	$17,798	$37,566	$49,134	$79,600	$79,600

Exhibit 5.6 State Association of Nonprofit Managers Version 1: Charted Cash Flow

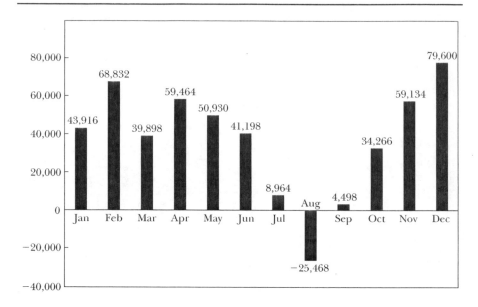

Exhibit 5.7 State Association of Nonprofit Managers Version 2: Charted Cash Flow

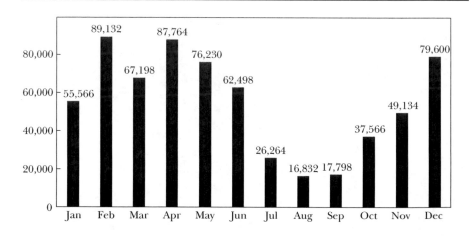

flow is yet another reason (in addition to those outlined later in Chapter 6 [Computerized Accounting]) to obtain a fully integrated accounting system that can update the cash flow budget automatically as a part of the monthly financial report process.

Exhibit 5.8 Church Cash Flow

HOLY SPIRIT CHURCH

CASH FLOW PROJECTED FOR YEAR 20XX

	January	February	March	April	May	June	July	August	September	October	November	December	Total
Receipts:													
Plate collections	$3,600	$3,600	$4,600	$4,400	$3,800	$2,000	$2,000	$2,000	$5,800	$6,000	$4,200	$6,000	$48,000
Annual pledge envelopes	3,000	3,500	3,500	6,000	3,500	2,000	2,000	2,000	3,500	3,500	3,500	6,000	42,000
Special gifts	600			6,500		2,000			4,000		900	10,000	24,000
After-school care fees	1,000	2,000	2,000	2,000	2,000				1,000	2,000	2,000	2,000	16,000
Total receipts	8,200	9,100	10,100	18,900	9,300	6,000	4,000	4,000	14,300	11,500	10,600	24,000	150,000
Disbursements:													
Clergy and vestry	4,000	4,000	4,000	4,000	4,000	4,000	4,000	4,000	4,000	4,000	4,000	6,000	50,000
After school programs	2,800	2,600	2,600	2,600	2,600	100	100	2,600	3,000	3,000	3,000	3,000	28,000
Music and Sunday school	400	400	400	600	400	300	300	300	400	400	400	700	5,000
Building costs	2,500	2,500	2,500	2,500	2,500	2,500	2,500	2,500	2,500	2,500	2,500	2,500	30,000
Church office	1,250	1,250	1,250	1,250	1,250	1,250	1,250	1,250	1,250	1,250	1,250	1,250	15,000

Exhibit 5.8 Church Cash Flow (*continued*)

Other	167	167	167	167	167	167	167	167	167	167	167	167	2,000
Total disbursements	11,117	10,917	10,917	11,117	10,917	8,317	8,317	10,817	11,317	11,317	11,317	13,617	130,000
Excess (deficit) of cash receipts over disbursements	(2,917)	(1,817)	(817)	7,783	(1,617)	(2,317)	(4,317)	(6,817)	2,983	183	(717)	10,383	0
Cash at beginning of month	6,600	3,683	1,867	1,050	8,833	7,217	4,900	583	(6,233)	(3,250)	(3,067)	(3,783)	
Cash at end of month	$3,683	$1,867	$1,050	$8,833	$7,217	$4,900	$583	($6,233)	($3,250)	($3,067)	($3,783)	$6,600	$18,400

BEYOND CASH FLOW IMBALANCES

Ideally, an organization always has cash in reserve for unforeseen conditions. Imagine how important that reserve was to an arts organization when the U.S. Congress slashed the National Endowment for the Arts budget. Contingency cash reserves can almost never be too high! A new organization particularly needs to budget for revenue surpluses in its early years until a sufficient level of cash is accumulated. To a young organization struggling to meet its payroll, building a cash reserve may seem like a luxury it can scarcely afford. Nevertheless, the fiscally prudent nonprofit plans from day one to build working capital reserves equivalent to several months, and preferably more, of operating expenses.

Whenever cash flow budgets indicate excess cash reserves, plans for temporary cash investments are in order. As much money as possible can be kept in interest-bearing federally insured accounts to maximize yield on cash. The choice of temporary investment—certificates of deposit, Treasury bills, or money market accounts—should be governed by a board-adopted investment policy following the prudent investor rules discussed later in this chapter (Prudent Investment Planning). Once the cash reserves exceed the current year's need, the opportunity for longer term investments arises. This resource management task requires even more complex decision making—ideally, by a finance committee with the assistance of professional investment managers. Investment policies must weigh the permissible level of risk to the organization's resources in relation to expected returns.

More Money in the Bank

The fiscally astute organization keeps its money in the bank as long as possible. Whether the organization is able to earn interest on the money or avoid paying interest on funds it must borrow or bills it pays late, money in the bank is obviously desirable. On the incoming cash side, when possible, revenue collection procedures should accelerate the time for receiving the money. Keeping in mind that there is no reason not to act like a business in this regard, a nonprofit may charge interest on late payments and offer discounts for early payment.

Many nonprofits accept credit cards for tuition, sales, services, and more. The accounting system should contain suitable information and the capability to bill promptly for services rendered. Similarly, the membership renewal system should remind members promptly that it is time to send their support. Submission of quarterly cost reports required to receive an installment on a grant receivable should never be late. Persons responsible for development should schedule the deadlines for submitting grant requests to potential funders well ahead of time. Typically, nonprofits with cash flow problems are slow in sending renewal notices or grant reports that would provide the funds to pay the staff to send the notices or prepare the reports.

On the outgo side, bills are scheduled to be paid when the terms for purchase require and not before. A regular cycle—say the first and fifteenth day of the month—can be established for bill payments. These established days are made known to the staff and creditors so that all can plan to receive their money based on the cycle. It is amazing how much effort is saved with this simple policy, in addition to interest earned on keeping the money in the bank.

To Borrow or Not

When the cash flow budget indicates a deficit in cash will occur during the year, the nonprofit faces a tough decision. Does the organization borrow the funds, can it possibly find new funding, or does it reduce the projected expenditures? The answer depends on the answers to many questions. Is the deficit temporary? Will it reverse itself in a few months? Before borrowing, an analysis of sources of funds to repay the debt should be made. For a new organization, interim borrowing may not be an option. For a mature one expecting to refurbish an old building, there may be alternatives. The decision is made in each case based on the particular facts and circumstances. This issue is one for which traditional business planning tools are particularly useful.

Securing a necessary loan takes good advance planning. In my experience, the nonprofit in a crisis mode gets loans only, if at all, from *angels*—patrons or funders who love the organization. But when the need for short-term indebtedness is recognized as a part of the budgeting process, solutions can be found. The budget itself probably indicates that the situation will reverse itself with money expected to be received later in the year. For an organization in this situation, preparation of a business plan to make a formal application to a bank is a good exercise. If a bank cannot be persuaded to make the loan, the nonprofit goes back to the drawing board and revises its budgets and/or finds new funding sources.

A cash deficit created by proposed capital acquisitions may have a simpler and easier solution. The physical and tangible nature of a capital asset makes it suitable to serve as collateral for a loan. Therefore, it may be possible, even for a new organization, to borrow the money needed to equip the organization. The lender expects they can get their computer, truck, or whatever back if the nonprofit defaults on the periodic payments. The questions to be answered in choosing to borrow money to buy versus leasing for capital additions are outlined later in Chapter 7 (Purchasing Procedures).

PRUDENT INVESTMENT PLANNING

Once a nonprofit organization accumulates cash assets beyond its operating needs for the coming year, it can begin to develop permanent investment plans. In managing the nonprofit's investments, the organization can be guided by the prudent investor rules compiled by the American Bar Association.[3] These standards say "a trustee is under a duty to the beneficiaries to invest and manage the funds of the trust as a prudent investor would, in light of the purposes, terms, distribution requirements, and other circumstances of the trust."[4] The business judgment rule, discussed in Chapter 2 (The Role of the Board), requires essentially the same standard for nonprofit corporate directors regarding the management of endowment funds, restricted gifts or bequests, and employee benefit plans as outlined in UMIFA (Uniform Management of Funds Act.[5]

The predecessor prudent man rule was first set forth in 1830 and directed trustees to "observe how men of prudence, discretion and intelligence manage their own affairs, not in regard to speculation, but in regard to the permanent disposition of their funds, considering the probable income, as well as the probable safety of the capital to be invested."[6] In explaining the rules, the guide cautions that the facts and circumstances of each investor (nonprofit organization) must be taken into account in choosing appropriate investments.

In June 2006, UMIFA was replaced with UPMIFA, or Uniform Prudent Management of Institutional Funds Act.[7] UPMIFA incorporates the experience

---

[3] *Prudent Investor Rules*, Restatement of the Law of Trusts adopted by The American Law Institute at Washington, D.C., May 18, 1990, American Law Institute Publishers, St. Paul, MN, 307 pages. The prudent investor standard of care is set forth in the Restatement of Trusts (Third) and incorporated in the Uniform Prudent Investor Act. Most states have adopted some variation of the Uniform Prudent Investor Act, as drafted by the National Conference of Commissioners on Uniform State Laws.

[4] Ibid, p. 8.

[5] George W. Overton (ed.), *Guidebook for Directors of Nonprofit Corporations*, Nonprofit Corporations Committee, Section of Business Law, American Bar Association, p. 41. In the context of investment decisions, most states have adopted some form of the 1972 Uniform Management of Institutional Funds Act (UMIFA). Under Section 5 of that Act the board of a nonprofit organization may delegate day-to-day investment management authority to committees or employees. Also, it may purchase investment advisory or management services. However, despite this delegation authority allowed by the Act, responsibility for investment policy and selection of competent agents remains firmly with the board. As of September 2 2007, seven states have adopted UPMIFA.

[6] *Harvard College v. Amory*, 9 Pick (26 Mass) 446, 461 (1830). In 1959, the rule was changed to direct trustees "to make such investment and only such investments as a prudent man would make of his own property having in view the preservation of the estate and the amount and regularity of the income to be derived."

[7] The National Conference of Commissioners on Uniform State Laws (NCCUSL) approved the Uniform Prudent Management of Institutional Funds Act (UPMIFA) and recommended it for enactment by the legislatures of the various states. UPMIFA is designed to replace the existing Uniform Management of Institutional Funds Act (UMIFA). Go to UPMIFA.org for more details.

gained in the last 35 years under UMIFA by providing even stronger guidance for investment management and enumerating a more exact set of rules for investing in a prudent manner. It requires investment "in good faith and with the care an ordinarily prudent person in a like position would exercise under similar circumstances." It requires prudence in incurring investment costs, authorizing "only costs that are appropriate and reasonable."

The nonprofit's financial planners must familiarize themselves with basic investment strategies and terms reflected in modern investment concepts and practices. Unless the trustees or directors individually possess expertise and time to manage the investments with care, skill, and caution, they have a duty to delegate management of such funds. The fees charged by professional investment managers are often modest when viewed in relation to the possibility of enhanced yield over a period of time and professional management provided. A formal investment policy setting out the organization's goals as it regards expected yields, the acceptable degree of risk to be taken, and resulting assets allocations can be adopted to guide the process and provide a structure for monitoring investments.[8]

To evaluate a nonprofit's funds suitable to be invested in a permanent fashion, the following five questions must first be carefully answered:

1. *For what length of time can the funds be invested?* The organization's liquidity needs must be projected into the future for a number of years. In choosing a suitable investment, the organization must know when or if the funds might be needed to pay future operating expenses, to build a new stadium, or to meet some other financial obligation.

2. *Can the organization afford to lose any of the money?* The answer to this question measures the level of risk the organization can take. The rate of return from interest, dividends, and/or increase in underlying value of the asset is related to the possibility that the original investment, also called principal sum, can be lost. The higher the risk of loss, the higher the expected return as explained below.

3. *How secure are the nonprofit's funding sources?* The organization must evaluate the stability of its funding sources to project the level of contingency or emergency reserves it may require. Such funds would be placed in investments with a low risk of loss of principal value.

4. *Are the organization's personnel or staff capable of overseeing the investments?* In the absence of a Midas touch, special talents and training are required to successfully manage a fully diversified investment portfolio. As evidenced by the stock market crashes in past years, no one knows

---

[8] www.ucop.edu/treasurer/invpol (University of California General Endowment Pool); www.hr-system.com/Investment_Policy_Statement (a 401(k) plan example).

whether the stock values will go up or down. A nonprofit's financial managers must evaluate their own knowledge and experience and consider the need to engage outside professional investment managers.

5. *How will the economic rate of inflation or deflation impact the investment?* Fixed money investments, such as certificates of deposit and U.S. Treasury obligations, do not fluctuate in face value according to the overall economy. Common stocks, real estate, and tangibles may be enhanced in value due to inflationary conditions and conversely lose value due to deflation. The nonprofit must project expected future inflation or deflation to properly diversify its investments.

Facing the Unknown

A healthy dose of skepticism and an appreciation of the uncertainty that abounds in regard to investments are important. As one writer noted in describing the Federal Reserve Board's deliberations about the interest rate, "No word seems to appear more frequently in the transcripts than uncertainty."[9] The financial markets in which a nonprofit must choose to place its funds are influenced daily by international forces beyond its control. Who knows if the stock market will go up, if a global stock fund will sustain its yield, or if the U.S. dollar will go up against the Japanese yen?

Diversification is a very important technique designed to face the unknown. It says essentially, "Don't put all the eggs in one basket." A prudently balanced investment portfolio contains a variety of financial instruments—stocks, bonds, real estate, and so on. The mix of investments assumes some go up, some go down, and in the long run the averages will provide a desirable stream of income. It is not necessarily conservative or prudent to maintain all the funds invested in fixed-money or interest-only bearing securities. Conserving the principal in its original dollar amount, inviolate and permanent into perpetuity, may not necessarily safeguard the fund for the donor's intentions. It should be remembered that fixed-return investments do have some inherent risk; in some, the value of some bonds falls or rises over 10%. The goal is to deliberately balance and continually rebalance what are called *asset allocations*.[10]

The investment alternatives available to a nonprofit organization are the same as those available to a for-profit investor. Because the nonprofit does not pay income tax on its income,[11] certain choices, such as municipal bonds or deferred annuities, may not be suitable. The types of investments from which the nonprofit chooses include those shown in Exhibit 5.9.

---

[9] Louis Uchitelle, "At the Fed It Looks Like Deja Vu, Again," *New York Times,* July 2, 1995, Section 4.

[10] This term brings up a wealth of models and discussion on the Internet.

[11] Except unrelated business income as discussed in Section 5.2(b).

Exhibit 5.9 Investment Alternatives

The following types of investments can be purchased directly from the issuing financial institution (the bank, the U.S. Treasury, or the company issuing the stock) or though mutual funds or other investment companies. To enhance diversification, investment issued by both domestic (U.S.) and international companies may be appropriate. Balancing risk might also include stock options and other hedging strategies.

Fixed-Money Value (principal dollar amount fixed):

> Interest-bearing checking account
> Money market account
> Certificate of deposit
> Treasury bills
> Series EE bonds
> Fixed annuities

Variable Money Value (principal value fluctuates with prevailing interest rates; but interest rate on investment usually fixed)

> Treasury notes and bonds
> Mortgage-backed bonds
> Corporate bonds
> Municipal bonds
> Annuities or universal life insurance policies

Equity Investments (principal value and dividend rate varies)

> Common stock (domestic and international)
> Preferred stock
> Bonds convertible into stock
> Stock options

Real Estate

> Commercial real estate (office, store, hotel, or factory building)
> Residential real estate (single-family or multiperson apartment)
> Raw land
> Agricultural or rural land

Tangibles (the first three are also called collectibles)

> Gold or silver
> Antiques
> Art
> Minerals
> Commodities

A classically diversified investment portfolio would contain some investments in several of the above categories. The portion of total investments held in each category depends on the organization's risk tolerance and life phase as shown in Exhibit 5.10. It is said that investment success depends on using good asset allocation techniques.[12] Each of the categories can be expended. For example, within the equities category, different types might be held (small-cap, mid-cap, and large-cap, for example) and both domestic and international equities could be held. One should keep in mind that one writer said, "Successful investing for the period 2004 through 2010 will require you to do things differently than you did in the 1980s and 1990s."[13]

Say a nonprofit organization has $1 million to permanently invest. If the board adopts a conservative approach, it would invest $250,000 in temporary cash, $350,000 in bonds, $350,000 in common stocks, and $50,000 in gold or commodities.

The investments within each category might be further diversified. A fixed-money portfolio, for example, would have debt instruments with staggered maturity dates and credit ratings, because fixed-return investments can also fluctuate widely in value and have some inherent risk of loss. The $350,000 in our example above might include $100,000 of 5-year bonds, $100,000 of

Exhibit 5.10 Classic Investment Ratios

	Conservative	Moderate	Aggressive
Cash and fixed money	25%	10%	5%
Fluctuating bonds	35	25	10
Equities	35	45	50
Absolute return strategies/options			10
Venture capital			10
Real estate		10	10
Tangibles	5	10	5
Total investments	100%	100%	100%

---

[12] www.da.ks.gov/ps/documents/ing/Asset%20Allocation.
[13] John F. Mauldin, *Bull's Eye Investing: Targeting Real Returns in a Smoke and Mirrors Market.* John Wiley & Sons, Hoboken, 2004.

7-year bonds, $150,000 of 30-year bonds. Similarly, a common stock portfolio would include stock of companies in different types of businesses—durable goods, drugs, computer software, home building, banking, and so on. One will find differences of opinion about the ratios presented above.

Many investment choices are available to fit a nonprofit's investment needs. Mutual funds and publicly traded partnerships that hold diversified types of investments can be purchased to achieve the desired balance of risk. What are referred to as *family of funds*, such as Fidelity, T. Rowe Price, and Vanguard, offer a wide variety of funds focused on the types of investments listed in Exhibit 5.5. An investment company founded in 1918 by Carnegie Foundation,[14] Teachers Insurance and Annuity Association–College Retirement Equities Fund (TIAA-CREF) is another possibility to study. Their web site says, "TIAA-CREF offers a wide range of investment products and services designed to meet our investors' specific financial needs, offering expert ways to help them control and manage income." An investment consortium created by major private foundations, The Investment Fund for Foundations (TIFF), is also available to §501(c)(3) organizations, though the minimum investment required is high. Information providing a look at how major nonprofit institutions invest their permanent funds can be found on the Internet.[15] Examples of investment policies can also be studied.[16]

Risk versus Return

A nonprofit must carefully identify those funds that are suitable for each category of investment type. The possibility for a higher yield or overall return provided by common stock may not always outweigh the inherent risk of the investment. A restricted grant to be spent over a three-year period certainly should earn some interest, but probably should not be invested in technology stocks.

The relationship of risk to investment return must be understood. The reason a six-month certificate of deposit pays the lowest available interest rate is that little risk is taken. Without question, the face amount of the certificate plus a stated amount of interest will be paid (unless there is a bank collapse or other banking system crisis). As the uncertainty about

---

[14] Established as the Teachers Insurance and Annuity Association to provide a fully funded system of pensions for professors.
[15] www.yale.edu/investments/Yale_Endowment_06; vpf-web.harvard.edu/annualfinancial/pdfs/2006.
[16] www.berea.edu/vpf/accounting/documents/InvestmentPolicy; www.investmentpolicy.com.

the final outcome of risk of loss increases, it is expected that the yield will increase. Correspondingly, the less uncertainty, the lower the yield. The conflict between risks the organization is willing (or reasonably able) to take and the return on investment needed to pay operating expenses is the same as for individuals or for-profit companies. In evaluating risk, however, the benefit of diversification, or holding investment of varying risks must be taken into account. The pyramid in Exhibit 5.11 illustrates the concept.

Investment Cycles

The categories of investment types chosen by a nonprofit organization can be based upon the phases of its financial growth cycles reflected in Exhibit 5.12. Phase 1 is the stage when the nonprofit has no cash reserves and needs to build its liquidity. During this phase, all the money would be invested in cash or near-cash securities, or those that can be converted to cash immediately without loss of principal value. Phase 2 represents the stage when the organization has begun to accumulate some working capital, maybe six months of operating expense in cash reserves, but still cannot afford to risk any loss of its principal. Phases 3 through 5 represent the three styles or investment philosophies a fully capitalized organization would follow when it is able to make permanent investments. There could

Exhibit 5.11   Investment Risk Pyramid

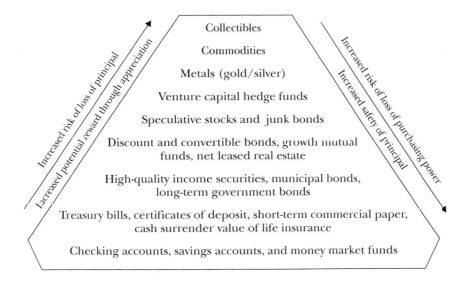

Exhibit 5.12   Investment Phases

	Short-Term Fixed-Income Securities	Long-Term Fixed-Income Securities	Growth and Income Stocks	Specu- lative Stocks	Real Estate	Other Types
Phase 1: Liquidity accumulation	100%					
Phase 2: Adequate liquidity, but no perma- nent funds	70	30				
Phase 3— Permanently capitalized organization						
Conservative growth	30	30	40			
Moderate growth	15	25	40	10	5	5
Aggressive growth	5	5	30	25	10	25

be significant variations on the patterns dependent on the investment knowledge and sophistication of the nonprofit's board members and advisors.

Measuring Investment Return

For some investments the return, or income earned, is easy to calculate. Investment return is calculated by dividing the current income received in a year—the interest paid or accrued, dividends, capital gain distributions, or other profit share (for partnership), plus the increase in value of the underlying investment less any decrease in value.

Fixed-money investments, whose principal values fluctuate with the prevailing interest rates, are purchased at what is called a premium (paying $102 for a $100 bond) or discount (paying $95 for a $100 bond). When a premium is paid, the stated yield on the bond is usually higher than the prevailing rate. Conversely a bond selling at a discount likely is paying a lower percentage than the current rate. Each year the bond is held, a ratable portion of the premium or discount is added to or deducted from income to reflect the true yield as shown in example 4. Similarly, a bond originally purchased with a coupon interest rate of 8 percent does not yield 8 percent in a year when its principal value declines 2 percent; instead it yields 6 percent as reflected in example 5.

Example 1: For a one-year certificate of deposit issued at 5 percent the yield is:

$$\frac{\text{Interest}}{\text{Principal of CD}} \quad \frac{\$5,000}{100,000} \quad 5\%$$

Example 2: Common stock worth $100,000 on first day of year, paying out $2,000 of dividends and selling for $110,000 at year end.

$$\frac{\text{Dividend} + \text{Increase in Value}}{\text{Value of Year's Beginning}} \quad \frac{\$12,000\,(2,000 + 10,000)}{100,000} \quad 12\%$$

Example 3: Same as example 2 except stock declined to $98,000 in value.

$$\frac{\text{Dividend} - \text{Decrease in Value}}{\text{Value of Year's Beginning}} \quad \frac{\$\text{-}0\text{-}\,(2,000 - 2,000)}{100,000} \quad 0\% \text{ (none)}$$

Example 4: A 5-year bond with principal sum of $100,000 bearing a 5 percent coupon is purchased for $95,000 and at year end is still worth $95,000. Note the brokerage or investment manager's report listing this bond would likely reflect that the yield is 5 percent, the face coupon amount.

$$\frac{\text{Interest Paid} + \text{Discount*}}{\text{Original Cost of Bond}} \quad \frac{\$6,000\,(5,000 + 1,000\text{*})}{\$95,000} \quad 6.3\%$$

(*The purchase discount of $5,000 is divided by five years.)

Example 5: A 5-year bond with principal sum of $100,000 bearing an 8 percent coupon is purchased for $100,000 on the day the bond is originally issued. By year-end the value of the bond has decreased to $98,000 (because the current rate rose).

$$\frac{\text{Interest Paid} - \text{Decline in Value}}{\text{Original Cost of Bond}} \quad \frac{\$6,000\,(8,000 - 2,000)}{100,000} \quad 6\%$$

Example 6: For the bond in example 5, assume in the second year the value increased to $99,000. Note that for the two year period, the overall total yield might be averaged to determine the cumulative yield was 7.6 percent (6% + 9.18% divided by 2).

$$\frac{\text{Interest Paid} + \text{Increase in Value}}{\text{Beginning of Year Value}} \quad \frac{\$9,000\,(8,000 + 1,000)}{98,000} \quad 9.2\%$$

Professional investment managers and mutual funds governed by the Securities and Exchange Commission must conform to a unified standard for reporting investment yield.

RESTRICTED GIFTS

The nonprofit organization that pursues restricted funding does so advisedly and fully aware of the accompanying responsibilities. Once the money is received, the funder's specific designation about its use must be respected, necessitating a high level of attention to details. The financial stability afforded by such funding customarily makes the effort worthwhile for those nonprofits fortunate enough to secure it.

Isolating Restricted Grants

A restricted gift is one subject to donor-imposed stipulations limiting its use. Some restrictions relate to a period of time that may expire, such as, "We pledge to give $100,000 to match any new foundation grants received in the next three years," or "to hold until the current pastor's retirement account is fully funded." Another common type of restriction grants the funds to be spent for a particular project, for example, to buy food for children, train the unemployed, or clean up the pollution.

Perhaps the most important financial issue concerning such gifts is the responsibility to isolate the money.[17] Under common law, the nonprofit owes a fiduciary duty to its contributors and grantors to use gifts for the purposes for which the funds are given. Accordingly, before accepting such funding, a mechanism for tracking the money must be in place. Because of this obligation, some organizations establish a separate bank account for each restricted fund. The fund accounting system discussed in Chapter 6 (Computerized Accounting) is designed to tag and track earmarked or restricted grants, and it should suffice to inform the financial managers on a regular basis of their obligation to have funds needed to meet the restrictions.

Administrative Costs

All too often, restricted grant funds come with little or no administrative cost component. The nonprofit must consider whether or not it can afford to manage such a gift; for example, should it accept a restricted grant to distribute food to the poor if the grant only funds the purchase and provides no money for delivering the food or evaluating qualified recipients? Can

---

[17] Not necessarily in a separate bank account, but clearly identified with corresponding expenses identified.

it afford to fund, from its other moneys, the staff position(s) necessary to actualize the program goals? Always consider the course of funds to manage the grant. Another cost factor is enhanced accounting expense; the grant expenditures must be specifically accounted for. Reporting to granting agencies and foundations may require special forms and reports. As described in Chapter 2 (Selecting Financial Reporting Services), the U.S. governmental Office of Management and Budget has a sophisticated separate auditing process and requires a special *Single Audit* for certain federal grants.

ENDOWMENTS

An endowment is a permanent gift intended to be kept intact, perhaps forever, to produce annual income to support the organization's activities. What is referred to as the principal amount of an endowment gift is preserved or safeguarded and not itself expended for the stipulated term of years, commonly the life of the organization. Sometimes an endowment gift is invested to produce income to fund a specific project, like scholarships or unspecified operational costs. Although such funding is a highly desirable resource, important policy issues regarding the terms of the endowment must be thoroughly discussed with the donors and agreed upon before such a gift is accepted.

The first question concerns the moment when the organization is ready to seek endowments. Potential endowment funders must perceive the organization to be sufficiently permanent or stable enough to exist a long time. Traditionally, universities, hospitals, and churches have attracted such funding. Recently cause-related organizations—some providing shelter to the disadvantaged, some dedicated to the environment, and others—have sought and received such permanent funding.

The other issues involve the terms governing the organization's use of the gift. In requesting endowment gifts, the informed nonprofit deliberates and suggests gift terms that will be to its best advantage. The issues that particularly should be agreed upon and stipulated in writing include the following, among others:

- *Endowment's life.* How long must the endowment remain restricted, for a term of years (5, 10, or 20) or forever? Can the funds be used for another purpose in a time of crisis? If so, what type of crisis? What happens to the endowment funds should the nonprofit—or the program(s) to be funded—cease to exist? Is the endowment subject to a life income interest? (See the section Planned Gifts earlier in this chapter.)

- *Definition of income.* Are realized gains (defined later) treated as current income? Is the endowment principal, defined as its original sum, a sum certain, or is it the original sum plus all appreciation less declines in underlying value?

- *Nature of investments.* Do the endowment creators wish the donated asset to be retained? Can it be sold? Must it be sold in a particular fashion? If sold for cash, is there any restraint on the fashion in which the cash is reinvested?

You can quickly see from the above questions that the meaning of the term *endowment* is complex and multifaceted. To illustrate how the questions arise, assume that a $1 million endowment gift made payable in shares of marketable securities is accepted. Historically, the common law of endowments considered the capital gains, that is, the gains realized from sale of shares over time, as additions to the principal, the original value of the shares. Thus, the principal value of the $1 million grew or shrank with market forces similar to the custom for private trusts. Only the current income (the dividends or interest) was expended currently on programs or operations. The structure of capital markets in the 1970s began to favor the treatment of capital gains as current income, and the nonprofit world was faced with a dilemma.

Who Gets the Appreciation?

The financial markets now expect low-dividend yields equal to a small portion of the company's annual income. This "current return" is accepted to allow the corporation to reinvest most of its earnings in expansion and conglomeration. The desired result is a consequential appreciation in underlying value of the securities. Most investment managers today anticipate that annual income will be earned from a combination of dividends and interest plus gains resulting from appreciation in the value of the underlying security. The objective is to achieve what is called *total return* on the capital invested. What formerly was treated as an addition to the principal—the appreciation in value of the asset(s)—is now treated of as income.

The trend toward following a *total return* concept for a nonprofit's endowment funds was encouraged by the Ford Foundation as early as 1969 in a study entitled *The Law and the Lore of Endowment Funds.*[18] The study said, "We find no authoritative support in the law for the widely held view that the realized gains on endowment funds can never be spent. Prudence would call for the retention of sufficient gains to maintain purchasing power in the face of inflation and to guard against potential losses, but subject to the standards

---

[18] *The Law and the Lore of Endowment Funds,* A Report to The Ford Foundation, New York, by William L. Cary and Craig B. Bright, 1969. The study was commissioned to review the law governing the endowment funds of colleges and universities with the goal of conveying new knowledge and informed commentary about charitable investments to strengthen the efforts of the institutions to improve their endowment income. The Uniform Management of Institutional Funds Act now recommends the total return concept. UMIFA has been adopted in all but 10 states and is applicable to nonprofit corporations.

that prudence dictates, the expenditure of gains should lie within the discretion of the institution's directors." The study investigated whether "the directors of an educational institution are circumscribed by the law or are free to adopt the investment policy they regard as soundest for their institution, unhampered by legal impediments, prohibitions or restrictions."

To Mark It to Market?

A number of parallel questions are faced by the nonprofit concerning its record keeping and financial reporting of its investment—endowment and otherwise. Among the issues to consider are the following:

1. Should investment assets be reported on the statement of net assets (balance sheet) at their original cost or at the current market value?

2. In which fund is the total return reported?

3. How is the increase or decrease in the value of the investments reported on the Statement of Net Assets and on the Statement of Activity?

The answer to question 1 is still debated, although the CPAs have now weighed in on the side of current value. The accounting profession struggled for a long time to arrive at its recommendation that readily marketable equity and debt securities be reported at their current fair market price.[19] Mortgage notes, real estate investments, oil and gas interests, venture capital funds, and partnership interests can be reported at original cost or appraised value. A purchased investment is recorded originally at its cost. Donated investment assets are reported at the fair market value on date of gift. Then, annually, those carrying values are adjusted up or down to reflect the current market value, and the result is reported as unrealized gains and losses.

Questions 2 and 3 are interrelated and more complicated to answer. First, one must ascertain whether local law or the donor stipulation say anything about the issue. The Uniform Management of Institutional Funds Act, now law in many states, sanctions the inclusion of gains (realized and unrealized) in currently spendable income alongside dividends and interest; said another way, total return is reported on the Statement of Activity (Income Statement). The National Association of College and University Business Officers (NACUBO) also recommends this policy. The *AICPA Audit and Accounting Guide for Audit of Certain Nonprofit Organizations* provides that a

---

[19] Statements of Financial Accounting Standards No. 124, *Accounting for Certain Investments Held by Not-for-Profit Organizations,* was issued November 1995, effective for fiscal years beginning after December 15, 1995.

governing board may make a portion of realized, and in some cases, unrealized, net gains available for current use.

The unexpended increase or decrease in value (appreciation) of the securities remaining in the investment portfolio are reported as temporarily restricted funds, rather than endowment funds, under Statement of Financial Accounting Standards (SFAS) 117. Note that this issue is evolving, requiring readers to seek the most current information. There are still choices about how the financial statements reflect the total return.[20]

How Income Is Measured

According to financial analysis theories, long-term investment income may be reported for financial purposes and correspondingly budgeted as expendable income in at least four different ways. The term *realized* is used to denote capital gain or loss from transactions that actually occurred. Realized capital gain is the excess of actual sale proceeds over the amount paid for a security. *Unrealized* capital gain is the hypothetical gain calculated assuming securities still held as investments were sold on the balance sheet date. Measures of long-term income include:

- *Current return method.* Using this method, actual interest, dividends, rents, or royalties paid are treated as income (unrestricted). Any realized or unrealized gains or losses added back to or subtracted from the principal fund (restricted).

- *The overall return method.* This method classifies the current return plus realized capital gains and losses (those resulting from actual sale of the investment asset) as operating (unrestricted) income.

- *The total return method.* This method reports overall return actually received plus or minus unrealized gains and losses as unrestricted income.

- *Constant return.* Based on a historical average amount, a fixed annual percentage of the value of the investment pool is treated as unrestricted income.

The *total return method* can be shown this way:

Total return = Dividends and interest ± Realized and unrealized gains (+) and losses (−)

---

[20] Reporting alternatives are very well illustrated and discussed in *Financial and Accounting Guide for Not-for-Profit Organizations*, 7th ed., Chapter 6.

Endowment and Restricted Fund Checklist

Management and protection of restricted and endowment funds present challenges and certainly involve significant policy decisions, as indicated by the above discussion. Again, tools are available to allow the prudent nonprofit and its directors and financial managers to exercise the fiduciary responsibility inherent in the acceptance of such funding. The checklist shown in Exhibit 5.13 is designed to be completed at least annually by the financial managers. Additionally, an adequate fund accounting system as explained in Chapter 6 must be used to monitor restricted fund flows and to ensure that such resources are devoted to the purposes for which they were given.

Exhibit 5.13   Endowment and Restricted Fund Checklist

This checklist contains questions to verify adherence to covenants and restrictions, if any, placed upon contributed funds. It suggests questions to evaluate investment policy and to check for private inurement. It is particularly designed for use by the chief financial officer and the board finance committee. Some questions have simple yes/no answers for actions taken personally and some ask if others have carried out responsibilities delegated to them.

A. Understanding General Information Endowment and Restricted Funds

To become familiar with the terms and restrictions on a nonprofit's endowment and restricted funds and the accounting procedures in place for tracking such funds, consider the following issues:

1. Does the organization have any endowment or restricted funds? ☐

2. If so, is there a master control for such funds? ☐

3. Verify maintenance of a permanent file for each endowment. ☐

4. Review the permanent files to familiarize yourself with each endowment's terms and restrictions. ☐

5. If the donor's terms are not clear, has there been a clarification made with the donor or his or her descendants; if not, has the board adopted a policy regarding the uncertainty? ☐

6. Is a fund accounting system used? ☐

7. Regarding endowment funds:

    a. Are the moneys separately invested and easily identifiable? ☐

Exhibit 5.13 Endowment and Restricted Fund Checklist *(continued)*

    b. Verify annual income required to be distributed or set aside.   ☐

    c. How is *income* defined? Do endowment terms allow
       allocation of capital gains to income?   ☐

B. Monitoring Compliance with Restricted Grand Covenants

To assess administrative ability to track restricted funds and measure availability of funds according to grant or endowment terms.

1. Can functional accounting reports, which identify costs
   allocable to grants, be prepared from the financial records?   ☐

2. Are detailed expense records maintained?

    a. Staff time reports   ☐

    b. Space usage allocations   ☐

    c. Direct and indirect cost-coding system in chart of accounts   ☐

3. Encumbrance system controls authorized expenditures under
   grant.   ☐

4. For government grants (both federal and state), are procedures
   of OMB Circular A-128 and A-133 followed?   ☐

5. Is income recognition properly timed?   ☐

6. Are funds held for future periods classified as temporarily or
   permanently restricted?   ☐

C. Permanently Restricted Land, Building, and Equipment (LBE)

To evaluate the nonprofit's ability to monitor permanently restricted gifts in the form of land, building or equipment (LBE), ask:

1. Is this fund being reported separately from the unrestricted
   funds because of donor restriction or accounting practice?   ☐

2. Does the LBE fund include unexpended donations? If so does
   their investment placement give regard to the expected timing of
   the building program?   ☐

3. Are transfers to cover depreciation made from the current
   unrestricted fund?   ☐

4. Is an asset inventory system used to control physical loss
of assets? ☐

D. Investment Policy

*To assess investment strategies in view of risks, potential for return, and profes-
sional investment management, explore such issues as the following:*

1. Are yields on investment assets monitored? ☐

2. Do yields furnish a return commensurate with the risk of
capital loss? ☐

3. Are funds managed by an independent professional manager? ☐

4. Is management fee commensurate with those charged in the
area for similar services? ☐

5. Consider propriety of having more than one manager. ☐

6. Does diversification of investments provide protection against
inflation, market forces, and other economic changes? ☐

E. Reliance on Restricted Gifts

To assess the nonprofit's dependence upon such gifts, consider the following:

1. What portion of annual operations are financed with income
from endowment funds or restricted grants? ☐

2. If income decreased substantially due to market forces, would the
organization's programs be jeopardized? ☐

3. Are governmental or United Way grants subject to decline in
current economic climate? ☐

F. Pooled Income Funds and Split-Interest Trusts

*To oversee adherence to trust provisions regarding private individual benefici-
ary's interest in restricted gifts, the nonprofit annually asks the following:*

1. Review reports of pooled income funds and split-interest trusts. ☐

2. Are terms of gift agreement adhered to? ☐

3. Is current income sufficient to make agreed payments to individual
beneficiaries? ☐

Exhibit 5.13   Endowment and Restricted Fund Checklist *(continued)*

    4. Is distinction between income and principal clear? ☐

    5. Were required annual reports prepared? ☐

    6. Review term endowments or charitable lead trust for termination dates. ☐

    7. Are annuity and unitrust computations evaluated by outside independent accountants? ☐

G. Suitability of Raising Endowment and Restricted Funds

To evaluate the benefit from endowment and restricted funds in view of the inherent costs and the potential fundraising alternatives, answer the following questions:

    1. Based on answers to the above questions, should the organization continue to solicit endowment and restricted grants? ☐

    2. Is time involved in record keeping excessive? ☐

    3. Could similar levels of support be raised as unrestricted grants? ☐

    4. Should existing endowment instruments be reformed to allow allocation of some or all capital gains to income? ☐

    5. Are donors still living? ☐

    6. Would benefit of reallocated funding deserve cost of court petition? ☐

    7. Should instruments for future endowment gifts and other restricted gifts be reformed? ☐

    8. Do the development department, staff, and the board adequately communicate regarding issues raised in this checklist? ☐

6

Nonprofit Accounting

The backbone of financial planning for a nonprofit
organization is a good accounting system.

This chapter outlines the basic elements of an accounting system. When and
why an accrual basis of accounting is used can be understood by comparing an accrual-based system to the simpler alternative, the cash method of
accounting. Factors indicating when a nonprofit goes beyond maintaining
its accounts on a computerized checkbook system, such as Quicken, are
presented. Illustrative financial statements append the chapter to reflect the
desired result of the accounting function. Information on how to design a
chart of accounts with samples can facilitate this critical process. Checklists
for choosing a computer accounting system, maintaining internal controls,
and minimal accounting system requirements complete the tools provided.

A broad range of data, both financial and nonfinancial, is used in making financial plans for a nonprofit organization. National and local economic performance, projections of future economic conditions, population
growth, surveys reflecting social preferences or the number of persons in
need of service, all may be useful data relevant to the planning process as
described in Chapter 1 (Comprehensive Financial Planning Checklist) and
Chapter 4 (Preparing Forecasts). By far the most accessible and typically the
most significant data is contained in the nonprofit's own accounting records
and financial statements. The desired result is an accounting system that
presents financial information in an understandable fashion that allows the
organization's managers to make astute financial decisions.

WHAT IS ACCOUNTING?

The accounting profession defines *accounting* as the art of recording, classifying, and summarizing in a significant manner and in terms of money,
transactions, and events that are, in part at least, of a financial character, and

interpreting the results thereof.[1] The United Way of America expands the definition and suggests that a nonprofit's accounting system records and summarizes the financial activities of the organization in a manner that:[2]

- Lends itself to revealing clearly and fully the organization's financial position, sources, and amounts of revenue, and nature and extent of expenditures, including per unit cost of the benefit, where feasible, and

- Complies with all legal and technical requirements of governmental and other authoritative organizations.

Budgeting serves as a financial guideline for future financial activity. The accounting process provides the financial data necessary to utilize a budget by capturing and recording the inflows and outflows of funds and presenting the nonprofit's resources in a meaningful presentation of budget and actual information for its management, volunteers and donors. From the resulting compilation of financial information, rational decisions can be made, aspirations can be tested against performance, and if necessary budgets as well as other plans can be adjusted to more accurately reflect the reality faced by the nonprofit organization. An accounting system for the typical nonprofit looks somewhat like that of a for-profit business, as shown in Exhibit 6.1. This section introduces the system components shared by all systems as well as the special attributes of a fund accounting system.

Exhibit 6.1 Bookkeeping and Accounting Process

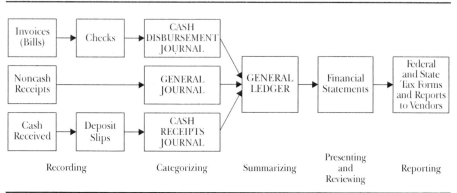

---

[1] Accounting Research and Terminology Bulletins, *Accounting Terminology Bulletin No. 1*, Final ed., American Institute of Certified Public Accountants, 1941, p. 9.
[2] *Accounting and Financial Reporting, A Guide for United Ways and Not-for-Profit Human-Service Organizations*, revised 2d ed., United Way of America, 1989, p. 9.

Cash Receiving Systems

Cash receipts may originate from several different sources such as receipts from customers on account or regular sales; program fees; fundraising special events; contributions; or investment income such as interest, dividends, or royalties. The cash receiving systems document all money received through mail, cash registers, and electronic transfers. Additionally, the cash receiving system may include a process to track and record money due to be received in the future, or accounts receivable, as described below. Whatever the level of sophistication of the receipt system, the objective is to have a chronological listing of all moneys flowing into the nonprofit, along with an appropriate paper trail evidencing the source of the funds. The cash receiving system records include the cash receipts journal, the accounts receivable ledger, and the sales journal.

Cash Receipts Journal   All nonprofits should keep one or more journals to record each cash receipt much like an individual enters deposits into a personal checkbook. A cash journal contains a chronological listing of each deposit, resulting in a monthly total that is reconciled to the deposits reported on the bank statement(s). For some organizations, a separate journal or record is maintained for each type of cash receipt, for example, each fundraising event, contribution type, program fees, and interest. Cash journals may be maintained manually or electronically through the use of specialized accounting software or customized databases. The monthly activity of the cash journals are recorded or posted into the general ledger.

Accounts Receivable Ledger   The nonprofit that sells publications, performs consulting services, treats patients, and has seminars and similar fee-based programs often provides goods and services before it receives payment. Likewise, members and grantors may pledge support or pay dues over a period of time. Such obligations to pay are called *accounts receivable*. A subsidiary ledger for accounts receivable is maintained and lists, either chronologically or alphabetically, the names of purchasers or donors, the amount due to be paid, and the date payment is due. For charities soliciting voluntary contributions, a contributions receivable ledger may be maintained in a donor database holding each contributor's history of giving, amounts pledged to be given in the future, contact information, and other data to aid fundraising efforts. These ledgers are called *subsidiary* ledgers and contain the detailed daily posting of activity. The monthly subsidiary ledger totals are recorded, or posted, into the general ledger.

Sales Journal   A nonprofit that makes over-the-counter sales through a bookstore, cafeteria, theater, and so forth may maintain a cash register-based sales journal. Whether the journal is a computerized sales register or manual one, it should contain a detailed listing of the sale by cash, bank check, or credit card. The sales journal information typically identifies the category of sale for purposes of recording the activity in the general ledger, for maintaining the cost of inventory on hand, cost of inventory goods sold, and sales revenue.

Cash Disbursement Systems

The steps followed in paying the expenses of the nonprofit comprise the cash disbursement system. A disbursement system serves to make certain that disbursements are made only for goods or services that are known to have been received and for other purposes that have been properly authorized. Disbursements should be made only after appropriate supporting documents have been reviewed and approved. When a budget is used, a proposed expenditure may be compared to the balance of unexpended moneys in the applicable budget category before approval of the disbursal of funds. Chapter 7 (Purchasing Procedures) explores this subject further and presents model purchasing forms. Three different systems are used as presented below beginning with the most thorough and complicated.

Purchase Orders   Under this system, the nonprofit establishes procedures for disbursing money based upon an advanced approval system. The prospective buyer first prepares a *purchase order* to seek authorization from a designated person(s). Ideally, the proposed purchase order is concurrently entered into the accounting system to verify available funds in the current-year approved budget. Only after this two-step approval system, the items or services are purchased. Upon the goods' arrival or service performance, a receiving report is received, and the liability or obligation to pay for what has been received is entered into the accounting system to be paid.

Accounts Payable System   A somewhat simpler system tracks *accounts payable*, or those bills due to be paid. The purchase first enters the accounting system when the supporting documentation for the disbursement, such as vendor invoice or statement, arrives and is approved by an authorized person. Thus, the obligation to disburse funds is recorded in the accounting system before the invoice is paid, but after the debt is incurred.

Check Writing System   Under the simplest system, the expense enters the accounting system as checks are prepared for payment directly from the invoice or statement as they are paid. The checks are registered in chronological and (optimally) numerical order, as they were issued.

Payroll Disbursement System

The details of salaries paid, federal or state taxes withheld for employees, the employer's matching federal taxes, employee benefits for child care or insurance, pension and other similar benefits, and other items affecting employees' compensation that is necessary for federal and state reporting are entered in a payroll journal. This information is accumulated for periodic tax depositing and reporting purposes. The journal may also categorize the payroll according to types of workers (full time versus part time, hourly versus monthly), by program, by location, or other suitable classification that summarizes personnel costs that may be useful in planning or financial reporting.

Some nonprofits outsource the payroll function to companies that specialize in keeping the records, preparing checks or direct employee bank deposits, and handling all of the federal and state tax reporting. Advantages of such services include facilitating confidentiality of personnel compensation, implementing current changes in federal and state tax rates, providing human resource services that may not otherwise be afforded by the nonprofit, and making timely payroll tax payments. The withheld portion of payroll taxes does not belong to the organization, but instead to the employees. A prudent board, whose members can in some circumstances be personally liable if the taxes go unpaid, might evaluate the usefulness of outsourcing the payroll reporting and accounting to ensure respect for employee funds. A record of vacation, sick, or compensatory time accrued and taken, plus all qualified and nonqualified pension or other deferred compensation should also be maintained. A nonprofit reporting on an accrual basis is expected to calculate and record the liability for its obligation for such unpaid employee benefits.

Other Useful Ledgers and Financial Files

Depending on the size and scope of the nonprofit's activity, many other ledgers, filing systems, or databases may be necessary to maintain adequate financial information. Exhibit 6.2 provides a checklist of minimal record-keeping requirements for use by a new and emerging organization. The types of detailed records that are useful include the following:

> *A general ledger* contains a record for each account listed in a chart of accounts beginning with cash as shown on the master listing in this chapter (Chart of Accounts). The detailed financial activity in each account is reflected chronologically throughout the year. When a detailed ledger, such as payroll or student tuition receivable, is separately maintained, its monthly totals are posted in the general ledger (rather than each item). At the end of each accounting period, the general ledger would be used to prepare a *trial balance* or listing of each account with its current balances for all accounts in the general ledger. General ledger journal entries are made when corrections or adjustments to accounts are required or noncash transactions are being recorded.

> *Investment records* may be maintained that list each separate investment held by the organization, the associated original cost or purchase price, number of shares, market value, and premium or discount information related to the investment. The expected revenue from dividend and interest might be noted alongside a comparison of the amounts actually received in a year or the prior year.

The property and equipment ledger, also called a *fixed-asset ledger,* contains a detailed listing of all tangible buildings, improvements, furniture, fixtures, or equipment and real properties owned by the nonprofit, plus intangibles such as copyrights or trademarks. At a minimum, the types of assets owned (computer, desk, truck, or building), dates purchased or received, purchase price or donated value, and depreciation information should be listed. Additionally, it may record serial numbers, insurance coverage, location, or other useful information pertaining to each property item. For internal control purposes, this ledger would be used to conduct an annual inventory of the property and equipment and their location.

The permanent asset files should be established to maintain original purchase invoices, insurance policies, guarantees or warranties, maintenance contracts, and similar documents. These files serve as companions to the property ledger and should always contain the original purchase invoice or contracts associated with the property as long as the asset is owned.

The paid bill files contain vendor invoices canceled or marked clearly as paid (preferably with the check number, account code, and date). There is a natural tendency to want to keep invoices for related expenditures grouped together—all the supplies, all the newsletter or meeting costs, for example. However, alphabetical filing by vendor is preferable because this method provides a third sort-and-retrieval system for the disbursements. Chronological retrieval is available from the check register contained in the cash disbursements journal. Accumulated costs associated with each category of expense are found in the accounting system's general ledger.

The personnel files contain records associated with employees or independent contractors, arranged in individual files for each person or firm. Such files include original engagement, hiring letter or contract, wage withholding form (W-4 or SS-9), periodic reviews, awards, complaints, vacation and sick records, continuing education records, and other employee-related information.

The grant files contain detail-relevant information for all grants: those to be received as a contribution or paid out by the nonprofit. Beginning with the grant request, the entire history of each grant is recorded and filed. Any information required for receiving or paying the grant and any information useful for grant renewal is noted. Considering the importance of grant documentation and the level of detail desired, a computer database (in addition to the manual record) can be very useful.

The noncash transaction ledger documents noncash gifts, a description of the property or services donated, the date received, and the value, if available, as of the gift date. Assigning value to noncash gifts, such as used clothing or other goods for resale or distributions to the needy, is not easy. If the goods are resold soon after receipt, the donation value is preferably recorded as the selling price. Professional services may or may not be valued following the rules explained in this chapter (FASB, GAAP, and Nonprofits). For those that are recorded, the nonprofit should obtain an invoice reflecting the value of the services donated.

Exhibit 6.2   Minimal Financial Record Keeping for a Nonprofit Organization

---

This checklist is a list of minimal record-keeping requirements for use by a new and emerging organization and suggests types of useful detailed records.

A. Organizational Documents

Create permanent files for the following organizational documents: ☐

1. State charter, bylaws, trust instruments, or articles of association.   ☐

2. Minutes of board meetings, finance, and other board committees.   ☐

3. Letters of exemption from federal, state, and local authorities, and applications file (Form 1023 or 1024).   ☐

4. Letters of intent, trust instruments, grant agreements, or other documents regarding restricted funds.   ☐

5. Agreements with event sponsors, fiscal agents, joint venturers, chapters, or other documents evidencing organizational obligations and entitlements.   ☐

6. Employment contracts, employee benefit plans, contracts for services, policy manuals, and other personnel files.   ☐

7. Leases, maintenance agreements, repair records, and other data regarding equipment and facilities.   ☐

8. Calendar of important organizational deadlines, such as IRS tax compliance returns and deposits, grant request, follow-up reports to funders, board and committee meetings, program announcements, and the like.   ☐

B. Banking Records

1. Check register or checkbook reflecting each transaction and the cash balance in each bank account is constantly maintained.   ☐

2. Bank statements opened and bank reconciliation prepared monthly by person not maintaining accounting records, preferably a non–check signer.   ☐

Exhibit 6.2   Minimal Financial Record Keeping for a Nonprofit Organization
(*continued*)

---

3. Bank statements kept intact (original canceled checks remain with statement) and reconciled monthly.   ☐

4. Consider need for separate accounts for restricted funds.   ☐

C. Revenues and Exempt Function Receipts

1. Deposit checks or cash, if possible, on day of receipt.   ☐

2. Enter the payer's name and describe nature of funds received, whether check or cash, on each deposit slip or create detailed report.   ☐

3. Record each contribution, sale, or service rendered in detailed ledger (student rolls or member receivables).   ☐

4. Maintain an alpha (by donor or client) file for copies of receipts with a deposit slip copy attached.   ☐

5. For events, canisters, or volunteer solicitations, maintain Public Fund Solicitation Control checklist (Exhibit 6.9).   ☐

6. Issue receipts or thank yous with donor disclosures if needed.   ☐

7. Calculate, charge, and report sales tax where applicable.   ☐

D. Disbursement of Funds

1. Pay bills on a regular basis, for example, the 5th and 20th or every Friday.   ☐

2. Design an approval system that provides internal control.   ☐

3. Maintain paid bills (invoices) in an alphabetical order by vendor, labeled with check number and date paid.   ☐

4. Establish a reporting system for employee/volunteer time worked, vacations, leave, expenses reimbursed, and licensing requirements.   ☐

5. Keep a file for permanent assets, including copies of original invoice, serial numbers, insurance, maintenance contracts, etc.   ☐

6. Keep files to document nature of activities and nonprofit purposes (copy of exhibition catalog, invitations, show announcements, patients seen, consulting provided, time expended on projects, training seminars, etc.).   ☐

7. For workers hired, classify as employee or contractor and complete checklist for employee tax requirements (Exhibits 7.12 and 7.13).   ☐

8. For independent contractors, obtain invoice and Form W-9 for all.   ☐

9. Obtain and use sales tax exemption certificate.   ☐

E. Accounting Records

1. Choose an accounting system, preferably a computerized one suitable for nonprofit's size and staff skills.   ☐

2. Develop a chart of accounts.   ☐

3. Establish system for documenting and recording noncash entries.   ☐

4. Preferably monthly, prepare financial statements of actual financial transactions compared to budgeted figures (Exhibit 6.6).   ☐

5. Maintain report of assets and debts (also called general ledger), preferably using a computerized financial statement program.   ☐

6. Prepare annual budget and compare actual results on accounting summaries to the budgeted amounts (see Chapter 4).   ☐

7. Prepare tax compliance checklist annually (see Chapter 8).   ☐

8. Develop a record retention system with advice of counsel.   ☐

9. Establish throw-away dates and label stored records accordingly.   ☐

Fund Accounting

A fund accounting system identifies the organization's resources according to the purpose for which it is holding the funds. The fund categories might include:

- Unrestricted general operating

- Unrestricted, but board-designated for a special purpose or reserve

- Restricted by the donor for some specific purposes or as an endowment

- Dedicated to land, building, and equipment (LBE)

As discussed further in Chapter 5 (Restricted Gifts; Endowments), different funds are created within the nonprofit's accounts to segregate and report transactions attributable to restrictions placed on the funding by outside donors and grantors. Such a system enables the organization to monitor funds entrusted to it. The system accumulates information for preparing reports to evidence compliance with any legal or donor restrictions placed on the expenditure of the funds.

A nonprofit using fund accounting designs its chart of accounts (considered in this chapter [Chart of Accounts]) to include subdivisions or sections for each fund for which it must separately account. The program or fund categories of a nonprofit will correspond to the departments or cost centers of a for-profit business.

COMPUTERIZED ACCOUNTING

The ledgers, files, and other elements of an accounting system discussed in this chapter (What Is Accounting?) can be maintained either with manual, or handwritten, financial records or a computerized accounting software package. Any nonprofit possessing a personal computer can and probably should computerize part or all of its accounting records. There is a dizzying array of programs available from simple checkbook/expense category programs, to customized fund accounting systems with integrated donor, member, asset, sales, or other necessary detailed ledgers. Because of this wide range of options, many find it difficult to choose an accounting program. Among the factors that complicate the decision are:

Computer skills. Do the nonprofit organization's personnel have the sophistication and skill to use and maintain the accounting software system?

Cost of an accounting software system. Is an accounting software system specially designed for the nonprofit the preferred choice? Such systems are more complex and the cost of such systems is also often higher and may prove too costly for some organizations. The logical choice for a modest organization may be off-the-shelf accounting software package with the capability of reporting by department or project code and comparing actual monthly results to budgeted numbers.

Number of modules. What functions should the accounting package be capable of performing? Integrating the detailed vendor, donor, member, and/or customer information with the accounting system is highly desirable. For example, both efficiency and an audit trail result when the donor's contribution is posted simultaneously in the donor database, as an increase in cash, and, correspondingly, entered in a revenue account as a contribution received.

Time savings. Will the system minimize the work involved in repetitive payments? The payroll processing system is a good example. The tax-calculating and reporting process becomes highly efficient using a computerized payroll system. Often, the compensation is fixed so that a person may receive a check of the same amount every other week throughout an entire year. Each paycheck is net of amounts to be paid to tax authorities, to an insurance company, to a retirement plan administrator, and others. The computer processing of payroll can save considerable time compared to a person repetitively performing this task every payday.

Computer capability. Will the computer hardware efficiently run the accounting software? Newer accounting software may require more computer memory.

Exhibit 6.3, a checklist designed by PriceWaterhouseCoopers, is an aid in the selection of a suitable accounting software system. The decision must be made carefully because the monetary and personnel costs involved in installing computer systems can be extensive. When the financial management is uncertain about the choice of hardware and software, a computer consultant may be helpful in making the decision. The nonprofit's independent accountants should always be asked about the choices. Many cities have management assistance programs staffed with volunteers knowledgeable about computers whose help can also be sought by the nonprofit organization.

Exhibit 6.3   Selecting Suitable Accounting Software

1. Determine the requirements that must be met by the software.

    — Include those who are to produce and use the information which is to be processed in the requirements determination process.

    — Concentrate on critical and unusual requirements.

    — Consider system-generated calculations.

    — Define all significant reporting requirements.

    — Consider nature and sources of transactions.

    — Consider required interfaces among modules and with other systems.

    — Consider any limitations on computer hardware or costs.

    — Prioritize requirements by importance.

2. Identify likely packages for detailed review.

    — Use requirements list to screen potential vendors for suitability.

    — Focus on critical and unusual requirements.

    — Eliminate obviously unsuitable packages based on requirements and/or cost.

    — Narrow the list to two or three vendors.

Exhibit 6.3   Selecting Suitable Accounting Software *(continued)*

3. Perform a detailed evaluation of the finalist vendors.

   — Prepare a detailed list of questions to ask each vendor.

   — Arrange to have the vendor provide a detailed demonstration of the accounting modules being considered.

   — Evaluate functionality and ease of use.

   — Obtain examples of reports produced by the system.

   — Obtain examples of documentation and manuals provided by the vendor.

   — Obtain financial information and business history of the vendor (especially if not well known).

   — Obtain at least three references from each vendor, preferably similar organizations.

4. Contact vendor references.

   Develop questions to ask references, including the following:

   — Perception of software strengths and weaknesses

   — Software problems encountered and limitations

   — Ease of use, ease of implementation

   — Report-writing capabilities and ease

   — Modifications made to the software

   — Availability and adequacy of vendor training and documentation

   — Vendor support and responsiveness (e.g., local presence, telephone assistance, response time to inquires)

   — Satisfaction with software performance

5. Obtain and compare cost information.Consider all potential costs and compare each candidate vendor:

   — Computer equipment requirements

   — Accounting modules

   — Other software (e.g., additional software required to operate the vendor's accounting software)

   — Cost for installation, modifications, data conversion, training, other additional costs to implement the system

   — Ongoing maintenance costs (annual expenses for both hardware and software)

6. Make a selection.

— Be willing to compromise.

— Consider alternatives for missing requirements.

— Select the software vendor with the best overall match.

— Base final decision on value, not just lowest cost.

Source: Malvern J. Gross, Jr., John H. McCarthy, and Nancy E. Shelmon, *Financial and Accounting Guide for Not-for-Profit Organizations,* 5th ed. Copyright © 1995, John Wiley & Sons, Inc. Reprinted with permission.

CHART OF ACCOUNTS

The chart of accounts is the master listing of the asset, liability, net asset or fund balance, revenue, and expense accounts used to record financial transactions. Exhibit 6.4 illustrates a suggested standard nonprofit chart of accounts with a description of the type of transactions recorded in each account. If you compare this chart to the IRS Annual Report of Exempt Organization, Form 990, you will note its listing of accounts mimics the order of Form 990 and is intended to encourage uniformity of reporting among all nonprofit organizations.

National Standard

Although an organization may design its chart of accounts to suit its particular needs, the standard system used by nonprofits throughout the country can be quite useful. Certainly a nonprofit planning to seek funding from the United Way should study their standard chart and consider using the system specifically provided in their accounting guide.[3] All nonprofits may find their budgetary projections and periodic financial reports understandable by more persons if the standard chart is used. Finally, for those self-preparing or seeking reduced fees for their Form 990 preparation, the compliance reporting is much easier to prepare when the year-end accounting reports follow the standard chart.

Functional Expense Categories

To assess flow of funds according to its programs—and to distinguish management and fundraising costs—the nonprofit must identify its expenditures by function or use. The label is built into the chart of accounts by appending or assigning a subcode or category. In the simplest fashion, the letters

---

[3] Ibid., note 2.

Exhibit 6.4 Standard Chart of Accounts

Assets and liabilities are listed in order of liquidity or maturity and may be further classified as current or noncurrent for financial statement purposes. The following definitions are based on using the accrual method of accounting.

Operating bank accounts	Separate number for each account.
Cash equivalents or short-term investments	Cash reserves available for current spending, which are invested for short periods of time.
Accounts receivable	Student, patient, member, customer amounts owed to the nonprofit, offset by amounts estimated to be uncollectable.
Pledges receivable	Contributions from individuals, foundations or corporations due to be paid to the nonprofit. These amounts may be offset by amounts estimated to be uncollectable.
Government grants or program service fee receivables	Grants from governments, or program service fees due to be paid to the nonprofit.
Other receivables	Due from employees, from purchasers of nonprofit's assets, or notes receivable from program related loans to exempt constituents.
Inventories	Publications, medicines, donated goods, crafts, handicapped worker products.
Prepaid expenses and deferred charges	Deposits, insurance premiums paid in advance.
Investments—marketable securities	Equity securities, bonds, and mutual funds.
Investments—Other or alternatives	Partnerships, hedge funds, joint ventures, real estate held for sales, etc.
Investments—land, buildings, and equipment (LBE)	Properties held for rent or for appreciation in value offset by reserves for depreciation.
Land, building, and equipment	Properties used by the nonprofit for its administrative offices, program facilities, or other direct exempt purpose, less accumulated depreciation.

| Other assets | Mineral interests, program-related investments, future value of interests in an estate or trust, and intangible assets such as trademarks, patents, etc. |

Liabilities

Accounts payable and accrued expenses	Bills received from creditors not yet paid and amounts due to be paid not yet billed, called accrued expenses.
Grants payable	Allotments or awards the nonprofit has committed to pay.
Deferred revenues	Prepayments, unearned program services fees or government grants.
Long-term debts	Debt such as bank loans, bonds or other financing agreements secured by purchased assets and commonly due to be paid over a period of years with interest.
Other liabilities	Loans advanced to nonprofit from directors or donors, capital lease obligations for the purchase of property or equipment, deferred compensation or pension obligations.

Net Assets or Fund Balances

Unrestricted net assets	Difference between assets and liabilities available as operating funds and not donor restricted for a particular purpose, can include board-designated funds.
Temporarily restricted net assets	Contributions or investment return specifically restricted by the donor and not yet used for their restricted purpose or time period.
Permanently restricted net assets	Endowment funds restricted by donors for investment in perpetuity to provide investment income for operations or for specific purposes.

Revenues

| Contributions and gifts | Voluntary, unconditional donations from individuals, corporations and foundations, includes dues of members receiving no membership benefits. |

Exhibit 6.4   Standard Chart of Accounts (*continued*)

Government grants or awards	Funding from government agencies or pass-through agencies to provide specific programs of benefit to the general public (rather than the government itself).
Program service fees	Fees for services provided to patients, students, members, performance tickets, tennis or swimming pool admission, consulting contract or research revenues, publication or patent royalties, conventions or trade shows ticket sales or booth rentals, etc. services.
Membership dues	Fees paid by members or affiliates to belong to the nonprofit and participate in the nonprofit's activities; also special member assessments.
Sales of goods, costs of goods sold	Sales of books, patient drugs, donated goods, or other properties held for sale and aggregate cost of goods being held for sale.
Investment income	Dividends, interest, realized and unrealized gains/losses from investments and cash equivalents.
Rents and royalties	Rental income and royalties paid from investments.
Fundraising revenues	Proceeds of galas, raffles, or special event activities.
Payments from affiliated nonprofits	Support from chapters or national affiliates.

Expenses (by Function)

Program services	Expenses incurred to fulfill the purpose or mission of the nonprofit resulting in goods or services being provided, such as to provide student learning, hospital services, membership benefits, present cultural performances, send newsletter, etc.
Management and general	Accounting, personnel, and administrative record keeping and supplies, board or staff meetings, investment manager fees and other

| | types of expenses which are not associated with a program of the nonprofit. |
| Fundraising expense | Costs incurred in raising money, seeking grants and gifts, also called development or donor solicitation. |

The categories of expenses listed above are called functional groupings; those below are specific, or natural, categories for expenses that are paid. The format for reporting the details varies by nonprofit type; but the following list matches the IRS Form 990, is recommended by the United Way of America, and is commonly adopted by many nonprofits. For internal accounting purposes, it is useful to adopt this standard format of functional expense designated by department.

Expenses (by Natural Classification)

Grants and allocations

Payments to affiliates

Salaries

Employee benefits

Payroll taxes

Professional fees

Supplies

Telephone

Postage/shipping

Occupancy (rent, utilities, maintenance of building—often separated)

Rental/maintenance equipment

Printing and publications

Travel

Conferences and meetings

Interest

Other expense

A, B, C, and so on, might be assigned to each program and function. Each disbursement attributable to a particular program is then assigned its natural, or generic, account code (for example, supplies or printing) plus a letter. Supplies purchased for program A are reportable at two levels: as supplies and also as supplies specifically associated with program A.

Exhibit 6.5   Functional Classification of Expenses

Line item or Natural Classifications	Functional Classification of Expenses					
	Program Services			Support Services		
	Program A	Program B	Program C	Mgt. and General	Fund Raising	Total
Salaries	X	X	X	X	X	X
Telephone	X	X	X	X	X	X
Supplies	X	X	X	X	X	X
Postage	X	X	X	X	X	X
Occupancy	X	X	X	X	X	X
Printing	X	X	X	X	X	X
Travel	X	X	X	X	X	X
Independent Contractors	X	X	X	X	X	X
Other Expenses	X	X	X	X	X	X
TOTAL COSTS	X	X	X	X	X	X

Computerized accounting systems make this dual coding system relatively easy. Luckily, the most basic of such systems have the capability to identify and sort the accounts by departments or subcodes. Exhibit 6.5 graphically depicts what is accomplished by using functional expense codes.

WHY A DOUBLE ENTRY?

The commonly used self-balancing system for recording financial transactions is called *double-entry accounting*. Each financial transaction is concurrently entered into two separate accounts as a *debit* and a *credit*, or a *plus* and a *minus*. This double-entry method provides a proof system by essentially adding and subtracting the same number at the same time from two different accounts. The books are said to be *out of balance* when the debits do not equal the credits. The system classifies financial transactions as those increasing or reducing an asset or liability and those impacting the income or expense for the year.

Study the financial statement categories illustrated in Exhibits 6.6 and 6.7, and consider how a payment for the organization's rent expense is entered. The check is entered both as a reduction (a credit) to the cash account, and correspondingly, as an increase (a debit) in the rental expense account, reflecting

Exhibit 6.6 Sample Accrual Basis Financials for Business League

STATE ASSOCIATION OF NONPROFIT MANAGERS
STATEMENT OF NET ASSETS

Assets	20XX	20XX
Cash and cash equivalents	$60,000	$17,000
Membership dues receivable	80,000	71,000
Inventory of publications	42,000	73,000
Prepayments	38,000	31,000
Total current assets	220,000	192,000
Office building	300,000	300,000
Computers and statewide network	80,000	62,000
Furnishings and equipment	90,000	80,000
Accumulated depreciation	(168,000)	(116,000)
Net fixed assets, at cost	302,000	326,000
Total assets	522,000	518,000
Current liabilities:		
Accounts payable	52,000	84,000
Deposits and prepaid dues	42,000	28,000
Current portion of mortgage	22,000	23,000
Total current liabilities	116,000	135,000
Mortgage on building	180,000	183,000
Total liabilities	296,000	318,000
Unrestricted Assets	226,000	200,000
Total liabilities and net assets	$522,000	$518,000

STATE ASSOCIATION OF NONPROFIT MANAGERS

Statement of Activity	20XX	20XX
Revenues:		
Chapter member dues	$249,700	$238,000
Members at large dues	78,600	76,000
Information services	120,000	40,000
Publication sales	204,000	180,000
Continuing education	106,000	98,000
Annual meeting	28,000	42,000
Royalty income	42,000	1,000

Exhibit 6.6   Sample Accrual Basis Financials for Business League *(continued)*

Interest income	1,000	3,000
Total revenues	829,300	678,000
Expenses:		
Member services	267,000	260,000
Publications	229,600	202,000
Continuing education	122,000	96,000
Management and general	184,700	172,000
Total expenses	803,300	730,000
Change in net assets	26,000	(52,000)
Net assets, beginning of year	200,000	25,000
Net assets, end of year	$226,000	$200,000

STATE ASSOCIATION OF NPO MANAGERS

Statement of Functional Income and Expenses

	Member Activities	Publications	Meetings and Classes	Management and General	Total	Budget	Variance
Revenues:							
Chapter member dues	$249,700				$249,700	$260,000	($10,300)
Members at large dues	78,600				78,600	100,000	(21,400)
Information services	120,000				120,000	80,000	40,000
Publication sales		$204,000			204,000	200,000	4,000
Continuing education			$106,000		106,000	100,000	6,000
Annual meeting			28,000		28,000	40,000	(12,000)
Royalty income	42,000				42,000	10,000	32,000
Interest income				$5,000	5,000	2,000	3,000
Total	490,300	204,000	134,000	5,000	833,300	792,000	41,300
Expenses:							
Salaries and payroll taxes	126,000	84,200	33,800	119,000	363,000	350,000	(13,000)
Retirement and medical benefits	6,000	3,800	1,400	14,100	25,300	26,000	700
Professional fees	12,000		8,000	12,000	32,000	28,000	(4,000)
Supplies	8,000	4,000	6,000	6,000	24,000	20,000	(4,000)

Telephone	8,000	4,000	2,000	4,000	18,000	16,000	(2,000)
Postage and shipping	4,000	10,000	2,000	2,000	18,000	16,000	(2,000)
Building costs	8,000	12,000	10,000	6,000	36,000	30,000	(6,000)
Equipment repair and insurance	2,000	4,000	2,000	4,000	12,000	10,000	(2,000)
Printing and publications	5,000	92,000	20,000	3,000	120,000	130,000	10,000
Travel	10,000		5,000	2,000	17,000	16,000	(1,000)
Meetings and classes	2,000		20,000		22,000	25,000	3,000
Information services	61,000				61,000	40,000	(21,000)
Depreciation on equipment and furnishings	14,400	12,800	10,200	4,600	42,000	40,000	(2,000)
Insurance	4,600	2,800	1,600	8,000	17,000	20,000	3,000
Total	271,000	229,600	122,000	184,700	807,300	767,000	(40,300)
Change in net assets	$219,300	($25,600)	$12,000	($179,700)	$26,000	$25,000	($1,000)

Note: Information service usage fees are substantially more than projected, and correspondingly, the eexpenses associated with the telecommunication systems are higher.

STATE ASSOCIATION OF NONPROFIT MANAGERS

Statement of Cash Flows for the Year 20XX

Cash flow from operations:

Excess of revenue over (expenses)	$26,000
+Add back noncash depreciation:	52,000
Adjust for accrual items:	
+(–) (Increase) in accounts receivable	(9,000)
+(–) Decrease in inventory and prepayments	24,000
+(–) (Decrease) in accounts payable	(32,000)
+(–) Increase in deferred revenues	14,000
= Net cash provided from (to) operations	75,000
Cash flow from investments:	
Net proceeds of sale (purchase) of securities	0
+(–) Sale of equipment	16,000
+(–) (Purchase) of equipment	(44,000)
= Net cash from (used for) investment:	(28,000)

Exhibit 6.6   Sample Accrual Basis Financials for Business League *(continued)*

Cash flow from financing:

+ Proceeds of new loan	0
= Payments of mortgage principal	(4,000)
= Net cash provided from (to) financing	(4,000)
Sum of net increases (decreases) in cash for year	43,000
+ Beginning cash balance	17,000
= Ending cash balance	$60,000

Exhibit 6.7   Sample Cash-Basis Financials for a Church

HOLY SPIRIT CHURCH

Statement of Activity

(with Comparison to Prior Year and Budget) for the Year 20XX

	Actual	Budget		Variance Favorable
	20XX	20XX	20XX	(Unfavorable)
Revenues:				
Plate collections	$48,000	$46,500	$48,000	($1,500)
Annual pledged contributions	38,000	54,000	42,000	12,000
Restricted contributions	12,400	16,400	24,000	(7,600)
Day care fees	16,000	18,000	16,000	2,000
Total revenue	$114,400	$134,900	$130,000	$4,900
Expenses:				
Clergy and vestry	57,000	63,000	50,000	(13,000)
Day care programs	19,000	28,700	28,000	(700)
Music and Sunday school	4,200	5,600	5,000	(600)
Building costs	22,400	36,800	30,000	(6,800)
Church office	14,100	18,200	15,000	(3,200)
Other	1,990	7,900	2,000	(5,900)
Total expenses	$118,690	$160,200	$130,000	($30,200)
Change in net assets	($4,290)	($25,300)	$0	($25,300)
Net assets, beginning of year	138,100	133,810		
Net assets, end of year	$133,810	$108,510		

HOLY SPIRIT CHURCH

Statement of Net Assets for the Year Ended August 31, 20XX

	20XX	20XX
Cash	$6,600	$1,850
U.S. Treasury note, at cost approximating market	9,140	12,400
Marketable securities at contributed cost (market $ 5,600)	4,260	4,260
Current assets	$20,000	$18,510
Building and land	250,000	250,000
Church fixtures, hymnals, and robes (net)	88,600	86,000
Computers and office furnishings, net of depreciation	31,400	26,700
Total fixed assets	$370,000	$362,700
Total assets	$390,000	$381,210
Accounts payable	81,490	47,400
Church bonds due in 10 years	200,000	200,000
Total liabilities	$281,490	$247,400
Net Assets	$108,510	$133,810

HOLY SPIRIT CHURCH

MONTHLY REVENUES AND EXPENSES, COMPARED TO BUDGET

For the Month of October, 20XX				Ten months ending October 31, 20XX		
Actual	Budget	Variance Favorable (Unfavorable)	REVENUES	Actual	Budget	Variance Favorable (Unfavorable)
$3,600	$4,000	($400)	Plate collections	$36,200	$40,000	($3,800)
3,400	3,500	(100)	Pledge contributions	33,000	35,000	(2,000)
500	2,000	(1,500)	Special gifts	12,800	20,000	(7,200)
2,200	1,333	867	After school care	14,400	13,333	1,067
		0	Contributions and gifts			
$9,700	$10,833	($1,133)	Total revenue	$96,400	$108,333	($11,933)
			EXPENSES			
5,200	4,167	(1,033)	Clergy and vestry	53,000	41,667	(11,333)

Exhibit 6.7   Sample Cash-Basis Financials for a Church *(continued)*

2,200	2,333	133	After school care	22,316	23,333	1,017
467	417	(50)	Music/Sunday school	4,666	4,163	(503)
2,433	2,500	67	Building costs	29,700	25,000	(4,700)
1,560	1,250	(310)	Church office	15,110	12,500	(2,610)
260	167	(93)	Other	1,900	1,670	(230)
$12,120	$10,833	($1,287)	Total expense	$126,692	$108,333	($18,359)
($2,420)	$0	($2,420)	Net asset change	($30,292)	$0	($30,292)

expense for how the money was spent. When a member's dues are deposited, the cash account is increased (debited) and the dues revenue account is credited (which, paradoxically, is for the revenue account an increase).

A computerized checkbook system, such as Quicken, is essentially a single-entry system because the entries impact only cash in the bank account. Such a one-sided system lacks the checks and balance inherent in a double-entry accounting system. The following chart of financial statement categories illustrates how the debits and credits interact. It is reasonable to be confused by the fact that an increase in an asset or expense account is a debit, whereas an increase in a liability or revenue account is a credit. The typical double entry for each major category of account is shown below.

	An increase in this category is entered normally as a:	A decrease in this category is normally entered as a:
Assets: Cash, investments, equipment.	Debit	Credit
Liabilities: Accounts payable, mortgages, deferred revenues	Credit	Debit
Revenues: Contributions, grants, program services fees	Credit	Debit
Expenses: Salaries, rent, insurance, etc.	Debit	Credit

CHOOSING A METHOD

An organization that records and reports financial transactions only when cash has been received or expended is said to use the *cash method of accounting*. If, instead, revenue is recorded when the commitment is received from the donor, fees and other revenue are recorded when earned, and expenses are recorded as incurred, the *accrual method of accounting* is used. In other words, revenues and expenses are accrued when "all events have occurred to evidence the obligation" without regard to the time of actual receipt or disbursement of the money.

The manner in which the two different methods function is best illustrated by examples. Under a cash-basis accounting system, office supplies ordered today and charged to the nonprofit's account are not reported as an expense until a check is written in payment of the bill. Under an accrual accounting system, the obligation to pay for the supply order is recorded as an obligation—an account payable—at the time the supplies are received.

Similarly, under accrual accounting systems, a promised gift to the building fund campaign to be paid over a three-year period is recorded as income when an unconditional pledge is made. The future portion of the gift is recorded as a pledge receivable—an asset. When each installment is actually received and put into the bank, the accounting entry is posted as a reduction to the receivable rather than to revenue (because the entire gift is recorded as revenue when it is pledged). A cash-basis system instead records the payments as revenue when received and never reflects the pledge receivable on its financial records.

Advantages of Cash Method

The cash method has the advantage of being simple and uncomplicated. Financial transactions are entered once when the money is deposited or paid out. Under the cash method, the nonprofit waits until the money is in hand or goes out of its hand to reflect the impact on its financial situation. For some organizations, little, if any, timing differences occur in the flow of their funds. They pay their bills before month-end and receive payments for services provided as the benefit or goods are delivered. The cash method of accounting may, in such situations, provide a relatively clear picture of finances.

Why Use the Accrual Method?

Many organizations have no choice in answering this question. Accrual-basis accounting is the recommended system under generally accepted accounting principles (GAAP) for fair presentation of financial position and results of operations. Organizations that hire an independent accountant to render an opinion on their financial statements in accordance with

GAAP must use the accrual basis of accounting. Aside from being required to follow the accrual method, a nonprofit chooses the method because it more precisely reflects the financial situation and results of operations. The system eliminates surprises and matches revenues with the expenses that produce the revenue. The goal of an accrual accounting system is to neutralize timing differences of the inflows and outflows. As an example, consider how the income on a one-year U.S. Treasury bill flows. Interest matures and is earned on a Treasury bill daily and can be realized if the bill is sold. The accrual method prescribes such income be calculated, shown as income, and correspondingly increase the carrying value of the investment regularly (usually monthly). Under the cash method, no entry is made until the bill matures or is sold. Because the bill can actually be sold for its original face price plus the accrued interest (plus or minus market fluctuations), the accrual method shows a more accurate picture of the nonprofit's resources.

DESIGN OF THE FINANCIALS

Financial statements are designed to reflect the fiscal condition by showing the means with which an organization finances its operations. The assets are distinguished between those that are readily available to pay the bills— current assets—and the more permanent assets, like investments held to produce income and like buildings and equipment, which are physically used in the activities. The titles and presentation of net assets or fund balances reflect the restricted or unrestricted nature of the nonprofit organization's assets. Four basic statements are contained in GAAP financial statements:

1. Statement of Financial Position (may still be called balance sheet)
2. Statement of Activity
3. Statement of Cash Flows
4. Statement of Function Expenses (required for voluntary health and welfare organizations; desirable for many nonprofit organizations)

The Statement of Financial Position reflects the assets owned by and the liabilities owed by the organization on a particular day, usually at year- or month-end. The report reflects the plus and minus scheme of the double-entry accounting system. The assets are essentially positive and presented first, as shown in Exhibit 6.6. The basic schematic balance reflects:

$$\text{Assets} - \text{liabilities} = \text{Net assets}$$

The financial resources are shown in the order of their liquidity or ability to be converted into cash. Most liquid assets come first and represent those assets that pay for daily operations—cash, receivables, and the like. The other assets—land and buildings, office equipment, and long-term investments, for example—support activities, but cannot be used to pay the light bill or next week's payroll.

The negative side of the balance sheet contains the debts or obligations as of the balance sheet date. Debts can be shown in due-date order, and the report may also show a separate subtotal of current liabilities or those due within one year, such as the light bill due next month, the undeposited payroll taxes from last month's salaries, and the portion of the long-term debt due within the coming year, for example.

Finally the remaining balance is the *net assets* representing the nonprofit's accumulated excess of revenues it has received over the years less expenses it has paid out. In a for-profit organization, this difference is called stockholder's equity and referred to as net worth or book value. As explained later in this chapter (Other Nonprofit Reporting), the net assets are further designated to identify restrictions on their use. Contributions received for a particular purpose, earmarked for a specific program, or otherwise restricted by the donor are identified with titles indicating the restrictions, if any, on expenditure or use of the resource.

It is useful to think of net assets as capital. Whether the nonprofit invests assets to produce income to pay for operations or uses assets directly in conducting operations, assets provide the financial capital needed to function financially. The net assets of a nonprofit organization are different in one important respect: Any profit generated is accumulated to accomplish exempt purposes rather than being paid out to owners.

The statement of activity is the equivalent of a for-profit's income statement and reflects the organization's revenues, gains, losses, and expenses for the period of time specified. Again, pluses (revenue) and minuses (expenses) and the difference (excess of revenue or expense) are shown. Because of the nonprofit motivation discussed in Chapter 1, the difference is called a change in net assets rather than profit or loss. The financial activities for the three major classes of net assets—permanently restricted, temporarily restricted, and unrestricted—are shown in a layered or columnar format. Additionally, expenses are required to be reported by functional classification as discussed earlier in the chapter (Functional Expense Categories) in categories for program, management, and general and fundraising. The reporting of expenses in functional categories provides information to assist donors, creditors, and others about the cost of program services provided and support for management and fundraising. Voluntary health and welfare organizations are required, and all nonprofits are encouraged, to present a statement of functional expenses, as shown in Exhibit 6.5.

Finally, GAAP financial reporting requires a statement of cash flows. The statement of cash flows show the nonprofit organization's cash receipts and disbursements categorized as operating, investing, and financing activities. It reflects where the cash comes from to finance a deficit, to purchase new equipment, or to repay debts. See Chapter 5 for more discussion of cash flows.

FASB, GAAP, AND NONPROFITS

Understanding the acronyms FASB and GAAP can help a financial manager communicate with the nonprofit's accountants and understand the basis of the standards applied in financial reporting for nonprofits. Certified public accountants (CPAs) are required by their profession to follow the GAAP standards promulgated by the FASB, the Financial Accounting Standards Board. The FASB is an independent division of the Financial Accounting Foundation created by the American Institute of Certified Public Accountants (AICPA) in 1973. The FASB's mission is to establish and improve standards of financial accounting and reporting for the guidance and education of the public, including issuers, auditors, and users of financial information. It is *the* authority in the CPA profession in defining GAAP. The standards are contained in pronouncements issued periodically.[4]

Specific Standards for Nonprofits

Nonprofit organizations are subject to many of the same accounting standards as for-profit organizations; however, their accounting and financial reporting is unique because the focus of reporting in not based on net income. Based on these differences, there are a number of pronouncements specifically written for nonprofit organizations. The following provides a list of a few of those unique aspects of financial reporting for nonprofit organizations:

> *Pledges or promises to give.* Pledges or promises to give are written or oral agreements to contribute cash or other assets to a nonprofit organization. Pledges received are recorded as an asset and contribution revenue when the promise to give is made or promised, rather than when paid in cash or other assets, if there is sufficient verifiable evidence that a promise was made by the donor and received by the nonprofit organization. Additionally, the pledge must be considered unconditional and not dependent on the occurrence of a specified future and uncertain event. Unconditional promises to give should be recorded as assets and contribution revenue even if the promise is not legally enforceable.[5]
>
> *Contributions.* Contributions are given by a donor as a nonreciprocal transfer of cash or other assets to a nonprofit organization. Unconditional contributions should be recognized as revenue when

---

[4] A list of principal standards can be found in PPC's Guide to Nonprofit GAAP, Practioners Publishing Company, Fort Worth, Texas, 2007 or on the web site www.fasb.org.
[5] FASB No. 116.

received. Unrestricted contributions received without explicit stipulation by the donor or "circumstances surrounding the receipt of the contribution that make clear the donor's implicit restriction on use" are reported as unrestricted. Contributions that are received with donor-imposed restrictions such as specific purposes or the passage of time are considered temporarily restricted or permanently restricted depending on the nature of the restriction.

Contributed services. Contributed services are to be recorded as contribution revenue and an asset or expense if the services received create or enhance nonfinancial (meaning equipment, buildings, theater sets, or other fixed) assets rather than cash or investments, and

- Would typically need to be purchased by the nonprofit organization, and

- The services require specialized skills, are provided by individuals possessing those skills, and would typically need to be purchased if not provided. Services requiring specialized skills are, among others, those provided by accountants, architects, carpenters, computer technologists, doctors, electricians, lawyers, nurses, plumbers, scientists, teachers, and other professionals and craftspeople.

Contributed facility use. The fair-rental value of facilities the nonprofit would otherwise have to rent are recorded as donated facilities expense and contribution revenue.

Permanently restricted net assets. These include the amount of those gifts or contributions subject to perpetual or everlasting conditions imposed by the donor on their use. The donor restrictions are those that cannot be removed by the organization's board of directors or management and do not expire with the passage of time. Gifts for creation of an endowment or construction of a building may be permanently restricted.[6]

Temporarily restricted assets. These are assets whose use by the organization is limited by donor-imposed stipulations that either expire by the passage of time or can be fulfilled by actions of the organization. A good example of such restricted funds would be grant moneys earmarked for a program to take place in the coming year. As of the financial statement date, the dollar amount of the remaining commitment or obligation to spend money for the program would be shown as a temporarily restricted net asset.

---

[6] FASB No. 117.

Unrestricted net assets. This is the category for all other resources of the nonprofit freely available for use in accomplishing the organization's purposes and whose use is not restricted by donor-imposed stipulations even though their use may be limited in other respects such as by contract or board designation.

Contributions or grants made. Contributions or grants made by the organization are to be recognized as an expense in the year the promise to pay is made, whether or not the cash or other asset is actually disbursed. If payments of the unconditional grant made are to be made to a recipient over several years a liability for the present value of the amount payable for the entire period should be recorded. Matching, conditional, or otherwise contingent grants made are recorded as a liability at the time the uncertainty is removed because the condition is satisfied.

Other Nonprofit Reporting

Several industry groups recommend reporting methods for their constituencies. The National Health Council, National Voluntary Health and Social Welfare Organizations, Inc., and the United Way of America issued their *Standards of Accounting and Financial Reporting for Voluntary Health and Welfare Organizations.* The National Association of College and University Business Officers (NACUBO) and the American Hospital Association have similarly prescribed standards of reporting for colleges and universities and hospitals, respectfully.

Government grant recipients are often subject to regulation from the Federal Office of Management and Budget and state and local government funding agencies. Federal grantees subject to such regulations receiving more than $500,000 a year must have an annual *A-133* or *single audit.*[7] A single audit must be performed by an independent CPA[8] and includes procedures to test compliance with certain rules and regulations in order to determine whether the nonprofit has expended the government funds for the purpose for which they were granted. The auditor also reviews compliance with nonfinancial federal grant requirements, such as maintaining a drug-free workplace and complying with civil rights requirements. The single audit is required to report findings about compliance, noncompliance, and weaknesses in internal controls.

---

[7] Office of Management and Budget (OMB), Circular A-133, *Audits of Institutions of Higher Education and Other Nonprofit Institutions.*
[8] See Chapter 2 (Inside and Outside Accountants; Selecting Financial Reporting Services).

INTERNAL CONTROLS

Internal controls protect the nonprofit's resources from intentional or unintentional misappropriation. The Committee of Sponsoring Organizations of the National Commission on Fraudulent Financial Reporting (COSO) defined internal control as a process, affected by an entity's board of directors, management and other personnel, designed to provide reasonable assurance regarding the achievement of control objectives in three categories:

1. Effectiveness and efficiency of operations

2. Reliability of financial reporting

3. Compliance with applicable laws and regulations

The keystone of a good internal control system is separation of certain duties to provide checks and balances. A good internal control system works because it sheds light on problems. Effective internal control requires that certain responsibilities (such as authorization of transactions, recording of transactions in the accounting records, custody and access to assets, and supervisory reviews) be assigned to separate individuals. If the person who receives and deposits the cash receipts is also the person who records and maintains the financial records, the possibility for hiding a theft is enhanced and the chance of discovering a mistake is reduced. The objective is to separate the assets themselves from the recording or accounting. Internal controls foster operational efficiencies as the roles people play are defined. Duties are delegated and responsibilities are spread among staff members subject to oversight by management. The planning processes described in Chapters 3 (Prioritizing Goals) and 4 are also an integral part of the process. This section focuses on the systems specially designed to assure that funds are properly received and expended and that the flow of funds is documented in the financial records. The way the accounting profession sees the function of internal controls is:

Internal control is a process—effected by an entity's board of directors, management, and other personnel—designed to provide reasonable assurance regarding the achievement of objectives in the following categories:

(a) Reliability of financial reporting

(b) Effectiveness and efficiency of operations, and

(c) Compliance with applicable laws and regulations.[9]

---

[9] *Statement on Auditing Standards 78, Consideration of the Internal Control Structure in a Financial Audit: An amendment to SAS No. 55.* New York: AICPA, 1995, p. 3.

Thus, an internal control system dictates the manner in which financial transactions are approved and completed by providing procedures to be followed. It can be thought of as a discipline system for organizational affairs.

The rules are designed to prevent the innocent or unintended misuse of funds, as well as deliberate misappropriation for any unauthorized use. Examples of problems that can occur in the absence of internal controls include:

- Falsification of the organization's financial records and reports

- Defalcations, such as embezzlement or theft of the organization's assets

- Unauthorized spending in excess of budgeted amounts by employees or volunteers

Exhibit 6.9 contains a checklist of procedures for establishing and maintaining a system of internal controls. Although the principles of separation of duties apply to all organizations, the checklist should be redesigned or tailored to suit the needs of each individual organization. No one system is suitable for all organizations. The many variables that determine the necessary steps include the size of the staff, nature of the activities, and the sources of funding. In addition, Exhibit 6.9 explores appropriate controls for public fund solicitations.

Exhibit 6.8   Internal Controls for Nonprofits

This checklist of internal control procedures presents the possibilities for minimizing errors and deliberate misrepresentations in accounting or other financial records. Space is provided to note where each control is currently used and to record relevant observations.

	Yes	No	Comments
A. Financial Reporting			
1. Monthly financial statements are prepared.	____	____	_____
2. Operational, cash flow, and capital budgets prepared and compared monthly to actual results.	____	____	_____
3. Departmentalized chart of account is used.	____	____	_____

4. Adequate accounting system is in place with appropriate subsidiary ledgers. _____ _____ _____

5. Written accounting policies and procedures. _____ _____ _____

B. Cash Receipts

1. Mail is opened in the presence of two persons (where staffing allows), with a cash receipt or ledger report prepared concurrently. _____ _____ _____

2. Checks are stamped immediately with proper endorsement. _____ _____ _____

3. Receipt system is in place to control cash from events or sales. (Complete Public Fund Solicitation Checklist) [Exhibit 6.9]. _____ _____ _____

4. Cash receipts handled by bonded employees, not volunteers. _____ _____ _____

5. Daily deposits are made to the bank. _____ _____ _____

6. Receipt records or ledgers are reconciled to monthly bank statements by someone other than those opening the mail. _____ _____ _____

7. Noncash gifts receipted with donated item described with value assigned, if available. _____ _____ _____

   Professional service invoice with value obtained. _____ _____ _____

   Goods subject to inventory control system. _____ _____ _____

C. Disbursement of Funds

1. Disbursements made with checks based on documentation and proper authorization. _____ _____ _____

2. Checks are prenumbered and accounted for monthly. _____ _____ _____

3. Voided checks are defaced and retained. _____ _____ _____

Exhibit 6.8   Internal Controls for Nonprofits *(continued)*

4. No checks are signed in advance or made payable to cash. _____ _____ _____

5. Check signer is not the bookkeeper, check preparer, or person responsible for authorizing disbursement. _____ _____ _____

Two signatures required for amounts >$500, 1,000, etc. _____ _____ _____

Board member is a signatory if staff size is limited. _____ _____ _____

6. Blank check stock is kept in a secure location. _____ _____ _____

7. Bank statements are reconciled by someone other than a check preparer or signer. _____ _____ _____

8. One person handles petty cash; receipts required for pay out. _____ _____ _____

D. Documentation

1. Supporting documentation, invoices, or statements are required for each expenditure and receipt of funds. _____ _____ _____

Time sheets for personal services— employees and volunteers. _____ _____ _____

Travel/meal/car usage/reimbursables voucher. _____ _____ _____

Receiving reports prepared for ordered goods. _____ _____ _____

Vendor invoices matched to receiving reports. _____ _____ _____

Petty cash voucher for impress fund. _____ _____ _____

Cash receiving report coded by type of income. _____ _____ _____

Vendor/contributor/member/student return slip. _____ _____ _____

Daily cash register reports. _____ _____ _____

2. Project manager or nonaccounting
   personnel approve expense.   ____   ____   _____

3. Purchase orders are used.   ____   ____   _____

4. Vendor statement reconciled to
   invoices with details of prices,
   quantity received, discounts, returns,
   and prior payments.   ____   ____   _____

5. There are established levels of
   approval for major expenditures.   ____   ____   _____

6. Invoices labeled (canceled) with
   check number and date paid.   ____   ____   _____

7. Personnel records document that:

   Time sheets, hirings, and
   terminations are approved by
   responsible parties.   ____   ____   _____

   Vacation, sick leave, and overtime
   accumulations are authorized.   ____   ____   _____

   Pay increases made only according
   to proper authorization.   ____   ____   _____

   Payroll taxes deposited on time.   ____   ____   _____

   Federal COBRA, civil rights,
   disability, and other codes followed. ____   ____   _____

E. Safeguarding Assets

Cash

1. Cash management system is in place
   to maximize interest earned.   ____   ____   _____

2. Bank statements of accounts are
   reconciled monthly and reviewed
   by the appropriate level of
   management.   ____   ____   _____

3. Bank accounts and check signers are
   authorized by the board of directors
   or top level management.   ____   ____   _____

4. Bank accounts are reconciled by
   individuals independent of cash
   receipts and disbursement functions. ____   ____   _____

5. Procedures are adequate for
   approving and recording interbank
   transfers.   ____   ____   _____

Exhibit 6.8   Internal Controls for Nonprofits *(continued)*

6. Certificates of deposit or money
   market accounts used for short-term
   cash funds.   _____   _____   _____

7. Personal cash or other assets of
   employees are not mingled with
   nonprofit's.   _____   _____   _____

8. Petty-cash fund replenishment
   requests are properly approved.   _____   _____   _____

Receivables and Revenue

1. Accounts receivable are monitored
   and reconciled to detail subsidiary
   ledger.   _____   _____   _____

   Work orders/sales/member service
   and dues invoices numbered.   _____   _____   _____

   Customer/donor/student ledgers
   balanced monthly.   _____   _____   _____

   Monthly statements sent for unpaid
   balances.   _____   _____   _____

   Uncollectable account write-offs and
   discounts approved by responsible
   employee not in business office.   _____   _____   _____

   Duties are segregated between credit
   authorization and collection.

2. Balances periodically verified
   independently from nonaccounting
   records.   _____   _____   _____

   Student tuition rolls are compared to
   registrar's office records.   _____   _____   _____

   Number of hours times tuition
   per hour equals student payment.   _____   _____   _____

   Dues receipts are traced to
   membership department lists.   _____   _____   _____

3. Interest or other charge made for
   late payment.   _____   _____   _____

4. Pledges or contributions receivable
   timetables are kept.   _____   _____   _____

Aged amounts receivable are
established and monitored. _____ _____ _____

Periodic reports are issued in time
for installment payments to be
received. _____ _____ _____

Grant requests for reimbursement are
submitted by their deadline. _____ _____ _____

5. Contributions restricted for specific
   purposes and future periods
   identified. _____ _____ _____

Gift letters reviewed for restrictions. _____ _____ _____

Expenditures analyzed to vouch
adherence to restricted purposes. _____ _____ _____

Procedures for return or use of
unexpended funds in place. _____ _____ _____

6. Program service fees and government
   grant contracts are monitored for
   timely billing and revenue is
   recorded when earned. Revenue is
   reconciled to appropriate underlying
   documentation such as general ledger
   cost centers, subsidiary ledgers, or
   contract provisions. _____ _____ _____

7. Monitor terms of charitable and
   remainder trust agreements. _____ _____ _____

Inventory

1. Detailed records are maintained for
   inventory. _____ _____ _____

2. Custody of inventory is independent
   of shipping, billing, and record
   keeping. _____ _____ _____

3. Periodic count is performed and
   compared to control records or
   perpetual records. _____ _____ _____

4. Management reviews comparison of
   physical count to control records. _____ _____ _____

5. Inventory is adequately safeguarded. _____ _____ _____

6. Inventory levels and product choices
   monitored with view to amount

Exhibit 6.8   Internal Controls for Nonprofits *(contined)*

invested and marketing
considerations.   ____   ____   _____

Property and Equipment

1. Detailed records are maintained
   for property assets.   ____   ____   _____

   Serial numbers listed separately.   ____   ____   _____

   Guarantees and service contracts
   controlled.   ____   ____   _____

   Purchase invoice copies kept in
   permanent files.   ____   ____   _____

   Detailed ledger of assets maintained.   ____   ____   _____

2. Assets are purchased only pursuant
   to a capital budget.   ____   ____   _____

3. Competitive bidding is conducted
   for major purchases.   ____   ____   _____

4. Borrowing to purchase must be
   approved by the board.   ____   ____   _____

5. A retirement policy assures a fair
   price for old assets sold, traded,
   or junked.   ____   ____   _____

   Outside appraisal is obtained for
   buildings or major equipment.   ____   ____   _____

6. Insurance coverage is adequate.   ____   ____   _____

7. Periodic physical inventory is taken.   ____   ____   _____

8. Property and equipment
   improvements costing less than an
   established amount are expensed.   ____   ____   _____

9. Reasonable depreciation reserve is
   calculated and recorded.   ____   ____   _____

Investments

1. Detailed investment record or ledger
   is maintained.   ____   ____   _____

   Purchase/sales reports or records are
   reconciled to investment activity
   monthly.   ____   ____   _____

Dividend and interest payment dates
are monitored for receipts.   _____   _____   _____

2. Investments are managed by
   knowledgeable person(s) such as an
   investment committee.   _____   _____   _____

   Investment return measured and
   compared to projections.   _____   _____   _____

   Management fees are analyzed for
   reasonableness.   _____   _____   _____

   Cash income being generated is
   sufficient for operations.   _____   _____   _____

   Board investment or finance
   committee monitors investments.   _____   _____   _____

   Diversification and inherent risk of
   investment reviewed.   _____   _____   _____

3. Endowment fund principal and
   income are recorded and balances
   maintained.   _____   _____   _____

4. Formal investment policies have
   been established.   _____   _____   _____

5. Changes in the valuation of
   investments are properly recorded
   on a regular basis.   _____   _____   _____

6. Safe custody is maintained.   _____   _____   _____

Liabilities

1. Accounts payable system is in use. _____   _____   _____

   Vendor invoices are recorded in an
   open invoice file.   _____   _____   _____

   Statements are vouched for invoices
   as paid.   _____   _____   _____

   Detailed accounts payable regularly
   reconciled to general ledger.   _____   _____   _____

   Lease terms are monitored.   _____   _____   _____

2. Interfund borrowing allowed only in
   limited circumstances and thoroughly
   documented for advances and
   repayments.   _____   _____   _____

Exhibit 6.8   Internal Controls for Nonprofits *(continued)*

Emergency situations policy.   _____   _____   _____

Board authorization.   _____   _____   _____

Formal record of loan and terms for
repayment.   _____   _____   _____

3. Payments on notes payable and other
debt agreements are made on time.   _____   _____   _____

4. Debt covenants monitored by
management regularly for
compliance.   _____   _____   _____

Exempt Functions

1. Program.   _____   _____   _____

2. Grant application process is efficient.   _____   _____   _____

Grantee forms complete and
approved before funds are
disbursed.   _____   _____   _____

Follow-up grantee reports required
before additional payments are
made.   _____   _____   _____

3. Fees for services, tuition, dues,
subscription rates, and the like are
published in catalogs, bulletins,
notices.   _____   _____   _____

4. Program activity archives
maintained.   _____   _____   _____

Weekly church bulletins filed
chronologically.   _____   _____   _____

Visiting nurse diary with patient
names and dates.   _____   _____   _____

Student handbooks or curriculum
catalog.   _____   _____   _____

Research reports and publications.   _____   _____   _____

Attendance records for programs.   _____   _____   _____

Other evidence of exempt activities.   _____   _____   _____

5. Tax exempt status is intact.
Complete tax compliance checklist.   _____   _____   _____

Exhibit 6.9 Public Fund Solicitation Controls

A. Door-to-Door Collections

1. Is campaign organized with chief, block captains, schedule for location and dates, and clear written materials instructions? ☐

2. Are receipts prenumbered with instructions for completion? ☐

3. For currency collections, is amount verified to prenumbered receipts at the time solicitor turns in money? ☐

4. Are solicitors informed about the nonprofit's mission? ☐

5. Do solicitors have proof of nonprofit's authorization to represent it? ☐

6. Are solicitor reports tallied and deposited daily? ☐

B. Festivals and Events

1. Is all money collected through ticket sales with tickets used to secure admission and purchase goods? ☐

2. Is monetary value or admission price printed on tickets? ☐

3. Are ticket numbers recorded as issued to solicitors of advanced sales? ☐

4. Is deadline and system for turning in advanced sale money written and deadlines provided? ☐

5. Are tickets collected at booths reconciled with number of items sold or food consumed? ☐

6. Is there a centralized payment booth with a cash register for entering ticket sales at the event? ☐

7. Are daily receipts tallied and deposited daily? ☐

8. Are unsold tickets reconciled to collection reports? ☐

C. Cash Canisters

1. Does nonprofit keep list of canister locations and person responsible for them? ☐

2. Are canisters replaced on regular schedule? ☐

3. Are canisters emptied in presence of two persons? ☐

4. Is currency report prepared and money deposited day of pickup? ☐

5. If risk of theft is high, can canisters be made more secure? ☐

Exhibit 6.9   Public Fund Solicitation Controls *(continued)*

D. Direct Mail Campaigns

1. Are two persons jointly controlling incoming mail receipts?   ☐

2. Is a daily receipt report prepared and approved by both persons?   ☐

3. Is the report compared to bank statements by someone else?   ☐

4. Should a bank lockbox service be used?   ☐

7

Special Financial Tools

*Specialized financial tools can allow a nonprofit to
be more fiscally astute and to make informed
decisions on issues with multiple, complex answers.*

This chapter expands the tools useful to a financial planner. Specialized
financial analyses and procedures can provide needed answers not evident
from the financial reports described in Chapters 4 and 6. Using ratio analysis to critique performance sheds a different light on resource flows and
allows evaluation of revenue sources. Cost accounting allows the nonprofit
to calculate its expenses by programs. Money spent is reclassified according to function categories—counseling, vaccinations, and food services—in
addition to generic type, such as supplies, salary, and rentals.

Comparing the numbers for leasing versus buying can be made a little
easier if one asks the appropriate questions suggested later. In this time of
reduced government funding, affiliating with other nonprofits to leverage
resources can be critical to a program's or even an organization's survival.
The section Affiliations and Agency Agreements in this chapter suggests
questions to ask and terms to consider in negotiating such partnerships. Classifying so-called contract or part-time people as nonsalaried workers is a
tempting choice many nonprofits make. A fiscally prudent organization will
complete the employment tax compliance checklists in this chapter (Who's
an Employee?) to ensure that it has no hidden tax liabilities from these
decisions.

FINANCIAL INDICATORS TO CRITIQUE PERFORMANCE

Ratio analysis permits financial planners to identify trends, recognize
strengths, and pinpoint weaknesses that may not be readily apparent. As an
addition to the financial statements and budgets, ratios provide a different
look at a nonprofit's fiscal health. Exhibit 7.1 illustrates some commonly
used ratios and comments on issues that the results might raise.

Exhibit 7.1   Using Ratio Analysis to Test Fiscal Health

This exhibit presents ratio analyses for testing an organization's fiscal situation. Financial conditions are measured with ratio calculations based partly on the sample financial statements found in Exhibits 6.6 and 6.7. Issues posed by the results are discussed.

Overall Fiscal Health
Current Ratio

	Holy Spirit Church	Ratio	Assn. of NPO Managers	Ratio
Expendable current assets* / Current liabilities**	$20,000 / 80,000	1/4	$220,000 / 116,000	1.9/1

*Unrestricted cash and assets convertible to cash.

**Debts payable within one year.

Issues: The current ratio compares the organization's resources available to pay the bills during the coming year. Classically, it is thought that the current ratio of assets to liabilities should be at least 2:1. A ratio lower than 2:1 means short-term liquidity problems. The church obviously has a serious problem with its 1:4 ratio. The Association of Nonprofit Managers, with its 1.9:1 ratio, can comfortably pay the bills and have some cash left over. What if the ratio were above 2:1? Too high a ratio sacrifices income for safety. The difference between current assets and current liabilities is also called working capital. When working capital is adequate, a nonprofit may be in a position to make long-term investments as discussed in Chapter 5 (Prudent Investment Planning). This formula can also be calculated and compared for restricted and unrestricted fund current ratios.

Acid-Test Ratio

	Holy Spirit Church	Ratio	Assn. of NPO Managers	Ratio
Cash or assets due in one month*** / Total expenses within same period	$20,000 / 40,000	1/2	$110,000 / 74,000	1.5/1

***Or three months.

Issues: The acid, or quick-ratio tests to see if the organization can pay its bills this month or this quarter. Ask this question: "Is the acid test or *quick ratio* at least 1 to 1? If the ratio is below 1:1, the planners asks, "Can the organization survive the month if receipt of funding is delayed?" The church finance committee may hope it had been asking these questions sooner as it faces what is now a serious financial situation—debts equaling two times its assets available to pay the debt.

Overall Liquidity Ratio

	Holy Spirit Church	Assn. of NPO Managers
$\dfrac{\text{Expendable fund balances}}{\text{Total monthly expenses}}$	$\dfrac{\$20,000}{10,833}$	$\dfrac{\$220,000}{67,000}$
Number of months	1.8	3.3

Issues: The overall liquidity ratio measures how long the organization could survive if it receives no new money. The Association of Nonprofit Managers has enough money available to pay its normal bills for a bit more than three months. The church only has 1.8 months of money. See Chapter 3 (Assessing the Resources) and Chapter 5 (Cash Flow Planning) for cash and resource planning ideas to evaluate the situation. For an organization with an endowment or other permanent funds, a similar calculation would be made to compare the permanently restricted, or unexpendable funds, to the total annual expenses.

Operational Indicators

Revenue Collection Results

		Good	Bad
1.	$\dfrac{\text{Average month end balance—unpaid pledges}}{\text{Annual member dues or donations received}}$	$\dfrac{\$50,000}{500,000}$	$\dfrac{\$150,000}{500,000}$
2.	$\dfrac{\text{Amount of pledges written off}}{\text{Annual member dues or donations received}}$	$\dfrac{\$12,000}{500,000}$	$\dfrac{\$80,000}{500,000}$
3.	$\dfrac{\text{Number of members not renewing}}{\text{Total number of members}}$	$\dfrac{26}{380}$	$\dfrac{140}{380}$

Issues: These ratios show how effectively the nonprofit collects promises of support it receives. Whether the result is good or bad actually must be determined by the particular facts in each situation. Ratio 1 essentially shows the time lag between the time the member makes a pledge and the organization actually collects the money. Ratio 2 reflects the bad debt experience and can be looked at as a percentage. The good ratio shows 2.4 percent of the pledges were not collected as compared to the bad ratio of 16 percent. In 3, a good renewal rate of 6.9 percent is shown and a bad rate of 38 percent.

A nonprofit's life blood comes from the collection of pledges from members and donors. An annual checkup of the sort shown in these ratios can be

---

Exhibit 7.1   Using Ratio Analysis to Test Fiscal Health *(continued)*

---

very helpful to spot "high blood pressure." Bad results should prompt the organization to take steps to heal the problem, such as:

- Analyze pledge collection policies and payment terms.

- Consider using software to track donors, send renewal notices, and otherwise improve the process.

- Change the nature of funding requests (mail versus phone).

- Use commercial credit card or Internet donor processing service.

- Following up with a paid staff instead of volunteers.

- Hire a professional fundraising consultant.

Revenue Source Comparison

Version 1

	Year 1	Year 2	Year 3	Year 4	Year 5
Members dues and donations	100,000	120,000	110,000	90,000	80,000
Total revenue and support	300,000	300,000	320,000	340,000	350,000
Ratio	33.3%	40%	34.4%	26.5%	22.9%

This ratio analyzes the percentage of the organization's support received from member dues and donations over a five-year period to see if the portion of this funding has changed significantly in relation to the whole. This example reflects a 10 percent decline over five years and could signal a serious problem unless the organization has deliberately focused to on increasing other sources of revenue.

Revenue Source Comparison

Version 2 (using Exhibit 6.6)

	Association of Nonprofit Managers	
	Prior Year	Current Year
Chapter member dues	$238,000	$249,700
Members-at-large dues	76,000	78,600
Information services sales	40,000	120,000
Publication sales	180,000	204,000
Continuing education	98,000	106,000
Annual meeting	42,000	28,000
Royalty income	1,000	42,000
Interest income	3,000	1,000
Total income	$678,000	$829,300

Issues: How does the current year's revenue portion for a particular revenue source compare with last year's? Is the change planned or expected? Should any action be taken in response or to analyze the reason for the change?

Cost Ratios

Version 1	Year 1	Year 2	Year 3	Year 4	Year 5
Dollars spent on:					
Direct program costs	$280,000	$300,000	$320,000	$304,000	$300,000
Management and general	100,000	110,000	120,000	140,000	150,000
Fund raising	10,000	20,000	40,000	50,000	55,000
Total	$390,000	$430,000	$480,000	$494,000	$505,000
Percentage ratio:					
Direct program costs	71.8	69.8	66.7	61.5	59.4
Management and general	25.6	25.6	25.0	28.3	29.7
Fundraising	2.6	4.7	8.3	10.1	10.9
Total	100%	100%	100%	100%	100%

Issues: On Form 990 and on a GAAP financial statement, the nonprofit's costs must be presented in the three categories shown above for this ratio—program or exempt function costs, management and general (administrative) expenses, and fundraising costs. It is, therefore, extremely important for a nonprofit to monitor this measurement annually. Funders prefer to pay for program expenditures. Some measure the worth of a proposed grantee according to the portion of the total expenditures devoted to programs. Some will not fund an organization whose combined management and general and fundraising costs exceed 25 percent of the total. The organization shown in this example has, in five years, gone from spending 71.9 percent of its budget on programs down to 59.4 percent. This situation may be troublesome and should again be monitored annually.

Cost Ratios

Version 2	Total Cost	Percentage
Project 1	$180,000	18.4%
Project 2	304,000	31.1
Project 3	242,000	24.7

Exhibit 7.1   Using Ratio Analysis to Test Fiscal Health *(continued)*

Project 4	189,000	19.3
Project 5	64,000	6.5
Totals	979,000	100%

Cost Ratios

More Versions	Number	Ratio
$\dfrac{\text{Average daily cost per patient (student, etc.)}}{\text{Average charges (income) per patient}}$	$\dfrac{\$129}{140}$	108.5%
$\dfrac{\text{Management and general (not counted in patient daily cost)}}{\text{Number of patients served in a year}}$	$\dfrac{\$250,000}{1,922}$	$130 each
$\dfrac{\text{Direct cost per participant—fundraising dinner}}{\text{Number of attendees at benefit}}$	$\dfrac{\$44}{75}$	1.7 times
$\dfrac{\text{Administrative costs plus value of volunteers}}{\text{Number of attendees at benefit}}$	$\dfrac{\$60,000}{1,200}$	$50 each
$\dfrac{\text{Total membership costs}}{\text{Number of members}}$	$\dfrac{\$267,000}{856}$	312 each
$\dfrac{\text{Cost of newsletter or other member services}}{\text{Annual membership fee}}$	$\dfrac{\$22}{\$200}$	11%
$\dfrac{\text{Fundraising costs}}{\text{Total annual support}}$	$\dfrac{\$28,000}{\$200,000}$	14%

Issues: These cost ratio variations provide a tool for the nonprofit to (1) see what portion of its funds it is spending on a particular project and (2) test profitability or lack of it for income-producing activities. Some of the ratios work in concert. The ratios can be useful in understanding and correcting financial difficulties. The numbers can be translated into fundraising goals, revenue increase targets, or a variety of other indicators.

The first hospital ratio looks positive, with 108.5 percent of direct patient costs being charged to patients. The second, though, shows an additional $130 per patient per year is spent on administration. Similarly, one might think benefit tickets sold at 1.7 times the direct cost of the event is acceptable until the fourth ratio shows the administrative cost is actually $50 per person in addition. When the intention is to balance costs with revenues, these ratios provide a useful tool. Some states regulate the percentage fee paid to fundraising consultants.

The member dues calculations might be used to analyze the need to raise prices or to report to members how much of their dues is spent on the types of services provided. Fundraising costs ratios must often be considered in relation to other data. What is the normal ratio for the type of nonprofit? Has the fundraising program just begun with too little time to bring results? Was a direct-mail campaign started just this year? Funders are interested in these ratios, as discussed in this chapter (Techniques for Capturing Costs).

Other Useful Ratios

Inventory Turnover: This ratio is calculated by dividing the total sales of the year by the inventory on hand at year end. If the answer is one-fifth, it is said the inventory turned five times. The average number of days items were unsold would be one-fifth of 365, or 73 days, or about two months.

Each day that inventory (items bought to be resold) remains unsold theoretically costs the organization money. If the goods had not been purchased, the money could be earning interest in the bank. Thus, it is important that inventory "turn" or remain as few days as possible in the hands of the seller. A low inventory turnover might also indicate poor buying decisions—the goods are in inventory because no one wants to buy them.

The overall fiscal condition of an organization can be measured with capital structure ratios. The current, or acid-test, ratios are widely used by banks and financial advisors to assess an entity's financial health. By comparing the ratio of available cash to the liabilities or debts to be paid, the outlook for continued operation is revealed. The higher the cash flow is in relation to total debt or expense, the better. The ratio of debt to net assets also indicates the degree of the nonprofit's ability to take on additional debt or to self-finance a new project. The ratio of existing debt to current assets also indicates the existing degree of leverage or ability to afford more debt. The lower the ratio, the better.

An endless array of operational indicators can be useful. Comparing the relative types of income received over a five-year period can reflect trends that could be meaningful. Knowing how much it costs to serve a patient is necessary to evaluate whether the price of services is appropriate and so on.

Economies of Scale

This important concept recognizes the fact that certain costs do not increase in relation to an increase in the number of persons served or the number of units sold. The payroll department with three persons might only need to add one more person to handle a payroll for twice as big a staff. Printing hills reflect dramatic economies of that sort. The price for 10,000 sheets of letterhead is typically less than 50 percent more than the price of 5,000. Calculating and keeping records necessary to achieve economies to scale can enhance financial results.

Break-Even Analysis

This calculation is similar to scaled economies. The idea is to calculate at what point a program or project pays for itself. Say a hospital wants to equip a new laboratory that it expects will cost $1 million annually; also assume the prevailing market price for a test performed by the equipment is $200 a session. The break-even point for the lab is 5,000 patients, or the number it takes to bring in the revenue to cover the expected costs. The 5,001st patient begins to bring in additional revenue typically needed to pay for supporting, administrative, or other management costs (referred to as indirect costs) attributable to the lab operation.

Performance Statistics

A nonprofit should be constantly aware of the number of persons it serves, how much they each pay, and the changing mix of such constituents. Student enrollment, church parishioners, persons receiving legal assistance, and similar details can be tracked and studied. Performance measurements related to constituents that can also be useful in analyzing performance include test scores, number of publications sold, awards received, diseases cured, attendees at performances and their reactions, student enrollment, and the like.

COST ACCOUNTING

Cost accounting identifies the money spent in connection with each program, product, or other specific purpose. Economies to scale, better pricing, and more realistic expectations can result for the nonprofit that keeps track of how the money is spent. It is the cost accounting system that allows the organization to prepare the functional expense reports shown in Chapter 6 (Functional Expense Categories).

By using a cost accounting system, revenues and costs are captured in generic categories (salaries or rent) and also by function (program 1, 2, or administration). When expenses are attributable to more than one function, the United Way says:

> Organizations are required to develop techniques that will provide verifiable bases on which expenses may be related to program or supporting service functions. The functional classification of expenses permits an agency to tell

the reader of the financial statements not only the nature of its expenses, but also the purpose for which they were made.[1]

More informed financial decisions are possible when functional expenses are captured in a cost accounting system. Other advantages stemming from the effort, to name a few, include:

- Charges for services can be evaluated for reasonableness.

- Indirect cost reimbursement grants can be accurately negotiated.

- Realistic overall cost of programs can be quantified to facilitate planning and, sometimes most importantly, to prepare grant funding requests, or to calculate member dues assessments.

- Deductions for unrelated business income tax purposes can be maximized.

Techniques for Capturing Costs

An extra layer of details is needed to effectively use a cost accounting system. To allocate the salary of a staff person that works, for example, on three different programs, a time-keeping system is required. Suggestions for gathering the necessary data include the following:

Staff Salary Allocation System   Records to quantify the time employees spend on task(s) performed each day should be prepared. The possibilities are endless. Most efficiently, each staff member maintains a records of time spent each day on a database designed to accumulate his or her work by function—in other words, fills out a time sheet. The reports should be completed often—while the memory is fresh—to assure accuracy, preferably weekly. Personnel performing repetitive tasks may only need to prepare a one-week report each month; or one month each year might be sufficient. Based on employee reports, percentages of time spent on various functions can be tabulated and used for cost allocations.

Office or Program Space Utilization Charts   Physical building space rented or owned is customarily allocated according to its usage, or functions performed in the space. Floor plans can be used to tabulate the square footage of the space allocable to each activity center. In some cases, the allocation

---

[1] *Standards of Accounting and Financial Reporting for Voluntary Health and Welfare Organizations*, Revised 1988—3rd ed. National Health Council, Inc., National Assembly of National Voluntary Health and Social Welfare Organization, Inc., United Way of America (called the Black Book). There is no more recent edition available.

is based on the time reports of the staff using the spaces. One way to allocate space used dually (by more than one program or activity) is to allocate space costs according to the number of hours or days the space is used for the respective purposes.

Direct Program or Activity Costs   To capture costs by function, or program, each financial transaction must be identified in the accounting system as being associated with a function. As discussed in Chapter 6 (Chart of Accounts), this process is accomplished with the design of chart of accounts. All expenditures and revenues are coded, or labeled, according to the titles from the chart for entry into the accounting system. When a purchase order system is used, the function codes are designated when an item is approved for purchase as shown in Exhibit 7.6. Separate departmental accounts can be established with vendors to facilitate identity of purchases.

Joint Projects Allocations   Allocations of joint costs must be made on a reasonable and fair basis recognizing the cause-and-effect relationship between the cost incurred and where it is allocated.[2] A joint project is one that embodies two or more programs or purposes. The classic example is a brochure containing both public health information (stop smoking or vaccinate your children) and a solicitation for contributions to support the dissemination of the information. At least four allocation methods provide an acceptable method for making the cost allocation as follows:

- Activity-based (identifying the inches of brochure devoted to health information and those containing the solicitation)

- Equal cost (when two projects share the cost, divide by two)

- Ratio of the total based on stand-alone cost (what it would cost if that department had to hire and buy independently)

- Cost saving (costs allocated in proportion to efficiency)

---

[2] Dennis P. Tishlian, "Nonprofit Organizations' Cost Allocations, The Implications of Madigan," *CPA Journal*, New York State Society of CPAs, July 2005; also Reasonable Joint Cost Allocations in Nonprofits, *Journal of Accountancy*, AICPA, November 1992 p. 66. Also see *AICPA Audit and Accounting Guide, Audits of Certain Nonprofit Organizations*, including *Statement of Position (SOP) 78-10*, as amended by SOP 87-2, *Accounting for Joint Costs of Informational Materials and Activities of Not-for-Profit Organizations That Include a Fund-Raising Appeal*, issued by the Accounting Standards Division of the American Institute of Certified Public Accountants. AICPA audit guides for hospitals, colleges, and universities and voluntary health and welfare organizations are also available.

Supporting, Administrative, or Other Management Costs   For many reasons, it is important that administrative costs be properly classified. Funders like to see their money spent on programs, not what people refer to as overhead or indirect costs. What percentage of supporting costs is excessive is arguable; but the Better Business Bureau (BBB) used to insist that any amount above 25 percent was too much, and the smaller the better. The BBB/Wise Giving Alliance has reformed this absolute rule, but the concept remains. Evaluations of charities available on the Internet sites for the BBB[3] and Charity Navigator[4] reveal this ratio. They rate nonprofits according to the percentage of program, management and general, and fundraising costs in relation to total costs plus other factors, such as executive salaries and finances of comparable organizations. The Charity Navigator system awards stars. On June 14, 2007, there were only 1,308 four-star charities listed.

Large nonprofits may have clearly identified administrative costs—a human resource or personnel department, a business office, and other independently functioning support staffs. In many nonprofits, however, support staff personnel are also involved in programs. Where the scope of such involvement can be measured, support function costs may be allocated partly to programs utilizing staff salary, space utilization, or other reasonable criteria. Staff salaries are most often allocable. Say, for example, the executive director is also the editor preparing articles for the quarterly journal. If a record of the time spent is maintained, his or her salary and associated costs could be attributed partly to the publication.

Cost Allocation Methods

Costs can be allocated using a variety of factors as listed below. The challenge is to identify the factor(s) that most suitably calculate relative costs associated with any particular program or activity. Once a method is chosen, it is advisable to use it consistently for some years so that comparable data is accumulated. The IRS manual instructs examining agents that any reasonable method resulting in identifying the relationship of the expenses to revenue produced is acceptable.[5] In an unrelated business income tax case, one court said there is no particular approved method that must be followed. The IRS says they prefer a system that allocates costs to all activities, similar to a GAAP functional expense statement. The various methods and factors to consider follow.

Actual time records should be maintained to evidence the portion of time staff and volunteers actually spend conducting various functions. In the

---

[3] See www.give.org/reports.
[4] See www.charitynavigator.org.
[5] *Exempt Organizations Examination Guidelines Handbook,* Internal Revenue Manual, Section 720(7).

absence of time records, or instead of them, an allocation based on relative gross income produced by each program might be used.

Direct and indirect expenses must be distinguished. Direct expenses are those that increase proportionately with the usage of a facility or the volume of activity and are also called *variable*. The number of persons attending an event influences the number of ushers or security guards and represent a *direct* cost of the event. In other words, the cost would not have been incurred *but for* the particular scheduled performance. *Indirect costs* are those incurred without regard to usage or frequency of participation, and are also called the *fixed expenses*. Building acquisition costs, for example, may not vary with usage.

The *fraction denominator* used in the formula for calculating cost allocations can impact the result significantly. Take, for example, a college football stadium with the following statistics concerning its usage:

		Divide by Days Used	Divide by Days in Year
No. of days used by the college	52	70%	14%
No. of days rented to others	22	30	6
Total days used	74		
No. of days idle	291		80
Total days in year	365	100%	100%

The gross-to-gross method of cost allocation is used to calculate the cost of goods sold when costs bear a relationship to the revenue produced from exempt and nonexempt factors. A proration based on the number of participants can also be used. This type of formula is used in calculating allocations for social clubs and publications charging different prices to members and nonmembers.

PURCHASING PROCEDURES

In the long run, a written plan or procedure to monitor spending saves money. Acquiring goods and services for a nonprofit involves both monetary and nonmonetary considerations. How complicated the purchasing procedures need to be depends on such factors as the size of the organization, the sheer number of transactions, the number of persons authorizing the purchases, the internal control system, and so on. Buying a copy machine for a three-person office that makes 4,000 copies a month might be relatively simple. Setting up a computerized communication network for an organization with 100 employees is more challenging.

Approval Systems

An efficient purchasing system contains at least three elements:

1. Approved vendors

2. Authorization policy

3. Uniform documentation system

For many reasons, it is more efficient to establish purchasing relationships with particular, or approved, vendors. Relying on approved vendors should result in better services, compatibility of equipment and supplies used throughout the organization, possibly more favorable credit terms, optimum prices, and realization of economies to scale. Considerable time may be saved because fewer checks are written for the many items purchased from approved vendors rather than an array of vendors. Staff and volunteer time is not wasted on duplicative shopping efforts.

Likewise, to maintain internal controls and respect budget constraints, purchases should only be made based on proper authorization. Specific persons to approve purchases and monitor the expenditures in relation to the budget should be designated, before any substantial commitment to purchase can be made. An adequate purchasing system establishes a hierarchy that requires the least possible red tape for recurring and modest purchases. The chart shown in Exhibit 7.2 would serve to communicate the policies to staff and volunteers and to govern commitments of funds.

Exhibit 7.2   Hometown Education Center: Purchase Procedure Reference Chart

Amount of Purchase	Approved Vendor Used?	Quotes Required	Written Bid Required	Special Approval Needed	Required Prior to Purchase
<$100	No	No	No	No	Petty cash req.
$100–500	Yes	No	No	No	Check request
$100–500	No	No	No	Yes	Check request
$500–5,000	Yes	Yes	No	No	Purchase order
$500–5,000	No	Yes	Yes	Yes*	Purchase order
Over $5,000	Yes or No	Yes	Yes	Yes*	Purchase order
Capital item	Yes or No	Yes	Yes	Yes*	Feasibility study + Purchase order

*By CFO

How Much Paperwork?

Documentation should be designed to evidence that the purchasing procedures are followed by all persons spending the nonprofit's money. Again, the documents needed varies, but the forms illustrated in Exhibits 7.3 through 7.6, for petty cash, check request, and capital expenditures, are a minimum. A large organization with far-flung purchasers would require purchase orders, might allow credit cards, and would design a bidding-process form. In all nonprofits, the purchasing system should be coordinated with the conflict-of-interest policy described in Chapter 2 (Conflict-of-Interest Policy).

Exhibit 7.3   Hometown Education Center: Petty Cash Reimbursement Request

Name _____   Amount $ _____
           (Petty Cash Custodian)   (Equals Sum
                                                                          of Receipts)

Expense Category	Program or Designated Fund	Description	Amount

_____   _____
Signature of Custodian   Approved by

Exhibit 7.4   Hometown Education Center: Petty Cash Log

Date	Name of Person Receiving Cash	Amount Advanced	Receipts Returned	Total of Receipts	Change Returned

Exhibit 7.5 Hometown Education Center: Petty Cash Request

Name _____ Amount $ _____
    (Person receiving cash)   (Equals Sum of Receipts)

Describe Reason for
Cash Advance   **Amount**   **Receipt Yes or No**

_____   _____
Signature of Custodian   Approved by

Exhibit 7.6 Hometown Education Center: Purchase Order # _____

Vendor: _____   Ship to   Hometown Community Center

        _____   1234 Main Street

        _____   Hometown Texas 77777

Quantity	Description	Program Function Code	Received	Unit Price	Total Price

Totals

Special Instructions: Authorized by:

Deliver no later than _____ (date)   _____

Contact person. _____ (name)   Cost center: ___

_____ Verify quantities received with purchase order and packing slip
(initial)   upon arrival.

_____ Packing slip or invoice then forwarded to business office.
(initial)

Measuring Lifetime Cost

Capital acquisitions, particularly major purchases, involve considerable costs in addition to the basic initial price. The affiliated costs for equipment might include theft insurance, maintenance and supplies, personnel time and expense for training, and additional occupancy costs for the space required for the equipment. In addition to the check request or purchase order form suggested above, the long-term cost of the item can be calculated as shown in Exhibit 7.7.

Exhibit 7.7   Hometown Education Center: Major Purchase Planning Matrix

Description of   _____

Equipment Needed   _____

Justify the Need: _____

                      _____

Quantify Its Original Cost:

   Purchase price $_____

   Shipping   _____

   Software, tools, accessories   _____

   Installation fees/programming   _____

   Training costs (hours × wage × 1.3)   _____

   Other   _____

   Total Purchase cost $_____

Annual cost (divide purchase by years
estimated to be of usefulness to NPO $_____

Add recurring annual costs: _____

Financing costs (or loss of income)   _____

Insurance   _____

Maintenance   _____

Training   _____

Expected annual cost for equipment $_____

Prepared by _____

                (Signature)   (Date)

To Lease or to Buy

A related financial consideration in acquiring new equipment or other long-term property is whether to lease or buy the property. The question is essentially a financing issue. Is it better to buy today for cash or to buy with a down payment plus borrowed funds, or is it better to lease? As with investment decisions, it is important to realize there is no absolute and precise answer. Interest rates are going to fluctuate, so the benefit of keeping the money in the bank is only a guess. The potential need for repairs is impossible to predict. New technologies may or may not be developed that will render the equipment obsolete.

Despite the uncertainty, the alternatives can be evaluated with the best information available. Exhibit 7.8 outlines some of the factors to consider.

Exhibit 7.8   Deciding Whether to Lease or Buy

There are potential advantages with both leasing and buying. No absolute answer to the question exists because facts are indeterminate. Six factors to consider and compare are outlined in this checklist.

Advantages of Leasing

- Leasing allows freedom to move easily if more space is needed, if another location is found more desirable, or to change facilities or equipment if it becomes obsolete or inadequate.

- Leasing has somewhat lower financial risk. It may be less costly (particularly where there is rent control); it requires less commitment of time, resources, and maintenance; and it does not tie up capital.

- The market may be at its peak. Leasing buys the time to judge whether prices will fall in the future.

- The nonprofit may be able to lease with an option to purchase, which leaves it free from commitment but retains the opportunity to buy.

Advantages of Buying

- The permanency of owning its own property can give the organization stability.

- If prices are rising, buying locks in the current price.

- Alterations and choices of space utilization are not restricted.

Exhibit 7.8   Deciding Whether to Lease or Buy *(continued)*

Space and Size Considerations

1. Prepare a needs assessment for people, projects, storage, and other uses. How much space or equipment must be provided for?   _____

2. Ask how far into the future plans can be made with reasonable certainty.   _____

Price Considerations

1. The prices of comparable property, whether the contemplated purchase is for a building, a computer, or a car, should be obtained (based on square feet, capacity, quality, or other relevant factors). Independent appraisals might be appropriate   _____

2. The condition of property must be considered: _____

    a. Are major repairs needed?   _____

    b. Are security and other services adequate?   _____

    c. How good is the location in relation to the nonprofit's constituents?   _____

3. The cost of occupying the property must be included in purchase price:

    a. Will the nonprofit need to remodel, rewire, paint, relocate?   _____

    b. Can skilled workers be found to perform the job?   _____

4. Consider the possibility of renting out excessive space or capacity.   _____

The Nonprofit's Financial Position

1. What are the consequences of using cash reserves?   _____

    a. What is the minimum amount of cash the nonprofit can afford to commit without jeopardizing operations?   _____

    b. Prepare cash flow projections for several years, including debt service and annual maintenance and occupancy costs.   _____

2. Can existing capital be allocated to major purchase?   _____

3. What other expenses would be reduced or eliminated?   _____

Local/State Sanctions

1. Can an occupancy permit be obtained for the purpose for which the nonprofit plans to use the property?   _____

2. Are there restrictive deed covenants?   _____

3. How much will it cost to satisfy building code ordinances?   _____

4. Will property tax exemptions be available?   _____

AFFILIATIONS AND AGENCY AGREEMENTS

For a number of reasons, a nonprofit organization may wish to join forces with another organization, a business, a volunteer guild, a student club, or an artist, for example. Such affiliations occur frequently in many different forms, including the joint operation of a mutually beneficial project (computer database), a fundraising or special-event sponsorship, or a fiscal agency in which the nonprofit serves to maintain the bank account (student or special grant). A number of issues need to be explored between the parties in forming such an affiliation. At least the following questions should be answered:

1. Whose money is it?

   - Will the nonprofit serve as fiscal agent, meaning it will receive moneys as pass-through gifts that will not be its property?

   - On whose financial statements will the financial activity be reported?

   - If a charity is involved, to whom is the charitable gift made for income tax deduction and donor disclosure purposes?

2. Who bears the risk of loss?

   - With whose money and in whose name will a bank account be opened?

   - In whose name will purchases be made or obligations entered into to rent a facility, engage a performer, or print a flyer?

   - If workers are hired, who is responsible for tax reporting?

3. What other terms should be agreed to?

   - How long will the agreement last?

   - Who is in control of what?

   - Whose staff and other assets will be actively involved?

   - Are prior approvals required for announcements or other use of the nonprofit's name?

To protect its interests and provide operational guidelines, the non-profit that serves as a fiscal agent should document such arrangements with written agreements.[6] The alliance may be permanent and deserve a formal prenuptial or partnership agreement, or it may be a one-time special event or project for which a simple letter reciting the understandings and setting forth the budget is sufficient. The parties to the association must describe the nature of the association and define the responsibilities of all involved. Exhibits 7.9 and 7.10 are models provided as examples, not as a legal document to be executed. They can serve, just as the preceding checklist is intended to, as a starting point for consideration in developing the facts and circumstances to document a nonprofit's particular affiliation agreement.

Documentation must be maintained by the sponsored project under this fiscal sponsorship agreement follows:

Exhibit 7.9   Sample Fundraising Event Sponsorship Agreement

Agreements should be prepared in consultation with a nonprofit's legal counsel. This model is intended only as an illustration.

Name of **Benefited Charity** _____

Name of **Event Sponsor**   _____

Description of purpose for which the funds raised will be expended

_____

_____

Description of Event _____

_____

_____

Financial Information:

Gross revenue expected to be raised (attach details)

  # of people × _____ (price per ticket)   _____

  In-kind contributions of food, facilities, etc.   _____

---

[6] Gregory L. Colvin has written an excellent booklet entitled, *Fiscal Sponsorship: 6 Ways to Do It Right*, published by Study Center Press, San Francisco, CA, 82 pages. The legal relationships among the parties are carefully illustrated and explored using six different models.

Total

Expenditures (attach details)   – _____

Projected net profit $_____

_____(Event Sponsor) hereby authorized by _____ (Benefited Charity) to sponsor a fund-raising event on its behalf on _____ (date) at _____ (place). Expenditures in connection with this event are authorized by sponsor in accordance with a budget mutually agreed upon prior to event's announcement. Sponsor agrees it is responsible for any expenditures in excess of revenues, if any, incurred in presenting the event.

Sponsor warrants that all proceeds of the event, less mutually agreed upon costs, belong to the Benefited Charity. Sponsor will control event funds by using the enclosed Public Fund Solicitation Controls Checklist (Exhibit 6.9). A bank account in the name of the Benefited Charity will be established for deposit and disbursement of funds. Checks will be made payable to the Benefited Charity and deposited on a daily basis during the fundraising period. Detailed records of the financial transactions, in accordance with the attached Record-Keeping Requirements, will be maintained by Sponsor's business office.

Use of Name: Sponsor agrees, in advance, to seek _____ (Benefited Charity)'s approval for all written announcements, press releases, tickets, and any other materials reflecting charity's name.

Termination: This agreement will cease once a full detailed accounting of revenues and expenses, along with copies of receipts and other required documentation, have been furnished to the benefited charity.

Agreed to on this _____ day of _____, 20XX.

_____   _____
For the Benefited Charity   For the Sponsor

Exhibit 7.10   Sample Fiscal Sponsorship Agreement

Agreements should be prepared in consultation with a nonprofit's legal counsel. This model is intended only as an illustration.

1. Parties to the Agreement. Hometown Artists Fund (HAF) is a public tax-exempt §501(c)(3) organization established to serve as sponsor for artist's projects in the Hometown area.

New Artist Project (NAP) is an unincorporated association created by Joan Fatcat and Alex Painter to honor emerging artists with exhibitions and to document their works with catalogs and similar educational materials. As its first project, NAP plans to curate an exhibition and catalog of the art work of Frank Creative in the spring of 20XX, at the Museum for New Art, Hometown, USA.

Exhibit 7.10 Sample Fiscal Sponsorship Agreement *(continued)*

2. Financial Information. NAP will seek donations from individuals, businesses, and foundations to provide financial support for the exhibition. A bank account has been opened for the project. NAP will satisfy the attached Record-Keeping Requirements (Exhibit 7.11) for moneys raised and expended in HAF's name and furnish a quarterly report of the financial activity. HAF will annually file Forms 990 reporting its overall activity to the Internal Revenue Service, furnish donor receipts, and take whatever other steps are necessary to keep its qualification as a charitable tax-exempt organization current and in good standing.

A preliminary budget for the project estimates $_____ will be raised in donations and $_____ will be expended to survey the work and prepare a catalog of Creative's work. The Museum of New Art has made an oral commitment to pay all of the costs of the exhibition. NAP hereby agrees not to commit HAF to any expenditures in excess of the moneys raised through voluntary contributions. A reasonably detailed accounting will be maintained by NAP to assure the spending is within the amount of funds available. The creators of NAP, not HAF, will be responsible for any cost overruns incurred. A budget for expenditures will be furnished for approval by HAF's board prior to NAP entering into any binding commitments to expend funds.

3. Rights and Ownership. NAP will be operated as a project of HAF. HAF will delegate to NAP's managers the authority to carry out the activity as described in the project proposal and within the approved budget. The managers of NAP will work without compensation but will engage one or more writers or curators to compose the catalog and design the exhibition. Those artists will be hired as independent contractors and will retain no ownership interest in the work product. HAF will be given a limited license for reproduction and exhibition of Frank Creative's art work. Mr. Creative will receive a fee as reflected in the budget for his work. Additionally HAF will request he receive a royalty (of up to 10%) interest in the catalog sales, if possible, in its negotiations with publishers.

Plans for the catalog are preliminary and specific ownership rights and responsibilities in that regard remain to be agreed upon. HAF's role is to assure that the catalog is used exclusively for educational purposes and that it receives the widest possible distribution and preferably as a publication of a university press.

4. Administrative Fee. HAF is managed by its creators, Molly Smart, CPA, and Joe Lucky, Attorney-at-Law. They respect and admire Frank Creative and wish to support NAP, whose managers are also unpaid volunteers. Thus, no administrative fee will be paid from NAP funds for handling the project through 20XX. It is presumed the managers of NAP will maintain the required fiscal records and keep the project expenditures within budget so as not to expose HAF to risk of creditor claims or manager travail.

5. Duration of Agreement. This agreement shall last until the exempt purposes for which NAP is raising funds are accomplished or until NAP establishes itself as independently qualified as an exempt charitable organization. Agreed to this day of _____ in _____, 20XX.

_____   _____
For Hometown Artists Fund   For New Artist Project

Exhibit 7.11   Sponsor or Agency Record-Keeping Requirements

BANKING RECORDS   Done By

- Open bank account in name of XYZ, a project of
  Hometown Artist Fund.   _____

- Keep a computerized checkbook, recording each transaction
  and the daily cash balance.   _____

- Prepare bank account reconciliation monthly.   _____

- Keep checks with statements intact (copy items if needed).   _____

REVENUES RECEIPTS

- Deposit checks or cash as soon as possible after receipt.   _____

- Keep a copy of each check received and any daily cash tally.   _____

- Identify the nature of payment received (donation, cost
  reimbursement, etc.).   _____

- Receipt or thank each contributor using standard HAF form.   _____

- Maintain a database of donors in alphabetical order.   _____

DISBURSEMENT OF FUNDS

- Identify each invoice or bill paid with check number, date paid,
  and budget category description.   _____

- Maintain bills and invoices in an alpha order by merchant.   _____

- Keep files to document the nature of activities, such as a copy
  of exhibition invitations, manuscripts, photos, and so on.   _____

- At least quarterly, prepare summary of income and expenses
  by categories in grant proposal.   _____

If workers are to be hired, ask for checklist to classify as contractors
versus employees. **Employees can be hired directly only by HAF**.
Obtain invoice and Form W-9 for all independent contractors.   _____

WHO'S AN EMPLOYEE?

Nonprofit organizations who have employees must satisfy Internal Revenue
Service withholding and filing requirements outlined below, as well as
requirements imposed by other regulatory agencies including the department of labor, workers' compensation statutes, Employee Retirement
Income Security Act of 1974 (ERISA) rules, and state employment taxes.

Most wages are subject to tax withholding except those paid to certain min-
isters, members of religious orders, student workers, and fellowship or grant
recipients. Exhibit 7.12 reviews the primary tax issues to be considered. The
most severe penalties in the tax code are imposed on failure to pay withheld
employment taxes, because such money does not belong to the organization
but instead to the employees. Of equal importance to nonprofit managers,
the IRS may consider them personally liable for unpaid payroll taxes

---

Exhibit 7.12   Employer Tax Checklist

---

*This checklist compiles local and federal tax filing requirements and outlines
types of compensation arrangements for which reporting may be required as well
as other employment law issues.*

1. Does the entity have a policy for distinguishing between employees
   and independent contractors?   ☐

   a. Complete Employee versus Independent Contractor Checklist.   ☐

   b. Does the entity have a contract with independent contractors
      (Exhibit 7.14)?   ☐

   c. Have vendors' Social Security numbers been secured with a
      signed Form W-9?   ☐

   d. Are vendor invoices obtained from independent contractors to
      prove their professionalism?   ☐

2. Are meals, cars, tuition, or housing allowances furnished to
   employees? If so, determine taxable portion, if any.   ☐

3. Does the pension plan adhere to ERISA rules?   ☐

4. Is Form 5500, 5500C, or 5500R required for the pension plan?   ☐

5. Are the terms of any qualified or nonqualified deferred
   compensation plan adhered to?   ☐

6. Do COBRA rules entitle former employees to continued medical
   benefit coverage?   ☐

7. Is workers' compensation coverage required?   ☐

8. Verify adherence to federal requirements. Study IRS Circular E,
   Employer's Tax Guide, for filing requirements, chart of wages
   subject to or exempt from taxes. Verify correctness of:

   a. Income tax withholding   ☐

   b. Social Security tax   ☐

c. Federal unemployment tax ☐

d. State and local income taxes ☐

9. Verify timely filing of the following IRS reports:

a. Form 941, employer's quarterly federal tax return ☐

b. W-2 Forms for all employees ☐

c. W-3 Form with copy of W-2s ☐

d. W-4 From placed in each employee's file ☐

e. Form 1099-MISC for all independent contractors ☐

f. Form W-9 placed in each contractor's file ☐

g. Form W-2G, Prizes and Awards ☐

h. Form W-2P, Statement for Recipients of Pensions ☐

i. Form 940, federal unemployment (not filed by §501(c)(3)s) ☐

10. Verify timely deposit of federal employment taxes. ☐

11. Are state employment commission or tax requirements satisfied? ☐

a. Are periodic returns filed and tax paid on time? ☐

b. If new employer, file status report to obtain account number. ☐

Exhibit 7.13 compares the attributes of employees—those for whom a nonprofit is responsible for withholding and paying taxes—versus independent contractors. There is no specific mathematical test applied to make the determination, although more than one-half on either side is a strong indication. The facts and circumstances of each payee/payor relationship are analyzed to identify an employee relationship. As a rule, classifying a worker as an employee is seldom challenged; it is finding justification for treating one as independent that is troublesome. For those treated as a contractor, a prudent nonprofit can enter into a contract of the type illustrated in Exhibit 7.14.

Making a distinction between employees and independent workers is important for two reasons. The costs associated with providing benefits and matching taxes for employees range between 10 percent and 30 percent of direct payroll costs; so classifying a worker as an employee is a costly decision. This factor tempts some nonprofits to treat workers as contractors, not subject to tax withholding and employee benefits. The wrong decision, however, can be costly. When the IRS finds that a worker should have been treated as an employee, they assess payroll taxes even though the organization withheld nothing from the worker's compensation.

Exhibit 7.13   Employee versus Independent Contractor Status:
A Comparison Checklist

This checklist lists the six primary characteristics distinguishing an employee (E) from an independent contractor (IC). The letter E identifies the predominate characteristic of an employee and IC describes the characteristics of an independent contractor. For each pair of factors, choose best description and check either E or IC. Upon completion, the factor with larger number of checks should be the correct classification of the worker.

| | | Check One | |
		Employee (E)	Independent Contractor (IC)
Factor	Attributes		
Instruction and Training	**E** required to comply with instructions as to when, where, and how work is performed, and training is provided either by formal program or work supervision.		
	IC free to perform work according to own professional standards, use their own methods, and receive no training from purchasers of their services.		
Payment Terms	**E** is paid by the hour, week, or month on a regular, indefinite, and continuous basis. **E's** business expenses are paid. Fringe benefits are usually provided.		
	IC is often paid by the engagement with fee calculated without regard to time spent. **IC** not paid for excess time to perform task nor given vacation or sick leave. **IC** pays expenses.		
Nature of Engagement	**E's** employer has the right to discharge an **E**; control is exerted with threat of dismissal. **E** has the right to quit without incurring liability.		

	IC may suffer damages if work is not performed as contracted. Payment still due if IC is fired.		
Relation to Entity	E's services are an integral part to the ongoing success and continuation of entity. Services are rendered personally by E. E works only for and has loyalty to and does not compete with employer. E is bonded and provided workers' compensation.		
	IC consults on per-job, limited, or special-project basis. IC can hire and pay assistants to perform the work. IC's service is available to others on a regular basis. IC works under a company name.		
Work Place and Hour	E works on business premises or is physically directed and supervised by employer. Hours of work established by employer.		
	IC may work at own place of business and usually sets own time for performing work.		
Investment	E is dependent on employer for tools and facilities, and usually makes no investment in the job. E bears no risk of loss for financial costs of entity.		
	IC buys own tools, hires workers, pays licensing fees, and is responsible for costs of engagement. Bears financial risk of losing money.		

Internal Revenue Ruling 87-41 provides the above characteristics. The checklist contains all of the 20 factors set out by the IRS hopefully organized in a fashion that makes the determination easier. A nonprofit that is uncertain and wants IRS sanction for their decision is invited by the IRS to submit a completed Form SS-8, entitled Information for Use in Determining Whether a Worker Is an Employee for Federal Employment Taxes and Income Tax Withholding, *to obtain the IRS opinion on the matter. Form SS-8 can also be used as a self-examination tool.*

Exhibit 7.14   Minimal Independent Contractor Agreement

Agreements should be prepared in consultation with a nonprofit's legal counsel. This model is intended only as an illustration.

Name of Organization: _____

_____

Contractor: _____

Price:

      Fixed fee

      _____

      Hourly rate $. per-hour times _____ hours =

      _____

      Reimbursable expenses:

      _____   _____

      _____   _____

Payments for professional services you perform will be made monthly, based upon invoices submitted by you, along with receipts and other documentation for reimbursable expenses described above.

For consideration, you agree to perform the following work:

_____

_____

_____

In consideration of our engagement of your services, you warrant that you are an independent contractor, not an employee, agent, or representative of our organizations. You are responsible for any and all federal and state payroll taxes and insurance or other levies due in respect to your fee for services.. You—on behalf of yourself, your assigns, and estate—waive and release any and all claims or rights whatsoever you may have against us. This agreement may be terminated by either party at any time, except that you will be paid for any unpaid services properly chargeable to us prior to termination. In acknowledgment of our understandings, we have both signed below.

By: _____   By: _____

Date: _____   Date: _____

8

Obtaining and Maintaining Tax-Exempt Status

> Although for-profits do not often give away food or house the poor, they do operate schools, hospitals, galleries, and other institutions serving the public good. If the work of for-profits and non-profits can be the same, why do only nonprofits get special tax treatment?

A nonprofit organization's financial planners need to know not only why it qualifies for tax exemptions, but also the breadth of activity such status allows. Nonprofits are fascinating because they are full of paradoxes and surprises. In this chapter, the unique nomenclature defining those organizations entitled to federal tax-exempt status is explored, and some of the contradictions are explained. The subject is complex, and tax rules are vague and gray, with few generally applicable rules; the answers are typically based on the facts of each particular organization, meaning the answers are not always clear. A thorough review of the tax issues can be found in the fourth edition of my book entitled *Tax Planning and Compliance for Tax-Exempt Organizations,* which contains 741 pages; the text is updated annually, with a supplemental text of over 200 pages.

The complexity of this subject is also illustrated by the fact that the Internal Revenue Code (IRC) does not contain the word *nonprofit*—it refers only to *tax-exempt organizations.* The term *nonprofit,* or *not-for-profit,* describes the type of organizations legally created in most states, and is widely used to identify tax-exempt organizations. The terms are commonly used interchangeably.

CHARACTERISTICS OF TAX-EXEMPT ORGANIZATIONS

A nonprofit organization is not necessarily a tax-exempt organization. Exempt organizations are by necessity nonprofits and are established under state laws as nonprofit, or not-for-profit organizations, which leads to a certain amount of confusion. A tax-exempt nonprofit organization (an EO or simply an exempt) is distinguished from a nonexempt nonprofit by its ownership structure, the nature of its activities, its sources of revenue to finance operations, and what happens to its assets upon dissolution. As discussed in Chapter 1, the term *nonprofit* is sometimes a contradictory term. To grow and be financially successful, a nonprofit can and often must generate profits, and may be required to pay income tax on investment or business income unrelated to its underlying exempt purposes.

Theoretical Basis for Exemption

Federal and state governments view nonprofits as relieving their burdens. Thus, many nonprofits are exempt from the levies that finance government, including income, sales, ad valorem, and other local property taxes. Tax exemption recognizes that such nonprofits essentially perform functions the government would otherwise have to perform. U.S. tax laws were traditionally designed to encourage private philanthropy. Other exempt organizations, such as social clubs or labor unions, are exempt because they are organized for the mutually beneficial purposes of their members, rather than the individual member's private financial gain. Another way to express this concept is that such groups are permitted tax exemption precisely because they are not formed to produce profits for owners.

The thread running through the various types of exempt organizations is the lack of private ownership and self-directed profit motive in their programs. A tax-exempt organization is a nonprofit entity operated without self-interest and with no intention to produce income or profit distributable to its members, directors, or officers. Most nonprofits are afforded special tax and legal status precisely because of the unselfish motivation behind their formation.

Categories of Exemption

Although nonprofit organizations are often perceived as charitable, IRC §501 exempts 28 specific types of nonprofit organizations, plus pension plans (IRC §401), from income tax. States themselves, labor unions, business leagues, social clubs, and employee benefit associations are included on the list. Each exemption category has its own distinct set of criteria for qualification. Form 1023 or 1024, the form filed with the IRS to request recognition of tax exemption, can be reviewed to gain an understanding of the basic criteria applied in determining that a particular nonprofit organization qualifies as a tax-exempt entity. A brief abstract of the five major categories of exemption in the federal tax code follows.

§*501(c)(3)* organizations are known as charities and include those nonprofits that qualify for the charitable contribution deduction for income tax purposes. A §501(c)(3) organization must under the terms of its charter permanently dedicate its assets to its charitable purposes. Upon dissolution, any assets remaining must be paid over to another charity and cannot be returned to its funders. A charity cannot electioneer or attempt to influence the choice of persons running for public office. On a very limited scale, a charity, other than a private foundation, can lobby or attempt to influence elected officials once they are in office. The code specifically says nonprofits who exclusively pursue the following purposes can qualify for this category of tax exemption:

1. Religious

2. Charitable

3. Scientific

4. Testing for public safety

5. Literary

6. Educational

7. Fostering national or international amateur sports competition

8. Preventing cruelty to children or animals

This category includes churches, schools, hospitals, united giving campaigns, private foundations, and a myriad of organizations providing services and benefits to members of the charitable class—or the constituents for whom the charity operates. For some categories of exemption, the class members must be underprivileged or needy—the hungry, poor, or homeless low-income families. Educational and literary organizations, however, may conceivably only serve those who can afford to pay for attending their functions—symphony societies and private schools, for example.

Each type of charitable organization has its own particular set of criteria. For example, most nonprofits that support youth activities, such as a local Little League team, can qualify as Type 1, or charitable. To qualify as a Type 7, a national amateur sports competition sponsor is prohibited from selling sports gear and is subject to other specific rules intended to distinguish it from commercial counterparts. Charitable hospitals are not necessarily (as of June 2007) required by the IRS to provide health care for those who cannot pay, as long as they can show that they promote community's health needs. What distinguishes a church from other religious organizations is similarly governed by a specific set of published criteria. To understand the rules pertaining to a particular nonprofit, it is important to again keep in mind that many nonprofits provide the same services as for-profit businesses—hospitals, scientific-research organizations, bookstores, theaters, and so on. Distinguishing such organizations that serve the general public from their commercial counterparts providing the same services for the economic gain of its owners is sometimes difficult.

§501(c)(4) organizations include two very different types of nonprofits:

1. Civic leagues

2. Local associations of employees

Civic leagues are nonprofits that promote the common good and general welfare of the people of a community by implementing programs designed to have an impact on community, state, or national policy making. A §501(c)(4) organization can spend an unlimited amount of its funds on legislative lobbying, as distinguished from a §501(c)(3), which may spend only a limited amount. Organizations established to defend the environment, to protect human and civil rights, to lessen neighborhood tension, to eliminate prejudices and discrimination in a pro-action fashion would seek exemption under §501(c)(4).

§501(c)(5) permits exempt status for labor unions and agricultural groups. The statute requires that such groups serve three purposes:

1. Betterment of conditions of those engaged in such pursuits

2. Improvement of the grade of their products

3. Development of a high degree of efficiency in their respective occupations

Labor organizations are defined by the tax regulations to include an "association of workmen who have combined to protect or promote the interests of the members by bargaining collectively with their employers to secure better working conditions, wages and similar benefits." Unions also are permitted to conduct peripheral activities intended to advance the workers, such as providing strike benefits, mutual sickness and death plans, seminars and training programs, and job-placement counseling. Unions can participate in election campaigns and lobby without specific limits, as long as the union basically operates to benefit its members' interests.

Agricultural organizations are dedicated to developing techniques for efficient product and betterment of conditions for those engaged in agriculture or horticulture, or the "art and science of cultivating the ground, preparing soil, planting seed, rearing, feeding, and managing livestock." Such groups operate to benefit their members as a whole, rather than as individuals. For example, an agricultural group can conduct seed-certification programs to maintain an industry standard, but it could not (except as an unrelated business activity) sell seeds to individual farmers.

§501(c)(6) provides exemption for business leagues, chambers of commerce, boards of trade, and professional football leagues. A business league is permitted exemption because it is a nonprofit association of persons having a common business interest. The league does not itself conduct a regular business or perform services for or provide benefits to its members. Instead, a business league seeks to improve conditions and maintain standards for one or more lines of business. A common business interest exists for lawyers who form the American Bar Association, physicians and the medical society, accountants and the CPA societies, and contractors and their association, for example. The American Automobile Association is not a qualifying business league, because its members have no common business interest; any individual motorist can join to serve his or her personal needs. Similarly, a computer users group open to all persons using a particular type of computer operating system, without regard to their business interests, was found not to qualify for exemption under this category.

§501(c)(7) grants exempt status to social clubs. Theoretically the social club exemption permits persons to join together on a mutual basis for pleasure and recreation without tax consequence. Clubs that seek exemption, however, are subject to very stringent rules governing the limited extent to which a club can provide services to nonmembers. A social club's investment income on property accumulated as reserves is taxed, although any profits from member activities is exempt.

Tax Deductibility

For reasons not always apparent, all nonprofits are not equal for tax deduction purposes and not all "donations" are deductible. For charitable nonprofits, labor unions, and certain business leagues, the deductibility of dues and donations granted to such organizations further evidence the government's willingness to forgo money in favor of such organizations. Deductibility is thought by some to provide a major fundraising tool for the nonprofits.

UNDERSTANDING THE NONPROFIT'S LEGAL FORM

The requirements for nonprofit status vary from state to state, and few generalizations apply. Exempt charitable institutions are called public benefit corporations in some states. Business leagues, social clubs, burial groups, and other membership organizations are sometimes called mutual benefit corporations. Rather than being organized to generate profits for owners or investors, nonprofits generate profits for their broadly based public or membership constituents.

The choice of organizational form is influenced by laws of the state(s) in which the nonprofit will operate. The federal tax-exemption rules overlap and sometimes contradict. For example, the model nonprofit corporation charter acceptable to the state of Texas is deficient for federal tax-exemption purposes, in several respects. The choice of legal form for certain categories of federal tax-exemption is also limited. A title-holding company, for example, must be a corporation to qualify for federal exemption. Social clubs, civic associations, and business leagues commonly function as corporations governed by their members. Nonprofits functioning as a branch of a national organization may be required to adhere to the form of organization prescribed by the central and controlling entity. The common organizational choices are corporation, trust, or unincorporated association. The need to coordinate local and federal law may make the initial choice of organizational form a challenge. Retaining an attorney experienced in nonprofit matters is advisable.

Corporation

Because corporate status is the most flexible, it is usually the form of choice in most states. The American Bar Association and, more recently, the Association of Attorneys General, have developed uniform procedures and rules that have been adopted by many states and can be used as a guideline.

Creating a corporation as a separate entity is said to provide a corporate veil that shields the individuals controlling the nonprofit from liabilities incurred by the organization (unless they are negligent or participate in tortuous acts). Some states have adopted immunity laws augmenting protection against liability for directors and officers. In Texas, the Charitable Immunity and Liability Act of 1987 applies to charitable trusts and nonprofit organizations conducting charitable programs. This statute protects a charity's officers, directors, trustees, and volunteers, regardless of the form of organization, thus obviating one of the advantages in establishing a corporation. In California, apparently only not-for-profit corporations are provided such immunity.

A nonprofit corporation can be formed with or without members. Unless the charter provides otherwise, some states presume the existence of members. The primary role of members is to elect the board of directors who, in turn, govern the organization. In a privately funded organization, the members may be family representatives whose job it is to retain control by naming the directors, or the founder of a charity can be named the sole member. In most public benefit corporations and certainly in churches, members serve to broaden the base of financial support and to involve the community in the organization's activities. In such cases, there may be hundreds or thousands of individual contributors (investors in the financial planning sense) who, as a group, control the organization because they elect the directors. Most mutual benefit societies, clubs, and the like are also controlled by their dues-paying members. When the democracy afforded by member control is not desirable, the nonprofit's charter can provide for a self-perpetuating board or a board appointed by another organization or other persons (e.g., the town mayor, the governor, or the school superintendent). Calling the supporters of a nonmembership nonprofit *members* can cause confusion.

Bylaws are adopted to provide rules of governance, such as the number of directors, duration of their terms, and procedures for electing and removing them. Bylaws typically also address the frequency of meetings, notice of meeting protocol, type and duties of officers, delegation of authority to committees, extent of member responsibility, and indemnity from liability for the directors. The manner in which the bylaws and the charter can be amended is prescribed. An advantage of the corporate form—as compared to a trust—is the ability to easily mold and change policies as the organization evolves. Usually, the currently serving board has authority to make changes to both the bylaws and the charter.

Trust

Individually or family-funded charitable organizations are often organized in trust form, either by testamentary bequest under a will or by creation of an *inter vivos* (among the living) trust. Unlike a corporation, a trust can be totally inflexible, with no provisions for change in purpose or trustees. Thus, a donor with specific wishes may prefer this potentially unalterable form for a substantial testamentary bequest. Another advantage of a trust is that some states require no registration. There is some argument that charitable trusts can violate the rule against perpetuities. To avoid this potential obstacle, a trust may contain a provision allowing the trustee(s) to convert the trust into a nonprofit corporation, with identical purposes and organizational restraints, if the trust form becomes disadvantageous.

Nonprofit organization immunity statutes do not apply to trusts in some states, and more stringent fiduciary standards are often imposed on trustees than on corporate directors. As a rule, trustees are thought to be more exposed to potential liability for their actions than are corporate directors. The federal income tax rates on unrelated business income are lower for a corporation than for a trust.

Unincorporated Association

An unincorporated association is said to be self-establishing. Two or more persons adopt an organizing instrument, usually called a constitution or articles of association, outlining the same basic information found in a corporate charter or trust instrument. For a short-term nonprofit project that does not intend to seek tax exemption, this form may be suitable. It is also used for a local branch of a statewide or national organization holding a group exemption. The central organization provides subordinates with a uniform set of documents and procedures to adopt. An unincorporated group faces substantial pitfalls. The primary concern is lack of protection from legal liability for officers and directors. Also banks and creditors may be reluctant to establish business relationships without personal guarantees by the officers or directors.

TESTING SUITABILITY FOR TAX EXEMPTION

Before embarking on financial planning for an exempt nonprofit, the reasons why the nonprofit is exempt from taxation should be clearly understood. Proposed projects or changes in operations, particularly those involving creative methods of raising money, should be tested to ensure their suitability for a tax-exempt organization. The basic questions to be addressed are similar to those one asks before creating a new organization. Although the rules are sometimes ambiguous, certain requirements are applied precisely. Five major questions can be asked to determine whether a proposed program or, by reference, a new organization is suitable for qualification for tax-exempt status.

Why a New Nonprofit?

The first question to ask is whether a new organization is really necessary. Or ask if the project, instead, could be carried out more efficiently under the auspices of an existing nonprofit? Several factors can indicate that a new organization is not necessary. If the purposes to be accomplished are short term or essentially in pursuit of a one-time project with no prospect for ongoing funding, the expense and effort involved in setting up a new, independent nonprofit may not be economically feasible. Similarly, the costs of launching the project within an existing organization may not be recoupable.

A good question to ask is whether the project could be operated as a branch of an existing nonprofit under an agency agreement, as discussed in Chapter 7 (Affiliations and Agency Agreements). Maybe a local branch of a national organization holding a group exemption can be established. Consider if there would be a costly duplication of administrative effort, or if the cost of obtaining and maintaining independent exemption would be excessive in relation to the total budget. It might make sense to find a fiscal sponsor, form an alliance with an existing group, or find a more financially viable manner in which to accomplish the objective.

What Category of Exemption?

If the proposed organization passes the first test, it is time to choose the category of exemption best suited to the goals and purposes of the project. The §501(c)(3) charitable exemption rules are very specific, somewhat rigid, and can limit some activities. As explained earlier in this chapter (Categories of Exemption), a §501(c)(3) organization cannot, for example, participate in a political campaign and may conduct only limited legislative and grassroots lobbying. A §501(c)(4) civic league, however, can spend all its money on lobbying, and it can have some electioneering efforts. If no profits are expected to be generated and no tax deductibility is desired, tax-exempt status might not be necessary, and the organizers might simply create a for-profit company.

If a project is not suitable for charitable exemption, the other categories of exemption should be studied. Some projects can conceivably qualify for more than one category. There are garden clubs classified as charities under §501(c)(3), civic welfare societies under §501(c)(4), and social clubs under §501(c)(7). An association of business persons, such as the Rotary Club or the Lions Club, most often qualifies as a business league. If the activities of the group involve educational and/or charitable efforts, §501(c)(3) status, rather than §501(c)(6) status, might be sought. A breakfast group composed of representatives of many different types of businesses may not qualify under §501(c)(6), but might instead qualify as a §501(c)(7) social club. The tax deductibility of member dues and taxability of income influences the desired choice of category.

How Is Money to Be Raised?

To be financially viable, a nonprofit organization needs sufficient capitalization similar to a for-profit organization but cannot sell shares of stock, as discussed in Chapter 1 (Capitalization: Philanthropists versus Investors). Before the final decision to establish a new organization is made, the nonprofit's future needs for capital and its ability to raise money must be projected. The reliability of funding sources should be evaluated to assure sustainable spending levels.

Nonprofits are normally expected to be supported by voluntary contributions, member dues, and charges for services rendered or goods provided to accomplish an exempt purpose, such as school tuition or ballet tickets. Moneys raised through services rendered or goods sold in competition with businesses, such as insurance or legal services, may be taxed as unrelated business income. Although unrelated revenue activities are not prohibited, exempt status can be revoked if such activity becomes excessive in relation to the exempt focus of the nonprofit as explained in Chapter 5 (Business Income).

A charitable nonprofit that receives the majority of its funding from a particular family or other small group of persons or that is supported by its endowment income may qualify for exemption as a §501(c)(3) organization. Such a privately funded charity, however, is designated as a "private foundation," and is subject to a separate set of rules designed to prevent the use of the organization for the creator's selfish purposes. All financial transactions, other than voluntary gifts to the private foundation, between the organization and its creators are prohibited by self-dealing rules. At least 5 percent of the average monthly fair market value of the foundation's investment assets must be paid out annually in charitable grants and projects. Other specific rules apply to penalize insiders who make jeopardizing investments with the foundation's money or who pay out funds for noncharitable purposes.

Will Insiders Benefit?

The last and sometimes most important issue is whether the organization's creators desire economic benefits from the formation or ongoing operation of the organization. Is there any personal greed involved? Will the organization be operated to serve the self-interested purposes of its creators? The one-way-street characteristic of nonprofits is crucial to ongoing qualification for tax exemption, as discussed in Chapter 1 (Capitalization: Philanthropists versus Investors). If the founders desire incentive compensation based on funds raised, or wish to gain from profits generated, a nonprofit organization may not be an appropriate entity in which to operate. Reasonable compensation for services actually and genuinely rendered, however, can be paid.

For a variety of reasons, it is sometimes desirable to convert a for-profit business into a nonprofit one. In the health and human service field, for example, funding is often available from both for-profit and nonprofit sources. An organization's direction may change or funds may become available only for tax-exempt organizations or vice versa. When a nonprofit is created to take over the assets and operations of a for-profit entity, the buy-out terms will be carefully scrutinized. Too high a price, ongoing payments having the appearance of dividends, and assumptions of liability that take the creators off the hook are among the issues faced in this situation.

Where Will Assets Go?

The resources of an exempt organization must be permanently dedicated to its exempt purposes. When it ceases to exist, the assets remaining upon dissolution must essentially be used for the same exempt purposes for which the organization was initially granted tax exemption. Charities exempt under §501(c)(3) can only distribute funds to another §501(c)(3) organization or a governmental unit, and their charters must require this. Again, the one-way-street concept is applicable. The creators must understand and intend from inception that they will gain no personal economic benefit from the organization's operations and benefits. Exhibit 8.1 summarizes the issues to be considered in forming a new exempt organization.

Exhibit 8.1   Suitability Checklist for Tax-Exempt Status

This checklist asks questions intended to tell those considering the formation of a new tax-exempt nonprofit organization whether the effort is financially viable.

Is a new organization necessary, or could the project be carried out as a branch of an existing organization?

- Life of the project is short term or indefinite.   ☐
- It is a one-time project with no prospect for ongoing funding.   ☐

- Project could operate under auspices of another exempt organization. ☐
- Duplication of administrative effort is too costly. ☐
- Cost of obtaining and maintaining independent nonprofit is excessive in relation to total budget. ☐
- Group exemption is available through a national nonprofit. ☐

Which §501(c) category of exemption is appropriate to the goals and purposes of the project?

- Are the activities in pursuit of an exempt purpose? ☐
- No involvement in political campaigns for §501(c)(3)s. ☐
- Legislative and grassroots lobbying activities may be limited. ☐
- Private foundation strictures on activities may apply. ☐
- Compare business versus social aspects of future activities. ☐

Are the sources of revenue suitable for a tax-exempt organization?

- Sales of goods produced by members. ☐
- Services to be rendered in competition with nonexempt businesses, such as legal or management consulting services. ☐
- Over half of revenues to come from unrelated businesses operated in competition with for-profit companies. ☐
- Will support come from a particular family so as to require classification as a private foundation? ☐

Do the creators desire economic benefits from the operation of the organization?

- What are the possibilities for private inurement? ☐
- Do the creators wish to be paid incentive compensation based on funds raised or profitability of the organization? ☐
- Are transactions with related parties anticipated? ☐
- Is this an insider bailout? Are assets being purchased or debts being assumed? ☐
- Will services or activities be available to a limited group of persons or members instead of a public class? ☐
- Who will use or benefit from the existence of the organization's physical facilities or other assets? ☐

Exhibit 8.1   Suitability Checklist for Tax-Exempt Status *(continued)*

Upon dissolution, where will the nonprofit's assets go?

- Do the organizational documents permanently dedicate
  the resources to its exempt purposes?   ☐

- If the nonprofit is a §501(c)(3), will remaining assets be paid
  over to a similarly exempt nonprofit when it ceases to exist?   ☐

- For a league or club, will the funds be rebated to members?   ☐

MAINTAINING RECOGNITION OF EXEMPT STATUS

To be officially recognized by the IRS as an exempt organization, the non-profit submits an Application for Recognition of Exemption, Form 1023 or 1024, with the IRS Exempt Organization District Office in Cincinnati, Ohio. With the form, the prospective exempt paints a picture of its future self with information that is similar to a business plan for a new venture. Using both words and numbers to describe proposed activities and funding sources, the applicant submits a wealth of information to allow the IRS to judge whether the proposed activities and financing methods qualify it to be exempt from federal income tax on its net income and to gain other special privileges. Recognition of exemption by the IRS typically is an automatic basis for exemption from a variety of state and local taxes.

The tax rules on which the IRS decides qualification are gray, and they are not necessarily made clear by the IRS regulations and rulings or by court decisions. As with most federal tax matters, the Internal Revenue Code expresses general concepts subject to endless interpretations. The categories of exempt nonprofits have expanded considerably since the Tariff Act of 1894 established a single category that included charitable, religious, educational, fraternal, and certain building and loan, savings, and insurance organizations. Since that time, the number of categories has expanded to include the 28 distinct types. The distinctions among the categories are not always clear or logical. For example, only scholars of legislative history can explain why agricultural organizations and labor unions are coupled together. Why are agricultural groups not considered business leagues? Why are agricultural auxiliaries classified as business leagues? Why was a separate category carved out for real estate title-holding companies with multiple parents, instead of placing them in the original §501(c)(2) for single-parent organizations? A discussion of these mysteries and rules that govern tax-exempt status can be found in the fourth edition of my book, *Tax Planning and Compliance for Tax-Exempt Organizations*. The book contains many checklists and exhibits to aid the critical goal of maintaining tax exemption.

To qualify for exemption, a nonprofit must be organized exclusively for exempt purposes within the specific terms described in the Code, and it must operate primarily for such purposes. *Exclusively* does not mean 100 percent, and *primarily* can mean a little more than 50 percent. The facts and circumstances are examined in each case because the IRS guidance and U.S. Treasury regulations provide very few specific numerical tests. When used, a numerical test is most often applied to gross revenues, but it can also be applied to net profits, direct costs, contributions in kind, and the like. In each case, the IRS examines the exact facts to determine whether exemption is in order. For example, a low-income housing project must provide a proscribed portion of the living units to the poor.[1]

Role of Internal Revenue Service

A special division of the IRS giveth and can taketh away a nonprofit's tax-exempt status.[2] Beginning in 1996 this division was reorganized and renamed the TE/GE (Tax Exempt and Government Entity) Unit. Responsibilities are assigned to four offices:

1. Washington, D.C., National Office for Customer Education & Outreach, Rulings & Agreements, and Technical Guidance & Quality Assurance

2. Cincinnati Ohio Office for Determinations

3. Dallas Texas Office for Examinations

4. Ogden Utah Office for Processing and Reviewing Form 990s

The TE/GE personnel are typically well-trained specialists with a number of years of experience, they are usually highly cooperative, and they view their role differently than the prototypical IRS agent. This division reviews applications for exemption and anoints properly organized and operated nonprofits as exempt organizations often before the nonprofit actually has any financial activity. Throughout the nonprofit's life, the TE/GE division receives and evaluates Forms 990 and, when it deems necessary (in the past, a rare occasion), examines the organization to ascertain that continued tax exemption is allowed. Changes in the nonprofit's purpose or scope of activity, public charity status, accounting methods, fiscal year, or similar issues necessitate a voluntary report back to the TE/GE division to obtain sanction or approval for the change. The telephone number for information and assistance is 1-877-829-5500 (as of July 1, 2007).

Only §501(c)(3) organizations are technically required to seek a determination by the IRS to qualify as exempt and are only treated as exempt if Form 1023 is filed. For all other categories of nonprofits, being established and operated according to the characteristics described in the tax code is technically sufficient. Those nonprofits, business leagues, and unions, for

---

[1] IRS Rev. Proc. 96-32, 1996-20 I.R.B. 1.
[2] Although this step occurs rather rarely.

example, often seek IRS determination to secure proof of their status for local authorities, members, and in some cases, the IRS itself, and to insure against penalties and interest due on their income if they do not qualify. The process by which application is made is thoroughly discussed and illustrated in a separate book.[3]

The administrative burden and expense of the determination process and annual compliance are at least equal to the annual filing burden of for-profit-motivated firms. Professional assistance from accountants and lawyers familiar with nonprofit matters will ease the process. If funds are limited, a qualified volunteer can be sought. In many states, pro bono assistance is available through CPA societies, bar associations, and other volunteer groups such as the Texas Accountants and Lawyers for the Arts.

Forms 990

Annual information returns—Form 990, 990-EZ, 990-T, or 990-PF—are filed by exempt nonprofits as an annual report to the Internal Revenue Service. Detailed balance sheets, income statements, lists of directors and officers and their compensation, and descriptions of activities are submitted, along with a report of any changes in the organization's form of organization, bylaws, purposes, activities, revenue sources, or so on occurring during the particular year. The returns contain descriptions of the organization's exempt activity along with financial information, and are open to public inspection upon request. Because of abuses by some exempts, there was ongoing pressure to enhance information disclosed on Forms 990, particularly as it regards compensation paid and transactions with insiders. The IRS expects the reports will be required to be filed electronically by 2009 and released a draft of a significantly revised Form 990 they hope will be used for filings for 2008 fiscal years. The availability of Forms 990 for anyone to see on Guidestar.org makes it important that the return be prepared in a thorough and careful fashion. To assure an organization is dotting it's I's and crossing the T's, readers can consult *IRS Form 990 Tax Preparation Guide for Nonprofits.*[4]

Forms 990 serve several purposes and should be prepared with care because it is often a nonprofit's most frequently viewed financial report. In addition to the initial filing with the IRS, Forms 990 are also filed in many states. Some funders request and review as a part of their grant-approval process. Anyone who asks is entitled to view a copy of Form 990 in the nonprofit's offices. Three years of 990s and Form 1023 or 1024 must be available for public inspection on request.

---

[3] Jody Blazek, *IRS Form 1023 Tax Preparation Guide*. Hoboken, NJ: John Wiley & Sons, 2005.
[4] Jody Blazek, *IRS Form 990 Tax Preparation Guide for Nonprofits*. Hoboken, NJ: John Wiley & Sons, 2004, to be updated in 2008.

Other Filings

A nonprofit organization has a number of periodic filing requirements as outlined in Exhibit 8.2. Accurate employment tax reports are particularly important. The penalties for failure to pay over taxes withheld from employees are very stiff. The money withheld from employees does not belong to the nonprofit and it certainly should not be spent for any other purpose. Finally, those nonprofit officers responsible for the failure to properly pay employment taxes can be held personally liable for the tax.

Exhibit 8.2   Annual Tax-Filing Requirements for Nonprofit Organizations

ANNUAL INFORMATION RETURNS

Form 990	Return of Organization Exempt from Tax. Filed annually by most §501 organizations with gross receipts greater than $100,000. §501(c)(3) also file Schedule A. Reports due by 15th day of 5th month following end of fiscal year.
Form 990-EZ	Short version filed by organization with gross receipts less than $25,000 and assets less than $250,000. Effective in 2008, an organization with less than $25,000 of annual revenue will be required to electronically file a post card annually. Failure to file the card for more than two years will result in revocation of exemption.
Form 990-PF	Filed by all private foundations annually by 15th day of 5th month following the end of the fiscal year.
Form 990-T	Income tax return to report unrelated business income and calculate tax due annually. Also reports lobby proxy tax.
State Reports	A copy of Form 990 or a version of it is filed in some states.

EMPLOYMENT TAXES

Form 941	Employment tax return reporting taxes withheld and due filed quarterly on April 30, July 31, October 31, and January 31.
Form 5500	Exempt organizations with employee benefit and pension plans must annually report its participant statistics and other details.
Depository Receipts	Federal, and some state, taxes are paid directly to a bank, not mailed to the IRS where tax due is greater than $500.

Exhibit 8.2   Annual Tax-Filing Requirements for Nonprofit Organizations
(continued)

Form W-2	On a calendar-year basis, employees' total wages and taxes are reported to individual employees on this form by January 31.
Form W-4	Completed (for exempt's files) by each employee that evidence number of exemptions claimed for income tax withholding.
W-9	Completed (for nonprofit's files) by each independent contractor claiming the nonprofit need not withhold tax from them.
Form 1099	Nonemployee fees, interest, rent, or other compensation paid to independent contractors is reported annually by January 31. If the nonprofit does not have Form W-9 verifying the Social Security number, backup withholding of 20 percent of each payment is required.
Form 1099G	Prizes and awards won in a raffle must be reported on this form or if the value is over $5,000, on W-2G (tax must be withheld).
Unemployment Tax	Both federal and state unemployment taxes may be due, depending upon the exemption category, number of employees, and registry as a reimbursing employer.

Other State Reports

Sales Tax	Sales of goods and services may be subject to sales tax. State and local exemptions and reporting requirements vary. Exemption from paying sales tax on purchases of goods to conduct exempt programs may be exempt under state law.
Local Property	Some states collect tax on real and intangible personal property.
Other State Filings	Many nonprofits are exempted from state income and corporate franchise taxes upon submission of evidence of federal exemption. In such states, a variety of other periodic filings, including a version of Form 990 are filed annually to maintain ongoing exemption.
Solicitation Registration	Organizations that conduct fundraising campaigns may have additional filings.

Resources

Books

AICPA Professional Standards Not-for-Profit Organizations; AICPA Not-for-Profit Audit and Accounting Guide. American Institute of Certified Public Accountants; others can be found at aicpa.org.

Blazek, Jody. *IRS Form 1023 Preparation Guide for Nonprofits.* John Wiley & Sons, 2005.

____. *Tax Planning and Compliance for Tax-Exempt Organizations,* 4th edition. John Wiley & Sons, 2004 (supplemented annually).

____. *IRS Form 990 Tax Preparation Guide for Nonprofits.* John Wiley & Sons, 2001.

____, and Bruce Hopkins. *Private Foundations: Tax Law and Compliance,* 2nd edition. John Wiley & Sons, 2003 (supplemented annually).

____, and Bruce Hopkins. *Legal Answer Book for Private Foundations.* John Wiley & Sons, 2001.

Board Source, Washington D.C., provides publications (pamphlets including *Nonprofit Governance Series* on governance issues and other books, monthly newsletter, bimonthly magazine) and consultations to increase the effectiveness of nonprofit organizations.

Colvin, Gregory L. *Fiscal Sponsorship: 6 Ways to Do It Right,* revised edition. Study Center Press, 2006.

Gross, Malvern J. Jr., John H. McCarthy, and Nancy E. Shelmon. *Financial and Accounting Guide for Not-for-Profit Organizations,* 7th edition. John Wiley & Sons, 2005.

Guide to Nonprofit Corporate Governance in the Wake of Sarbanes-Oxley. American Bar Association Coordinating Committee on Nonprofit Governance, 2005.

Hill, Frances R., Barbara L. Kirschten, Robin Atkinson, Wendell R. Bird, and Bonnie S. Brier. *Federal and State Taxation of Exempt Organizations.* Warren, Gorham & Lamont, 1994.

Hopkins, Bruce R. *Charity, Advocacy, and the Law.* John Wiley & Sons, 1992.
____. *The Law of Tax-Exempt Organizations,* 6th edition. John Wiley & Sons, 1992.
____. *The Law of Fund-Raising.* John Wiley & Sons, 1991.
____. *The Nonprofit Counsel.* John Wiley & Sons, monthly newsletter.
Independent Sector reports of the Panel on the Nonprofit Sector, available at www.nonprofitpanel.org/selfreg/Index.:
Principles for Effective Practice was released for comments, as of June 17, 2007.
Strengthening Transparency Governance Accountability of Charitable Organizations, a final report to Congress and the Nonprofit Sector, issued June 2005.
Jackson, Peggy M., and Toni E. Fogarty. *Sarbanes-Oxley for Nonprofits.* John Wiley & Sons, 2005.
McLaughlin, Thomas A. Streetsmart Financial Basics for Nonprofit Managers. John Wiley & Sons, 1995.
Overton, George W., and Jeannie Carmedelle Frey (Editors.). *Guidebook for Directors of Nonprofit Corporations,* 2nd edition. American Bar Association, Section of Business Law, Nonprofit Corporations Committee, 2002.
Rachlin, Robert, and H. W. Allen Sweeney. *Handbook of Budgeting,* 3rd edition. John Wiley & Sons, 1996.
Ruppel, Warren. *Not-for-Profit Accounting Made Easy.* John Wiley & Sons, 2002.
Siegel, Jack B., A Desktop Guide for Nonprofit Directors, Officers, and Advisors. John Wiley & Sons, 2006.
Standards of Accounting and Financial Reporting for Voluntary Health and Welfare Organizations, last rev. ed. National Health Council, Inc., National Assembly of Voluntary Health and Social Welfare Organizations, United Way of America, 1988.
United Way of America. Accounting and Financial Reporting, A Guide for United Ways and Not-for-Profit Organizations, 2nd ed. rev. United Way Institute, 1989.
U.S. Department of the Treasury, Internal Revenue Service. *Exempt Organizations Continuing Professional Education Technical Instruction Programs.* (issued through 2004 and available www.irs.gov/charities/article.
____. *Exempt Organizations Handbook.* Internal Revenue Manual 7751, www.irs.gov/charities.
____. *Private Foundations Handbook.* Internal Revenue Manual 7752, www.irs.gov.charities.
U.S. General Accounting Office, *Government Auditing Standards (GAAS)* (known as the Yellow Book). Revised January 2007 (GAO-07–162G).

PERIODICALS

The Chronicle of Philanthropy. Washington, DC: weekly journal.
The Exempt Organization Tax Review. Arlington, VA: Tax Analysts, monthly journal.

EXEMPTS, The Journal of Taxation of Exempt Organizations. New York: Warren, Gorham & Lamont, bimonthly journal.

Foundation News. Washington, DC: Council on Foundations, published bimonthly.

Giving USA. The American Association of Fundraising Counsel publishes an annual report that provides the latest facts and figures on philanthropic giving across the United States.

Paul Streckfus' Exempt Organization Tax Journal. Pasadena, MD: monthly journal.

Taxation of Exempts. New York: Warren Gorham & Lamont of RIA, published bimonthly.

WEB SITES OF ORGANIZATIONS SERVING NONPROFITS

Allianceonline.org. The Alliance for Nonprofit Management is the professional association of individuals and organizations devoted to improving the management and governance capacity of nonprofits—to assist nonprofits in fulfilling their mission.

Boardsource.org. BoardSource features articles related to nonprofit governance, information about upcoming conferences and events for leaders. The "Board Q & A" section of their site is useful for new nonprofit board members with questions about nonprofit governance.

cof.org. The Council on Foundations works to support foundations by promoting knowledge, growth, and action in philanthropy. Their site offers workshops, publications, and tools. Members have access to virtual resources. Recent books that can be ordered from their site include *Guide for Community Foundation Board Members, Understanding Philanthropy,* and *How to Calculate the Public Support Test.*

fasb.org. The Financial Accounting Standards Board web site contains full test, summary, and explanation of FASB standards for financial accounting for nonprofit organizations.

foundationcenter.org. The Foundation Center is the nation's leading authority on institutional philanthropy and is dedicated to serving grant seekers, grant makers, researchers, policy makers, the media, and the general public through its web site, print and electronic publications, five library/learning centers, and a national network of cooperating collections.

giftsinkind.org. Gifts In Kind International links donor resources to enhance, empower, and restore communities and people in need. Gifts In Kind receives donations from thousands of large and small companies and distributed technology, retail, and consumer goods to more than 150,000 community charities across the United States and throughout the world during 2006.

Give.org. The BBB/Wise Giving Alliance site displays its Standards for Charity Accountability developed to assist donors in making sound giving decisions and to foster public confidence in charitable organizations.

Guidestar.org. This site displays Forms 990 and 990-PF filed by §501(c)(3) organizations. For members, the site also contains financial information on individual nonprofit organizations, as well as articles and information of general interest.

IndependentSector.org. Independent Sector is a nonpartisan coalition of approximately 600 organizations dedicated to advancing the common good in America and around the world.

IRS.org. The IRS web site posts tax information for charities and non-profits.

nacubo.org. The National Association of College and University Business Officers serves a membership of more than 2,500 colleges, universities, and higher education service providers across the country. NACUBO represents chief administrative and financial officers through a collaboration of *knowledge, professional development,* and *advocacy.* Publications can be ordered from their site, including farm (financial accounting and reporting manual) and annual endowment study.

smallfoundations.org. The Association of Small Foundations is a membership organization of foundations with five or fewer staff. It helps in all aspects of foundation work: public relations, writing letters, cutting checks, mailing and processing grant applications, working with trustees and grantees, doing site visits and evaluations, managing assets, tax matters, and so on.

upmifa.org. The National Conference of Commissioners on Uniform State Laws (NCCUSL) approved the Uniform Prudent Management of Institutional Funds Act (UPMIFA) and recommended it for enactment by the legislatures of the various states. UPMIFA is designed to replace the existing Uniform Management of Institutional Funds Act (UMIFA).

urbaninstitute.org. The Urban Institute was created in the mid-1960s as a nonpartisan organization to study problems facing America's cities and their residents. UI gathers and analyzes data, conducts policy research, evaluates programs and services, and educates Americans on critical issues and trends. The Center for Nonprofits and Philanthropy (CNP), an arm of UI, maintains data on the nonprofit sector. UI created the Panel on the Nonprofit Sector in 2005 to address. CNP maintains the National Center for Charitable Statistics, a national clearinghouse of data on the nonprofit sector in the United States.

Index